Fredric Remington

Cowboys and Indians:
An Illustrated History

ROYAL B. HASSRICK

Cowboys and Indians:
An Illustrated History

ROYAL B. HASSRICK

octopus

Contents

This edition first published 1976 by
Octopus Books Limited
59 Grosvenor Street, London W1

ISBN 0 7064 0552 8

©1974, 1975, 1976, Octopus Books Limited

Reprinted 1981

Produced by Mandarin Publishers Ltd.,
22a Westlands Road, Quarry Bay, Hong Kong

Printed in Hong Kong

Introduction

HALF TITLE: Sheriff Wild
Bill Hickok, one of the
most famous gunslingers
of the West, and the
Apache leader
Geronimo, whose
defeat of General Custer
is still celebrated today
TITLE PAGE: *The Buffalo
Hunt*, painting by
Charles Russell
CONTENTS PAGE: Steer-
roping in California
PREVIOUS PAGES:
Chieftain at the
Gallup Inter-Tribal
Ceremonial gathering
ENDPAPERS: Frederic
Remington's painting
entitled *Stampede*

THE STORY OF the American West is a national
drama. It tells of an unique era in history
when men seemed to hold destiny in their
hands. It began as a dream in the minds of the
colonists, a dream in which hope for new and better
life was a driving force. And it was a force that
sustained itself for well over two centuries.

The characters in this saga begin with the intrepid
explorers, the noble American Indians, solitary fur
trappers and valiant pioneers. It ends with a cast of
arch brigands, heroic cattlemen, drudging miners
and tycoon empire-builders. It was a fabulous time
wherein heroes and villains seemed to join in a
national bonanza, the like of which has never before
nor since been witnessed. Few times in history have
so many diverse individuals pitted their wits, their
energies, their very lives to weld a new nation.

This two hundred years of achievement was not
without its share of tragedy, failure and sudden
death. Wars between Indians and whites, between

sheepherders and cattlemen and between cattlemen
and settlers took their toll. Pioneers lost their lives
by drowning, pestilence, even starvation. Bad men
prowled the West stealing horses, robbing banks,
looting trains and killing law men: the early West
was not the safest place to be and the men and women
who first ventured there had a raw kind of courage.

Of all the heroes, however, the Cowboys and the
Indians stood foremost. The Indian, proud and
colourful, came from many tribes and many nations.
Some, like the peaceful Pueblos, lived in the far
Southwest in great adobe apartment complexes
surrounded by their fields of corn, beans and
squash. Near them were the war-like Apaches and
the sheep-herding Navahos, bedecked in their
wealth of silver and turquoise. Others were sea-
farers, hunting ocean mammals and fishing along
the Pacific northwest coast. They lived in great
plank houses, and erected huge totem poles honoring
their animal ancestors. No Indians, however, were

more dramatic than the buffalo-hunting, tipi-dwelling warriors of the Great Plains. None has captured the fancy more than the painted men in war bonnets, who destroyed the flamboyant General Custer at the Battle of the Little Big Horn. And yet, though the Indians fought with unmatched valor to defend their homelands and won many brilliant battles, they finally lost the wars to an overwhelming enemy.

While the American Indians often symbolize the wild and mysterious men of the West, the American cowboys have come to typify the ideal of masculine prowess and Western romance. Once trailing great herds of Longhorn hundreds of miles from south Texas to the railheads, later riding range on huge ranches, enduring the hazards of stampedes, torrential lightning storms, howling blizzards, here were men whose hard and lonely and dangerous and often monotonous work made them archetypal American folk heroes.

Wild West—romance and reality
ABOVE: An anonymous painting entitled *The Rocky Mountains, Emigrants Crossing the Plains*
LEFT: In Tombstone, Arizona, the pioneers' justice was often rough

CHAPTER I

The Cowboy, One Man Alone

WHEN THE ROMANTIC history of the American West was finally recorded – after almost four centuries of colorful action and conquest – the story's hero turned out to be, strangely, not the indomitable explorer, the hardy trapper, the colorful Plains Indian in warbonnet and paint, nor even the pioneer girded with fortitude, but the lonesome cowboy.

The truth is that little real romance exists in the story of the cowboy; it is simply a saga of courageous men who don't know they are brave. It is basically the history of the American cattle industry in all its ramifications; nevertheless it is a story filled with adventure and drama, with ambition and harsh justice. No one group of men holds such a fascination for so many as do these hard-working horsemen, whose stoicism and

loyalty, whose taciturn demeanor combined with boisterous exuberance give them a charisma matched by no other men. They are *the* American folk heroes and their pre-eminence is unquestionable.

The vastness of the Western cattle lands, the toughness of the country and the nature of the work has always called for men of endurance — and men who could endure a great deal of their own company. An individual ranch might be as big as a 1,000 squares miles, and tending cows often means day after day spent in solitary (though not confinement). Any cowman worth his salt, who has had to shoot his horse because it broke his leg, or has seen his calves die like flies from an epidemic, or seen the price drop just when he must sell his calf crop to pay the bills, would feel like crying. To be thrown from a horse and have

The loner personified
Under Colorado skies a solitary cowboy plies his trade, alone except for several hundred four-footed friends

OVERLEAF:
Dust Storm, painting
by Roger Musick

**All in the day's work
for a cowboy**
FAR LEFT: Urging cow
ponies toward the
corral, in mesquite
country
FAR LEFT BELOW:
Pushing cows through
brush with the help of
some alert dogs
LEFT: Making tracks
for home across the
wide desert lands
BELOW: *Roping a
maverick* from the
painting by Charlie Dye

your sternum torn apart, to be gored by a maddened cow and be on a crutch for three weeks, to have your face torn apart by flying parts of a broken machine, could bring some people to tears; but not the cowboy. It's no job for a crybaby.

It takes more than equipment, rope and saddle, spurs and hat and horse, to make a cowboy. It takes practiced skill and cold courage. As one definition has it, "A cowboy is a man with guts and a horse."

Of all American culture heroes, the cowboy stands alone – or rather sits, astride his horse, his constant companion during the long lonely hours. One old cowpoke said to another as they turned their horses out in the night pasture after ten hours in the saddle, "You know, by God, Walt, I love that damn horse so much I like him."

But no cowboy wastes time on sentiment. If a horse steps on his toe, he does not say "Please, dear horse, remove your foot from my boot as you're hurting my toe and spoiling the shine." He simply yells, "Get the hell off my foot, you son-of-a-bitch."

A cowhand might or might not own his horse, but he surely owns a saddle. In a way it is his work bench and from it he does nearly all his chores. Like a well broken-in pair of boots, a saddle fits a man. Since the cowboy spends from eight to ten hours a day in it, it must fit well. A man might lend his hat, his sixshooter, his chaps, even his horse, but his saddle never. And while he might lose his shirt gambling, it's almost certain he won't get in so deep as to put up his saddle as a stake. The term "he sold his saddle" is the equivalent out West of saying a man has "sold his soul."

The cowboy is a man of few words, often succinct and more often rough. His statements are frequently punctuated with so many "dammits" and "oh hells" that one must listen carefully to get the gist of the sentence.

When this loner does get together with his

fellow men in a rough sort of camaraderie, his main means of communication is a crude kind of bantering and practical jokes of the hardest nature that help to make the job bearable. From earliest days, the cowboy has had his own wry brand of humor which is found to this day.

Above all, he is a man of "horse sense." Such a man does not suffer fools gladly.

There's the story of a rancher whose newborn calves were being decimated by an especially virulent disease known as "scours." The veterinarian was called in. While he prescribed preventative medication, he also strongly urged burying the little victims in hopes of reducing contamination. "Well," said a cowhand who was looking on, "you didn't think we were so dumb as to bury the live ones."

Cowboys have always had a reputation as hard drinkers, and they have earned it. "Sour mash," a corn liquor, used to be their favorite, partly because that was all that was available. When they came to town, the saloon became their club. If they weren't gambling at their popular card game of faro, they lounged at the bar telling tall tales.

And when a group of cowboys gather to put a foot on the rail, never was such a collection of bowlegged characters gathered at one spot — their knees bent from years in the saddle. A cowboy is a very awkward man when on foot. Walking is not only unnatural, it is immoral, and the only sensible human form of locomotion is astride a horse. This bent-legged, hunchbacked cowboy may barely be able to navigate on foot — but on a horse he is transformed into a gallant, dashing character, hero of every Western story both in fact and fiction.

ABOVE: *Pushing cattle through bush*, a particularly tedious task
FAR LEFT: *The Cowboy*, Frederic Remington's famous painting
BELOW: *Dramatic monument* to the cowboy by Frederic Remington

CHAPTER II

Indians, Men in Tribes

OVERLEAF:
Plains Indian Village, painting by A. A. Janssen
ABOVE: *Algonquian Village Life* on the banks of the St Lawrence River, depicted by T. Davies
CENTRE: *Seminole family* in "chickee," dressed in traditional patchwork costumes

UNLIKE THE SOLITARY cowboy, whose world is the relatively small area we call "the West," an Indian is one member of a tribe which is itself one element in a larger group. For while they are in many senses one people (and are classified by anthropologists as one race) North American Indians are of many "nations" spread over the north and south, east and west of the vast continent from Mexico and Florida to the far frozen North.

At the time of the Europeans' first arrival in America, it is estimated that between 1,000,000 and 2,000,000 Indians occupied what is now the United States and Canada. There were more than 200 tribes, speaking scores of different languages (of five distinct types) from New England to Florida, from California across Canada to Alaska. The different nations of Indians had widely varying customs and ways of life, so diverse that the details could fill many more volumes than this one.

The Northwest Coast

An especially sizable population of Indians lived in the area extending along the continent's west coast from the upper part of California northward of Alaska, a thickly wooded region of heavy rainfall. Typical tribes were the Kwakiutl, the Haida, the Nootka and the Tsimshian. They lived largely on fish, particularly salmon, and built their houses and canoes of wood.

Their illustrious gods and ancestors they honored with elaborately carved art works.

Theirs was a materialistic and classified society. Their customs, which included a bit of cannibalism, remained unaffected by European influences until the fur trappers first invaded the area in the 1700s.

The Plateau

The Plateau area covers much of California and the Rocky Mountains and extends up beyond the Canadian border. The Indians here spoke a wide variety of languages. A great many of them had no art whatsoever and an uncomplicated social structure. Tribes here included the Paiute, Shoshone and Nez Percé.

The Plains

In the Plains area stretching from Texas up into Canada and from the Mississippi River to the

Rocky Mountains, lived nomadic tribes and others who stayed put, in earth-lodge villages, raising corn, squash and beans. Trade between them and the nomadic tribes was active. After the introduction of the horse by the Spaniards in about 1700, many of the sedentary Indians became nomadic, living in tepees which they carried about with them on horseback.

Of all the Indians of the Plains, the Sioux probably best typified the dramatic character of these nomadic tepee-dwellers. The buffalo-hunting Sioux commanded a territory which included the western half of what is now South Dakota, the southern half of North Dakota bordering the Missouri River, and parts of Nebraska and eastern Wyoming.

LEFT: *Making a sand painting* in preparation for a cuting ceremony

BELOW: *Crow men,* dressed in their finest regalia.

The North

In the Northern area, which includes most of Canada from the Rocky Mountains to Hudson's Bay, an area of frigid weather, the typical tribe was the Chipewyan. Here the snowshoes made by the Indians were perhaps the most important of all their material items, along with their various tools of hunting.

The Southwest

In the Southwest area – Arizona, New Mexico and parts of Colorado and Utah – there were several distinct periods of Indian development. A thousand years before Christ, semi-nomads, called the Basketmakers, lived by hunting, which they accomplished with a spear thrower, or *atlatl.* They made unfired pottery. Three hundred years later, they were still making true pottery.

Two centuries after that, a new people arrived, the ancestors of the cliff-dwelling Pueblo Indians. Later came the Hopi and Zuni developments of these same Pueblos, whose way of life remained relatively undisturbed until recent times.

The Eastern Woodlands

The eastern woodlands area of North America stretches from the Gulf of Mexico in the South up into Canada, and from the Eastern Coast inland to the Mississippi River, and includes the Great Lakes. Thr Appalachian Mountains, steep and rugged, bisect the area north-south. In the 1500s it was a dense, verdant and often impenetrable forest wilderness cut by rivulets, streams and deep rivers. The reign was lush with fruits and vegetables; grapes, cherries and persimmons, onions, potatoes and artichokes grew in profusion. Rich, too, was the supply of

Tribal customs

RIGHT: *Indian Warfare*, by Karl Bodmer, showing a combined force of Assinibo'n and Cree attacking a band of Blackfeet at Fort McKenzie

BELOW: Algonquian Indians of the Atlantic Seaboard celebrated victories with singing accompanied by rattles

wild game. Deer, bear, rabbits and wildfowl were abundant, as were the small woodland buffalo. The creeks and rivers teemed with fish as well as clams and oysters.

The Indians of the eastern woodlands were agriculturists and it was the women who tilled the fields, raising corn, beans, squash and tobacco.

The Indians set their villages along the rivers which served as their principal routes of travel The chief occupation of the men was hunting, although waging war was equally important.

Far south in the Woodlands area, in Florida, lived the Calusa, the Timucua and the Apalachee, while to their north were such tribes as the Creek, Cherokee and Shawnee, the Tuscarora and the Powhatans of Virginia, and powerful and highly sophisticated groups like the Choctaws, Chicasaws and Natchez.

In what is now New Jersey and eastern Pennsylvania lived the Delaware or Leni Lenapi. New England was the home of many small tribes with such fascinating names as Narraganset, Wampanoag, Pequot, Massachuset, Penobscot and Mohican. The region of the Great Lakes was the realm of the Ottawa and Huron, the Erie and to their west the Potowatomi, Menonini, Sauk and Fox. Farther south dwelt the Kickapoo and Winnebago, the

Miami and the Illinois.

The Cherokee living in the western regions of North Carolina and parts of Tennessee were typical of the Indians of the Southeast though they were an unusually powerful and populous nation of some twenty thousand souls. Governed by a council of elders whose decisions were reached only in unanimity, the Cherokee were an orderly people.

LEFT: *The Buffalo Dance* by Charles Wimar. The Indians were little understood by the early pioneers, and their many and varied customs and ways of life invariably seemed strange – even savage
BELOW: Nomad Plains Indians on the move, in Seth Eastman's painting *Indians Traveling*

Nations of Iroquois

In the North, the woodlands that were to become New York State were the land of the Iroquois. These Indians had come to the area from the South in the distant past and had driven a wedge between such tribes as the Delawares to the east and the Hurons, Eries and Ottawas to the northwest. These men formed a remarkable confederacy known as the Five Nations. Spurred by the visionary concept of one Hiawatha (not Longfellow's hero), the Seneca, Mohawk, Onondaga, Cayuga and Oneida formed a league both for defense and aggression. And it was handsomely successful. By the mid-eighteenth century the Iroquois had almost annihilated the Huron and were now overlords of the Delaware and the Eries. At the same time,

they welcomed the Iroquois-speaking Tuscaroras from the South into their confederacy. It thus became the Six Nations of the Iroquois: the Onondaga (central tribe of the group), Mohawk, Seneca, Cayuga, Oneida and Tuscarora.

Women of Influence

As was true in many Indian societies, the Iroquois women were highly influential. Descent was reckoned through the female line as was property. It was the women who owned the bark houses, the utensils and the fields. Moreover, it was the women who arranged the marriages. The practice was to choose an older matron for a young man, and for a young girl an older man. Such a system had advantages: the girl was mated with a man experienced in hunting, well able to provide for her, besides being already acknowledged as a warrior with status. On the other hand, a young man married to an older woman acquired a wife skilled in the arts of housekeeping, child rearing and farming. In addition to these virtues, she had usually accumulated much property.

Iroquois men were not only the hunters and warriors, but some achieved recognition as shamans and councilmen. As sachems, the elders met in the "Longhouses," making decisions through unanimous vote on matters of war and peace.

By the Great Lakes

Prosperous people living along the western shores of Lake Michigan were the Sauk and Fox. The women, as the farmers, tilled the fields. The men were the hunters and warriors. And the Sauk and Fox were extremely warlike.

Desirous of the fertile bottomlands owned by the neighboring Illinois, they forthrightly made war, drove the Illinois from their valleys and simply took over.

The land of the Sauk and Fox was rich. Not only was the soil fertile, producing an abundance of corn, beans and squash, but the forests were alive with game. In the early fall, the Sauk and Fox left their bark house villages and migrated to the prairies to the west. Here they hunted buffalo and elk, collecting for themselves a winter's store of hides and meat. And when the signs of winter appeared, when the leaves were blown off the trees and the first snowflakes came to whiten the pine boughs, they would rekindle the fires and sit out the winter beside them.

Missouri River Tribes

Along the banks of the Missouri River and its tributaries lived a number of tribes. Among these were small groups like the Oto, Kansa, Ponca and Omaha. Others, the Pawnee and Arikara, the Mandan and the Hidatsa, were large and strong. Some, like the tiny Missouri and the powerful Osage, lived a semi-woodland life, venturing onto the open plains only for an annual buffalo hunt. All were farmers and like

ABOVE: *Members* of the Sia Giant Society curing a sick boy
LEFT: A *Sauk and Fox war dance*, usually performed to celebrate a victory

the Osage tended their fields in the summer and after harvest went hunting in the fall. With the exception of the Osage and Missouri, who preferred bark-covered wigwams and longhouses, their villages were an assemblage of large dome-shaped earth lodges protected by a stockade.

Most northerly of these Indians dwelling along the Missouri River were the Mandans, who divided themselves into two groups or moieties, the Lefts and the Rights. The moieties were unevenly subdivided into thirteen clans. The tribe was governed by a council of priests and elders: two headmen, one peace chief and one war chief.

CHAPTER III

The Origins

**Spectacular
semicircular city**
Models of the tiered
city-fortress of Chaco
Canyon, in north-
western New Mexico

IN THE MISTS of a long and forgotten past, possibly as much as 50,000 years ago, men, tiny groups of hunters, small families, began to leave northern Asia. They moved towards the rising sun, exploring and following game across the land bridge that once connected Siberia to what is now Alaska.

Mammoths and Mestodons

During the warm interglacial periods of the Pleistocene Age parts of what are now arctic tundra were quite lush and could support a variety of animal life, such as the mammoths and mastodons, the early horse and other animals not associated with frigid climes. A vestigial form of humpless camel remained in South America as the llama and alpaca, but the mammoths and mastodons became extinct at the end of the Pleistocene, some 12,000 years ago.

It may well have been the ancient mammoth with its massive tusks and bounteous supply of meat that lured the daring hunters to Alaska. Armed only with rudimentary spears, the men had to attack and kill these huge beasts if they were to survive. And somehow they did survive, even though they had not yet discovered fire.

Waves of Newcomers

As the centuries passed, more and more hunters came, and with each new wave, those who had come earlier were pushed, or more probably driven, farther and farther inland. Over a period of 20,000 years, scattered groups of people camped here and there throughout the entire continent of America.

At Santa Rosa, an island off the coast of California, dressed mammoth bones have been found in what appears to have been a barbecue pit. Radio carbon dating estimates them to be around 29,650 years old. Presumably by this time man had discovered how to make fire. In a cave at Sandia, New Mexico, a mammoth tusk has been dated at more than 20,000 years. Distinctive stone spearpoints, named for the site where they were discovered, exhibit a single shoulder form. Points like this have been found at sites as far apart as Alabama and Alberta. In the Sandia cave the bones of prehistoric and now extinct types of camels, horses and mastodons were also found.

At Clovis, New Mexico, featherlike stone points as well as bone points have been dis-

covered in association with the remains of mammoths which have been assigned an age of 15,000 years by some scholars, and at Gypsum Cave, Nevada, were found the signs of the extinct giant sloth. It is believed these monstrous beasts were herded in pens by the early men, between 8,000 and 10,000 years ago.

Mutual Relationship

As the years passed, other men appeared and in time were joined by the dog, the first animal to be domesticated. In all probability the dog tamed himself, scavenging around the camp-sites; then man learned that this animal could be of inestimable help, not only as an aid in hunting, but as a beast of burden. The relationship proved mutually helpful.

With the ending of the glacial period, the elephants and saber-toothed tigers, the camels and horses disappeared. At Folsom, New Mexico, a beautifully worked fluted point was found wedged in the rib of a *Bison Antiquus,* a huge and now extinct variety of the American buffalo. Similar points, dated as 8,000 years old, have been found throughout the Great Plains from Texas to Canada.

Diversity of Peoples

The people who migrated to the New World were not all of one kind, and while the ancestors of the Indians were predominantly mongoloid with the characteristic black hair, brown eyes and tawny skin, there were many variations.

Stone Effigy Pipe found at the ancient mound near Spiro, in eastern Oklahoma

Man and nature
BELOW: Wooden deer
mask from an
Oklahoma mound
FAR RIGHT: *The Rocky
Mountains* by James
Lanmon

north and east in the forest lands of the Great Lakes, men were fashioning tools of copper: spearpoints, axes, knives and chisel-like *celts*. Possibly the hammered copper points were designed for arrows, the bow and arrow perhaps by now having been introduced from the North.

A thousand years elapsed and in the desert lands of the Southwest descendants of the early Cochise farmers of Bat Cave built pit houses near their fields. Here they cultivated not only a variety of corn, but beans and squash. Around 300 B.C. the women made the first decorated pottery, now identified as Mogollon and Hohokam. By A.D. 1000, the latter had devised an impressive system of canals for irrigating their crops and had gradually moved from the pit houses to great tiered buildings of stone and adobe.

The Ancient Ones
To the north of the Mogollon and Hohokam people there appeared another group of farmers referred to as Anasazi or "Ancient Ones." At about the time of Christ, these people, too, raised crops of corn, beans and squash. Theirs was a basketmaking culture, but by A.D. 500 they also had learned the art of pottery making. Within the following 800 years, these people left their pit houses and began constructing masonry dwellings. By A.D. 1000, possibly for defense against marauding Athabascan-speaking people – Navaho and Apaches – the Anasazi retreated from the open country of Arizona and New Mexico, Utah and Colorado and built great fortified towns. These they made safe in the majestic rock cliffs along the canyons that cut the region, and for nearly three centuries the people at Mesa Verde, Betatkin and Canyon de Chelly flourished. Others, rather than seeking refuge in the cliffs, built huge multistoreyed structures of cut stone formed to provide a defense against their enemies. Like the cliff dwellers, the people at Aztec and Chaco Canyon, New Mexico, also thrived.

Birds for Plumage
The people of this time, known as the Great Pueblo period, were now skilful farmers. They raised a variety of corn, as well as squash, beans and cotton. They domesticated the turkey and kept eagles and colorful macaws imported from Mexico for their plumage. The men tilled the fields, hunted the small game, deer and rabbits. They also wove mantas, which they embroidered, and diamond- and twill-pattern shawls and dresses for the women, kilts and sashes for their own costumes. The ancient pit-houses now became circular ceremonial rooms or *kivas*. It was in these that the men held clan meetings and emerged from them as the masked gods or *kachinas* to perform ritualistic dances before the people.

Some were tall while others were stocky, some were longheaded, others round, some were quite fairskinned, others very dark. And they brought with them various languages. Six distinct language families have been isolated which can give clues as to the successive waves of population. The dialects within a single family group are more often than not unintelligible from one tribe to another. As for diversities between families, some are as different as Japanese is from Portuguese.

At Bat Cave, New Mexico, rudimentary maize – a primitive corn that popped – has been discovered dating back some 5,000 to 6,000 years. Although the Southwest had become a vast desert marked by stark mesas, brilliant and dry against the searing sun, it appears likely that here the first attempts at agriculture north of Mexico took place. Concurrently, yet far to the

Artefacts in ceramic, stone and textiles
TOP: Bowl made by early Pueblo Indians at Mimbres intended for burial with a hole punched in it but found intact
ABOVE FAR RIGHT: Effigy bowl made of diorite rock uncovered in an Alabama mound
ABOVE RIGHT: The blanket of a Navaho chief. Often considered the most colorful of all American Indians, the Navaho are still famous for their crafts

The Pueblo women ground the corn in stone *manas* and fashioned handsome decorated pottery in black and white designs, usually geometric, although those at Mimbres embellished their pottery with whimsical life forms – men, birds and animals.

Abandoned Cities
And then, mysteriously, the spectacular cliff dwellings, the fabulous circular cities, like Chaco Canyon, were abandoned. Evidence suggests that a cruel drought lasting over a period of twenty years and resulting in severe erosion forced the Pueblo farmers to search out new locations where they could find water for their crops. All this happened about A.D. 1250.

Far to the east of the arid lands of the Mogollons and Hohokams lay the dank forest regions of the Mississippi valley and the woodlands of the Southeast. Here pottery has been discovered which is believed to have been made over 4,000 years ago. Unlike the vessels of the Southwest which were painted, this was decorated with a kind of engraving called stamping, a decorative form that was to dominate the entire eastern two-thirds of North America.

The discovery of pottery some 2,500 years older than that of the Southwest suggests that very early these Indians were practising agriculture and probably living in permanent communities. Pottery, used both for cooking and the storage of grains and dried vegetables, like beans and corn, is not readily transportable and its presence suggests a sedentary way of life. Only with an agricultural economy can such a community exist.

Mound Builders
Here in the Mississippi valley and its tributaries the centuries passed. It was not until about 400

Camouflaged for the kill
LEFT: Florida Indians dressed in deerskins and hunting deer, by the early artist Jacques Semoyne
BELOW: Spear shafts and bindings used by the Anasazi *c.* 1000 AD, found in the San Juan Highlands, Utah

B.C. that any significant culture manifested itself. Now, from the Gulf as far west as Kansas, north to Wisconsin and east to New York, men began building burial mounds, sometimes in the form of an animal effigy. At Hopewell, Ohio, findings of handsome stone-carved pipes in the form of animals and birds attest to their skill as artisans. From copper traded from the Great Lakes they fashioned large snake-head ornaments and double-headed birds. From mica, too, they made similar forms, many of which were sewn to their clothing.

Little is known that can account for the widespread influence of the mound builders. Whether a new religious concept or a confederation of inter-tribal traders or some other factors inspired this development is not known. Whatever the cohesive force, it appears to have been a strong one, for it lasted for over 800 years.

Sacred-Fire Temples

At a much later date, far to the south, people living along the waterways that flow into the Mississippi acquired a combination of cultural traits with a distinct flavor of the people of Yucatan and the Toltecs of Mexico. As early as A.D. 1300, temples were being erected atop large earth pyramids, diminutive replicas of the great Mayan, Toltec and Aztec edifices. These Temple Mound people perpetually maintained a sacred fire in their temples, built their towns around a ceremonial plaza, cleaned their villages once a year. They appointed priests to guard the idols in their temples, carried their kings and nobles on litters, often maintained a rigid caste system and always hideously tortured their war captives. So many southern traits combine to suggest not

only influence, but very likely a colonization by southerners themselves.

Short-Lived Cult

It was among these Temple Mound people that a strange and macabre Death Cult was either developed or introduced. Again and again there appear in their shell and copper ornaments motifs of skulls, men with weeping eyes, a single weeping eye and vultures. No one knows yet what it implied, this obsession with what appears completely morbid. Perhaps they were frightened to death. In any case, the cult was relatively short-lived and died out as mysteriously as it came into being. The Temple Mound complex did continue, though in diminished form, into the early eighteenth century, among such groups as the Natchez and Apalachee, the Chitimacha, the Creeks and Cherokee and Caddos. And were it not for the European conquerors determined to destroy everything Indian, it might exist today.

RIGHT: *Burial bowl* of the Mimbres culture, made about the 11th century, of pottery with drawing representing childbirth. The bowl has been broken to allow the soul to be released

Invaders from Europe

The first step into the New World by European feet – a step that was to mark the end of the Indians' old ways – came at the end of the fifteenth century.

Christopher Columbus, sure that the world was round, believed that by sailing west he could more easily reach the rich ports of India and the Orient. Having successfully convinced Queen Isabella of Spain that the idea was practical he made a slight and understandable miscalculation and never reached India.

The Spaniards however capitalized upon his Western discovery. It proved to be a fabulous windfall. They proceeded to conquer the mysterious and majestic New World civilizations of the Aztecs and Incas. So complete was the conquest that they not only plundered the victims of their wealth in gold and imposed on the natives the avid proselytizing of the Franciscan fathers, but even plunged them into slavery. To those Indians who proved recalcitrant, the Spanish went to the extremes of cutting off their hands and feet to convince them of Christianity's omnipotence.

The Fountain of Youth

In 1513, Juan Ponce de Leon, seeking a mythical Fountain of Youth, made his first voyage to Florida. Later, in 1521, he was commissioned to conquer the "Isle of Florida" in the name of Spain. With two hundred men, fifty horses and farm implements, he set out from Puerto Rico in two ships. Reaching the West Coast, his party was savagely attacked by Indians. Ponce was shot in the back by a poisoned arrow. Turning his expedition around, he headed for Cuba where he shortly afterwards died.

It was a black Moroccan named Estevanico who, in the spring of 1539, was the first foreigner to enter the Southwest. Leading an army of 300

At home in a cliff
CENTER: *The cliff face* at Mesa Verde National Park, Colorado
LEFT: *Spearpoint* from Cloris, New Mexico
BELOW: *Cliff dweller's* window on the world, at Mesa Verde

wanted no part of Estevanico or his demands. They promptly shot the arrogant Moor through with arrows, and his Mexican companions hastily departed for home.

Legend of Seven Cities

The following summer Don Francisco Vasquez de Coronado, lured by the imagined wealth of the fabled Seven Cities of Cibola, arrived in the land of the Zunis. With him he brought mounted soldiers astride horses, beasts the Zunis had never seen. When the Zunis refused to submit to the Spaniard's imperious demands, Coronado attacked. The Indians retaliated, shooting arrows and throwing stones. They dented Coronado's shining helmet with so many rocks that the conquistador was at first dragged away for dead. In less than an hour, however, the Zunis were subdued.

Illusion and Disillusion

By September of the same year, more of Coronado's troops arrived, together with an entourage of cattle, sheep, swine and horses. Besides the troops, there were also other white men, women and children. In no time these interlopers had usurped the land of the Pueblos. They commandeered the Indians' dwellings,

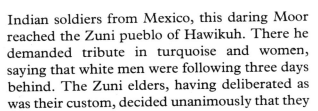

Indian soldiers from Mexico, this daring Moor reached the Zuni pueblo of Hawikuh. There he demanded tribute in turquoise and women, saying that white men were following three days behind. The Zuni elders, having deliberated as was their custom, decided unanimously that they

Invaders from Europe
RIGHT: Woodcut showing Indian village attacked by Spaniards
FAR RIGHT: Indians fall before the armored, mounted and gunpowder-equipped troops of Francisco Vasquez de Coronado

their food, even their women, and subjected the Indian men to the kind of slavery in which the Spanish were specialists.

Coronado was greedy and restless. The Cities of Cibola proved disappointing. Looting the Pueblos yielded nothing whatsoever by way of riches. The Indians simply had no gold. But tantalizing rumors reached the Spaniards of fabulous wealth to be found to the northeast, including a report of a wealthy city called Quivira. In the summer of 1541 Coronado set out to go there, guided by a Plains Indian called "The Turk." It was a grueling expedition. When they finally reached the dry flats of what is now southwestern Oklahoma and Kansas, all they found were the grass lodges of the Wichita Indians or Pawnee Picts.

The golden cities of Quivira were also a myth. Disillusioned, Coronado at last gave up. He turned around, collected his hogs and horses, his cattle and people and returned thoroughly disheartened to Mexico.

Another Conquistador
During the same period, Hernando de Soto was authorized by Spain's Charles V to conquer Florida, which really meant the entire continent of North America. His mission was to search for gold and precious stones and to claim the land for Spain. Landing in Florida in 1539, the conquistador marched his men north through Georgia to what is now Tennessee, then southwest to Alabama. Here in one of his many

ruthless engagements with the Indians, he was wounded.

Undaunted, he pressed westward, crossed the Mississippi and trecked up the Arkansas River as far as Oklahoma. Finding no treasure, he gave up and turned south, making his way back to the Mississippi. Here he died of his wounds and was buried in the river. His men traveled on, finally reaching Vera Cruz in 1543. Despite his untimely demise – he was only 42 years old – de Soto's trip had been monumental. He had explored more of North America than any other European before him. Like Coronado, he had found no wealth; lust for other people's property, land and lives had in fact brought him to financial ruin.

A Swarm of Spaniards
The Spaniards, however, were as hard to discourage as a swarm of hornets determined to build a nest. Forty years later they returned to the shimmering desert lands of the Pueblos, 400 strong, bringing over 7,000 rooting hogs and smelly sheep, bellowing cattle and rambunctious horses.

Led by a villainous governor, Don Juan de Oñate, they subjugated the Pueblos, taking special vengeance on the Acomas at Sky City who had dared to resist. Oñate ordered that those Indian men he did not kill should have one foot chopped off. Then he herded them into slavery for twenty years. Women and children were given slightly less harsh terms.

By now the Spaniards had planted their colony firmly, or so they thought, building their dried mud capital at Santa Fe. Here and there they set their little rancheros along the rivers which cut the land of towering mesas and rugged canyons. Franciscan friars in their somber black robes invaded the Pueblos, Taos and Picuris. San Ildefonso, Hemez and San Felipe, brought Christianity to the heathens, gained souls for the Catholic Church and strove to abolish the worship of the evil gods the Indians revered.

Pueblo Uprising

The period of Spanish domination, when they established their haciendas and enriched themselves by the labors of the Indian serfs, lasted nearly a century. And then one summer day in 1680 the Pueblos arose. Led by Popé, a man from San Juan who had brooded and schemed during a year in the Spaniards' prison at Santa Fe, the Indians joined forces. They attacked the rancheros, the tiny settlements, the capital itself. Enraged, they drove from their homes some twenty-five hundred Spaniards, including the governor from his adobe palace. Nearly five hundred settlers were killed as were many of the friars. With this swift and telling revolt, the Spanish colonial control of the Southwest was temporarily ended. The conquerors had at long last been given more than a little taste of their own savagery.

CHAPTER IV
Indian Life

Nalte Chief of San Carlos Apac.

A T THE TIME of Columbus there dwelt in the Southwest many native groups exhibiting a variety of life-styles.

Far to the South, in what is now southern Arizona, were the Pima and Papago, descendants, without much doubt, of the ancient Hohokam and Mogollon farmers. Their life was not greatly changed from that of their ancestors.

To have selected so arid a region as a place to farm at first appears inconceivable. Here the rainfall averages only about thirteen inches a year and when the rains do come it is often as cloudbursts filling the normally dry washes with surging torrents of water. The Pimans didn't actually choose the land. Their ancestors, the Cochise, chose it and the Pimans just stayed.

Like their forefathers, they cultivated crops of corn, beans and pumpkins, but by now had added cotton. The edible staples were supplemented by many wild fruits and berries, cactus buds and mesquite together with the meat of rabbits, deer, bear, antelope and the bighorn sheep. The Pimans lived in scattered villages, first in semi-subterranean pit houses, later in upstanding solid-walled structures. They wove blankets of rabbit skins, the men favoring skin ponchos and shirts of cotton, the women aprons of woven yucca fiber. They smoked clay pipes and even cigarettes, fashioned handsome pottery and superbly woven baskets.

The government was simple, unstructured and entirely democratic. A council of elders might choose one from among themselves as leader. Since tribal decisions demanded the unanimous agreement of the council, a principle that held true for the great majority of tribes throughout America, the chief was in reality the "voice" of the council.

Peace and Harmony

These were a peaceful people having learned to live in harmony with themselves and rarely going to battle save in self-defense. So abhorrent was war that a returning warrior who had taken a scalp had to blacken his face in shame and be ceremonially purified.

To the Northeast along the Rio Grande River flowing through New Mexico lay the towns of the great Pueblos. They, too, were experienced farming peoples, descendants of the Anasazi and the Cliff Dwellers. These were America's first apartment house dwellers. And to their west were other villages, the Acoma, Zuni and Hopi, high atop shimmering mesas, those fabled landmarks of the Southwest.

Theirs was a life of toil and ceremony and peace. As the men labored in the fields, often far distant from the village, with their digging sticks and hoes, the women ground corn and made handsome painted pottery, now in multicolors. Like their forefathers, the men wove the textiles for garments and hunted deer and rabbits, sometimes alone and sometimes in groups, driving rabbits before them and killing them with throwing clubs.

Farming was a man's summer occupation and weaving was his winter task. On an upright loom he wove cotton dresses with diamond and diagonal twill patterns. For himself he made white kilts in simple weave and embroidered the borders with red and black geometric designs.

The tradition of basketmaking among the Pueblos is an ancient one, dating as far back as the early Basketmakers, long before the Pueblos ever dreamed of apartment dwelling. The early Basketmakers wove sandals of yucca fiber and made basketry vessels woven so tightly that they could be used for cooking – throwing in hot

stones to make the water boil. Dyed in mute colors, bundles of grass were coiled to make trays with whirlwind, kachina and geometric designs. Baskets of wicker were designed as trays, dishes, even cradles. Today, except among the Hopis, the art of basketry has disappeared from the Pueblos.

Pueblo pottery was made by coiling rolls of moist clay one upon the other, to form a dish or bowl. Smoothed with a wooden paddle, the vessel was fired in a kiln composed of a pile of dried wood stacked over the pot. When the firing

OVERLEAF:
Prairie Indian Encampment, painting by J. M. Stanley
FAR LEFT: *Naite*, chief of the San Carlos Apaches, as he appears in an early photograph
CENTRE: *Papago grass house* in the Arizona desert
LEFT: *Sioux woman* wearing a painted robe whose designs symbolize the buffalo, with a child dressed in a typical outfit of the Assiniboins; engraving by the Swiss artist Karl Bodmer

45

Body painting
BELOW: Indians from
the Mohave desert in
the Southwest wearing
traditional clothes and
decorations

FAR RIGHT: A chief of
the Pamlico after a
painting by John White

painting them selues when
they goe to their generall
huntings, or at theire
Solemne feasts.

was completed, the pot was smoothed and polished with a round stone. Next it was painted. The designs, most often geometric, were achieved freehand, the artisans' designs coming out amazingly symmetrical even without any trial sketching.

While all pottery was low-fired and hence porous, some was burnished with stone to assume a brightly polished effect. Some, like the Santa Clara water jars, had a symbolic bear's paw impressed near the rim, for it was the bear who first led the people to water. The porosity of the jars permitted moisture to reach the outside surface which, in the arid climate of the desert Southwest, evaporated rapidly, thus cooling the water.

Whether at Taos, the most northerly of the Rio Grande Pueblos, which rises as much as four stories high against the backdrop of the Taos Mountains, or at Hopi, the most westerly of the Pueblos perched high on the edges of their barren mesas, the people's lives followed a regimen as certain as the seasons.

Spring was the time of planting and ceremonies were held to insure the germination of the seeds. More ceremonies, formal songs and dances by men representing the gods accompanied by rows of female attendants were held to ask for rain, and for bountiful harvests. New houses were blessed in the same way. These life-renewing ceremonies were a colorful, festive and sociable aspect of Pueblo life.

Many Gods

Among the Pueblos' hierarchy of many gods were the "Fun Makers," the clowns. It was they, with black-and-white striped painted bodies and horned masks or as earth-daubed figures called "Mud Heads," who spoofed and ridiculed a delinquent member of the community. They would frighten and scold a naughty child or pantomime the foibles of men, even jesting in lusty antic at the sexual activities of the people, a subject otherwise tabooed in a prim and proper society.

Pueblo society was very organized. Conformity to the norm was demanded for the good of all; individuality was suspect, dangerous, if not evil. The ceremonies themselves were

CENTRE: *Cape of chief Powhatan*, leader of the Powhatan tribe
BELOW: *Symbols of North, South, East and West* – Apache dancers wearing masks and headgear to represent the four directions together with a boy of the tribe, whose role is that of the invisible Great Spirit

Desert dwelling, Taos
Pueblo, one of
America's oldest
continually inhabited
apartment complexes

variations on the theme of life renewal. Subtle differences in costuming, in song, in dance steps were designed to fit the occasion.

To the untutored, the ceremonial dancing consisted of a monotonous ballet composed of strange masked gods and a long line of women wearing colorful *tablitas* chanting repetitious words in a singsong monotone for hours on end. But all had meaning, and they felt that as a result the rains came, the corn sprouted, the harvests were gathered. The system was tried and true. Any deviation might spell disaster; strict adherence to custom had proved effective for hundreds of years.

Pueblo boys as young as eight years old were harshly initiated into the realm of the supernatural by being thoroughly thrashed by the kachinas, not as punishment, but to cleanse and purify them. Sometime later boys were introduced to the mysteries of the kivas, learned something of the secrets of the clans, the roles of the gods, the meaning of the ceremonies. And they learned their duties with respect to them.

The kivas were the seat of Pueblo government. Generally owned by the clans, it was here the priests met. In some Pueblos, like Hopi and Zuni, men inherited the exalted positions, in others men voluntarily entered the realm of priesthood. In any case, men studied and became versed in the tribal rituals, the lore of the ancient gods, the skill of curing the sick. It was these men who became the leaders, the *caciques* of the Pueblos and as such the rulers of the theocracies.

Sickness was a fearsome matter. In general, it was the priests who specialized in curing. This was attended by much ceremony, for only through supplication could the sickness be exorcised. Before an elaborate altar, offerings and an intricately complex earth painting of colored sand, the patient sat facing the doctor-priest, who by means of chants endeavored to remove the cause of the illness.

It is believed by some authorities that very early Athabascan men from the north invaded the territory of the Great Pueblos, possibly as early as A.D. 700, probably as small marauding bands of hunting warriors. No one really knows. They called themselves "Diné," the "People," and their warlike ferocity may have been the cause of the Anasazis' building fortlike dwellings under the protection of the huge southwestern cliffs.

A Better Bow

Their descendants, the Navaho and Apache of New Mexico and Arizona, surrounded the Pueblos in their own country. As hunters they brought with them a powerful, newly designed bow – one reinforced with sinew – as well as a better method of arrow release. The simple method of holding the arrow's nock against the

bowstring pinched between the thumb and forefinger was now improved by pressing the nock against the side of the forefinger and then using the tips of the third and fourth fingers to pull against the bowstring. Equipped with these technical improvements, the Athabascans became efficient hunters and effective raiders, no doubt delighting in the pillage of the Pueblos' crops.

The history of the Apaches is that of a warlike group. They lived in scattered camps composed of brush-covered *wickiups* like bristling, overturned baskets. The Apaches completely ravished the countryside. Stealthy stalking and sudden raid were their manner of attack. Success was measured in booty and glory.

Some of the Apaches tended small gardens; it was generally the women who raised the crops. The women also made baskets, watertight canteens covered with pitch, as well as coiled storage bins and trays of willow and devil's claw. These were handsomely decorated either in geometric patterns or human and animal motifs. When the men weren't raiding, they hunted deer, rabbits and small game.

A Coming-Out Party

Each year the Apaches held a "coming-out" party for the young girls who had reached puberty. Elaborately attired in painted and beaded costumes fringed with dangling cones of jingling tin, the young women made music as they danced at their presentation. Strange masked dancers representing gods of the four directions – East, West, North and South – and a small boy personifying the invisible Great Spirit blessed the young girls.

Division of labor
FAR LEFT: A Papago woman making baskets
BELOW: Men must hunt and fight, as shown in this painting of Navaho Indians by H. B. Molehausen

Tribal chiefs
BELOW: Narbona
Primero, a Navaho
headman
FAR RIGHT: Geronimo,
the famous Apache who
fought long to preserve
his people's freedom

Unlike the Pueblos, the Apaches were anything but theocratic. Leadership was dependent solely upon individual initiative – some men were more or less granted a position of authority, others merely assumed it by personal dominance.

To the north and west of Apache country was the land of the Navaho. These hunters were milder in nature than their Apache cousins, a little more willing to adopt the ways of their peaceful neighbors, the Pueblos. From them they learned the techniques of farming, weaving, basketmaking; they even embraced aspects of the Pueblo religion. From the Spanish and Mexicans they acquired the knowledge of sheep herding and the skills of silversmithing. The Navahos incorporated the techniques of their neighbors and then added to them a special quality of their own.

In small log huts, some daubed and chinked with clay, the Navaho lived in scattered communities nestled along the hidden waterways

which cut the deep, red sandstone canyons of the Southwest. Young men and boys tended little flocks of sheep and hunted small game, while the women wove woolen textiles on an upright loom copied from the Pueblos. They made dresses, black with red borders, that were similar to the Pueblos', but instead of a single wraparound blanket, the Navaho fashioned two smaller rectangles and then stitched them together to form a simple tube. Around their waists they wore a belt of silver conchos and, as foot covering, bootlike moccasins which buttoned up the sides with silver buttons. Both men and women adorned themselves with shining silver necklaces and bracelets.

The Far West
Nowhere was the struggle for life harder than in the Great Basin region of the West. It was a vast area including what is now western Colorado and Wyoming, parts of Arizona and most of Nevada and Utah. It was a parched and desolate country and places like Death Valley and the Great Salt Lake attest to the barrenness of this cruel desert. And it was here that the most primitive of all Indians lived.

People like the Paiutes and Western Shoshoni best typify the simple life of these poor Indians. The women devoted their lives to gathering seeds and berries in great baskets and digging for roots with sticks. White men on first seeing these Indians dubbed them "Diggers," and so disdainful were they of these primitive folk that when there was nothing better to do they organized hunting parties to kill Indians as sport.

Food resources were scarce. While some deer and antelope were present, rabbits and grasshoppers seem to have been the staple. Rabbits were often snared in huge nets, while to catch grasshoppers a long trench was dug several feet deep. The insects were then flushed and driven along until they hopped into the trench. Here they were roasted alive. According to these people they made excellent flour. Lizards and caterpillars were considered delicacies and rats were eaten too.

The Indians lived in little wickiups of sticks and brush, always moving their tiny camps in an unending search for food. Their clothing was scant. Men wore only a breechcloth, if that much, while the women wore short fore-and-aft aprons of cedar bark and a basket hat. Both sexes wore sandals and in winter rabbit-skin robes.

These Indians had no government as such, but when decisions needed to be made with respect to a hunt, an elder might be appointed to be "talker." With regard to marriage, a man might have two wives, but if there was a shortage of women, a wife might have two husbands. When an Indian died, his hut was burned and the name of the deceased never spoken lest the voice of the dead return.

BELOW: *Easy transport*, a present-day Navaho woman carries a sheep home on the reservation
FAR RIGHT: *Ermine for a brave*, Big Knife, a Flathead, wearing an ermine-trimmed bonnet and holding an eagle-winged fan

A Peaceful People

Like the Pueblos of the Southwest, these were a peaceful people, fighting only to defend themselves. Isolated and moving only in small groups, they were rarely bothered by enemies.

In the valley shelves of the Grand Canyon of Arizona, the Havasupai hid, protected by the massive walls of rock. Their way of life was similar to that of the Basin peoples, but like their naked neighbors, the Mohave farther down the Colorado River, they had little gardens and raised crops.

The Havasupai had a particular concern, when twins were born, about determining which of the two was the elder. This was easily resolved, however, by the assumption that the older, in deference to the younger, would stand aside just prior to birth, allowing the second born to come into the world first. Hence the last born was considered the elder.

North of the Great Basin was the Plateau region, somewhat less inhospitable than the Basin, yet still anything but lush. This was the country of the Flatheads and Bannocks, the Coeur d'Alène and Nez Percé. Here the hunting was better. Deer, elk and mountain sheep were plentiful in some areas. Fish, especially salmon, were abundant along the Snake and Columbia Rivers during the spring season. When smoked, large quantities could be preserved. The women, like the Paiutes, gathered berries and wild plants and dug for bulbs and roots. They, too, wore aprons and basket hats which later they embellished with beads. In the winter the people wore robes of rabbit skins and sought shelter in pit houses covered with brush or mats. While life was better than in the Basin, it was hardly luxurious for the Indians of the Plateau.

Quest for Visions

Seeking visions was highly important to these people, for only through this quest could one obtain a guardian spirit. Both boys and girls sought this gift, but young men were much more determined. All manner of trials were endured; scratching oneself with thorns, diving into icy water and fasting at a lonely vigil were commonplace. It was only later in life that the spirit informed the individual of his blessing.

Some men became shamans endowed with the power to cure. Sickness was believed caused by worms or sticks entering the body or sometimes by the loss of one's soul. Medicine men were skilful in sucking out the foreign matter with tubes as well as in recapturing a lost soul.

The Utes, whose territory embraced what is now western Colorado and southeastern Utah, formerly lived much as their western relatives, the Paiutes. Theirs was the rugged mountain country of the Rockies. But for an amazing event, they might well have remained a simple hunting and gathering people, poor and struggling.

RIGHT: *A shaman making medicine*; sacred songs accompanied by rattles ensured the efficacy of the potion
BELOW: *Medicine man* of the Navaho tribe, a shaman named Hastobiga
FAR RIGHT: *A Plains Indian travois*, a device used to transport possessions; engraving by Frederic Remington

Sometime around 1650, the horse appeared. Strays from Coronado's legions and later from Spanish rancheros formed herds of wild mustangs. It was possibly these the Utes first saw or they may have obtained them from Apaches and Comanches who had got them earlier. In any event, with the introduction of the horse the Utes' whole life-style blossomed. Mounted on horseback, they became fearsome marauders. They could leave their mountain fastness and successfully hunt the buffalo on the plains below.

At a later date, the Shoshonis of Wyoming obtained horses. They, too, now hunted in the grasslands of the Rockies' eastern slopes. The Umatilla received horses in the late 1730s, as did most of the Plateau people. With this advantage their lot improved. Many of the little tribes assumed the attributes of the Plains Indians in costume, hunting techniques, even to adopting the tepee. One group, the Palouse, became particularly adept at horse raising; the breed of horses known as Appaloosa was named for them.

Medley of Tribes
California, before the coming of the Spaniards, was a medley of colorful little tribes. They occupied themselves in hunting small game, gathering acorns and wild vegetables, making exquisite baskets and celebrating life with

elaborate ceremonies. In this fabulous region were representatives of nearly every linguistic stock found in North America. Even then, everybody seemed to like to go to California.

Acorns were the staple, but the bitter tannic acid in the nuts required cracking them, grinding them several times, leaching and roasting them in order to make a palatable flour. This was the work of the women. In addition to their ingenuity in food preparation, the women fashioned baskets of superb beauty, unrivaled throughout America.

They made huge baskets for holding mush, four feet and more in diameter, and others as tiny as pinheads, with stitches so fine that they

can be counted only under a magnifying glass. Some baskets were coated with ugly pitch to make them watertight, others were interwoven with brilliant feathers and adorned with suspended shells to create veritable jewels of artistry.

As hunters and warriors, the men were equally clever. In hunting waterfowl, for example, men would float large gourds downstream past a flock of sitting ducks. When the birds became accustomed to the presence of the strange objects, the hunter would place a gourd over his own head and submerge himself in the water. When close to a duck, he would grab the bird by the feet, pull it under and drown it. A careful hunter could collect quite a few birds using this trick. Another stratagem the hunters figured out was that, by using a reed straw through which to breathe, a man could sink below the surface, approach the waterfowl and pull under as many birds as he could manage to hold in his hands.

The Californians were a very belligerent people, assiduously guarding their territories, and repulsing trespassers with vigor. Miniature wars broke out continuously, mostly over disputes about their borders. On occasion, to settle matters, the opponents chose two of their most able warriors who then battled among themselves. The group whose man was victorious decided and settled the issue.

Money and Death

The Californians had two overriding interests: money and death. They acquired and carefully accumulated shells: clam shells cut to the size of a thumbnail and dentalium. The latter was a white, curved, cone-shaped shell and its value depended on its length. Shells were used for the payment of all obligations as well as for trade. So widespread was their use that the well-to-do Sioux women of the Plains bartered for them to decorate the yokes of their dresses, thereby displaying their wealth. This, parenthetically, exemplifies one of the many complex trade routes the Indians had developed throughout all the continent.

Among most California tribes, death prescribed elaborate ceremonies. The Californians divided themselves into moieties or opposites. When death occurred, relatives of the deceased sent emissaries to the opposite branch. Bearing shell money, the bereaved requested members of the other moiety to officiate at the funeral lest the family, by being in too close contact with the dead, might be adversely affected. At the funeral, the house was burned, the body cremated and the name of the deceased never spoken again.

At the end of a year more death ceremonies were held. Myths about the Eagle, one of the first ancestors, and his untiring search for life, only to find death, were recounted in great detail.

Havasupa: dwelling hut in the shadow of a great rock cliff in Arizona

BELOW: *The primitive Paiutes*, for whom life was always a harsh struggle in an uncompromising environment
FAR RIGHT: *Women of four tribes* – a Mohave water-carrier with her child and a young woman of the Papago tribe and, on the bottom row, a Maricopa girl and a Pima matron

The Great Plains

High and barren, windswept and arid, the Great Plains are a hostile and forbidding region. In the north the winters are frigid, with howling blizzards piling snowdrifts in all the cuts and coulees. Summers on the southern plains are unbearably hot with dry winds searing the grasses and drying up the streams. Along the wide and shallow rivers, which can become raging torrents from the flash floods of summer, are groves of cottonwood and box elders, chokecherries and wild plums. To the west along the high ridges are stands of Ponderosa pine and cedar.

Once, huge herds of buffalo roamed by the millions up and down the unending sea of grass. Mule deer browsed in the wooded areas while antelope grazed the high, rolling ground. The black bear and grizzly rummaged everywhere in search of berries, fish and honey, while wolves and coyotes and fox grew fat from an abundance of jack-rabbits and prairie dogs. Golden eagles soared in the high, blue sky, ducks and geese made their flyways above the land and prairie chickens strutted their strange mating dance in dusty circles on the flats. It was a big country, a rich country and the men who wrested a living from it had to be of hardy stuff. The Indians of the Plains measured up handsomely.

Among the earliest settlers in recent times to venture onto the Plains were pioneers from the East. Southward, it was the Caddoan-speaking Wichita who inched their villages west along the rivers. Here in grass-thatched beehivelike lodges,

these farmers set their towns in what is now Kansas, Arkansas and Oklahoma. Some called themselves Kichai and Tawehash, Tawoconi and Waco. All were closely related, all lived in a land rich in buffalo, all were referred to as "Pawnee Picts" because of their custom of elaborate tattooing.

Siouan-speaking people, the Omaha and Ponca spread west from the Mississippi valley to parts of Kansas, Nebraska and the Dakotas. Here they built great earth lodges, domelike structures of logs covered with sod. Outside the stockaded villages, the women tilled the fields.

The fact that the women were the farmers has somehow led to the mistaken belief that the Indian woman's status was inferior. Other factors, too, added to this misconception. It was the women who carried the burdens, the cradled infants, the loads of firewood. When the people moved, it was the women who followed behind the men in single file, an apparently subservient position. Polygamy, too, at first glance, suggests a male chauvinism. Indian men might marry from two to six or even more women, depending solely upon how many they could provide for and keep happy. And that included the children.

Off with her Nose

Divorce, too, was easy. A man displeased with his wife often needed to do little more than go to the center of the village, beat on a drum and announce something to the effect of "I don't want her, you can have her, she's too fat for me!" And an outraged husband, learning of his wife's infidelity, was entitled summarily to cut off the end of her nose. Without a doubt, this act to some extent reduced her allure.

The women performed the backbreaking labor of farming in large measure because the men's responsibility was to provide meat from the hunt and protection from marauding enemies. The Indian village was an armed camp. Men slept with their weapons at their sides. Except during the deepest of blizzards, no night was safe from attack. More significantly, women were associated with the birth of newborns, not only humans, but the sprouting of seeds, the product of the Earth Mother, the very source of all men's sustenance and well-being.

In a great many Indian societies, war was for men the motivating factor of life. The inevitable consequence of a war-oriented pattern was a reduction in the male population. If women were to find husbands, they must be shared. Indians seem not to have believed in spinsterhood. Polygamy was a forthright solution. That the woman should carry the burdens, that she should follow behind her menfolk on the trail was only logical. Men led the way as scouts and guides. Armed with bow and arrow, it was the men who could ward off an unsuspected enemy and defend his women against an unexpected danger.

Divorce was easy, but since property, in so many of the tribes, belonged exclusively to the women – the lodge, the utensils, the fields, even the children – a man who was determined to divorce his wife had no place to go save back home to his mother. And about the only things he might take were the clothes on his back and his bow and arrow.

Disfiguring one's wife for an indiscretion was forthright, but a pretty risky business. In many tribes a man married into his wife's family. His go-between asked not only the girl's parents, but representatives of her family, in many instances her brothers. If the wife's family was a powerful one, mistreatment of one of its women could very well mean retaliation, sometimes in the stark form of murder.

Matriarchs or Patriarchs

The Indian family was of an extended nature and, depending on the tribe, traced its descent from either the female or male line. Matriarchs or patriarchs were the recognized heads of the family and as such were accorded respect and reverence. One married into his or her spouse's family and became part of that group. The idea of a man and wife setting out on their own as a conjugal family was not considered. The consanguine family wherein persons were related by blood rather than by marriage was the Indian pattern.

The consanguine family has some interesting ramifications. In certain societies, children called not only their own father "Father," but also their father's brother "Father." In the same way, they called their mother's sisters "Mother." And these tangential parents called

Different types of shelter
RIGHT: An Arapaho tepee ornamented with a quarter moon and a ceremonial calumet
BELOW: A Pawnee village of earth lodges at Loup Fork, Nebraska

these children "Son" or "Daughter." There were variations on this theme among the many tribes, of several "fathers" and several "mothers." This worked in a very practical manner. In the event that a parent was lost because of divorce or death, the child never suffered as the victim of a broken home. Rather he would still have several mothers and fathers who were responsible for him, for he was a member of a large and indestructible family.

One of the most westerly farmer tribes of the Plains were the Pawnee. As earth-lodge dwellers, they set their villages along the rivers of what is now Nebraska. Here they grew crops in the summer, while in the autumn they left their towns to hunt buffalo. The Pawnee were rich in ceremony and their most dramatic – the Sacrifice to the Morning Star – harked back to a far and ancient southern origin.

At the time of the summer solstice, just as the new corn began to sprout, a hereditary priest who was the keeper of the bundle (a packet of objects sacred to the tribe) would ceremonially open it. Now, too, a captive, a young maiden selected for the ceremony, was stripped of her clothing and her body symbolically painted. For several days she was accorded the greatest of deference and honor. But on the fourth day she was led to a platform where priests tied her and feigned to torture her. Then, just as the morning star rose, a warrior shot an arrow in her breast as another man at her back clubbed her to death on the head. Next, her heart was removed as a sacrifice to the morning star, whereupon all the men and boys filled her body with arrows. This was propitiation with a vengeance.

End of a Tradition

Early in the mid-nineteenth century, the practice was dramatically stopped. A young and respected warrior, indignant at the cruelty, dashed in on horseback, cut the binding thongs and rescued the victim. Rather than being punished, he was much honored for his bravery. The ceremony was discontinued and the Pawnees actually seemed relieved.

The Mandan and Hidatsa living far up the Missouri River, like their neighbors, the Caddoan-speaking Arikara to the south, were earth-lodge dwellers. The Mandan and Hidatsa believed that the great, all-powerful "Wakanda," the Sun, imbued various animal emissaries with his power. Furthermore, if man was to be successful in his endeavors, he too must possess this power. Rapport with the animal agent, therefore, became essential.

Self Torture

For the Mandan, a more direct way of acquiring power was to undergo self-torture during the Okipa ceremony. Here men, under the direction of their mentor-priests, allowed wooden skewers to be thrust under the chest muscles. Thongs attached to the skewers were then drawn over the great long beams in the earth lodge. The participants were next pulled up so that they hung suspended several feet above the ground, all this amidst the singing of the spectators. With intermissions, when the performers were let down to rest, the ceremony lasted many hours to be concluded when the supplicants tore themselves loose. Painful as it was, the Okipa was the accepted way to communicate directly with Wakanda.

The Mandan believed, as did nearly all Indians, that the individual owed his existence to a thorough understanding of and ability to communicate with the world around him. Failure to comprehend the habits of the planets, the forces of nature, the customs of animals, the desires and purgatives of the supernatural – the stars, the winds, the thunder and lightning, the causes of sickness – could bring disaster and woe. The Indian believed himself to be an integral though infinitesimal part of the system of things. He did not command, rather he propitiated, gave offerings and thanks to nature for its every blessing. Through auspicious ceremony he tried to control nature, insuring its beneficence and allaying its wrath, all toward the end of existing within its demands and understanding its complexities, all for his own security and well-being. His aim was to draw power from the order of things, never to disrupt that order.

"Lefts" and "Rights"

In the late eighteenth century, the Mandan were a prosperous people living in as many as thirteen stockaded villages with an estimated population of 3,600. They split themselves into two parts, the "Lefts" and the "Rights" and these were in

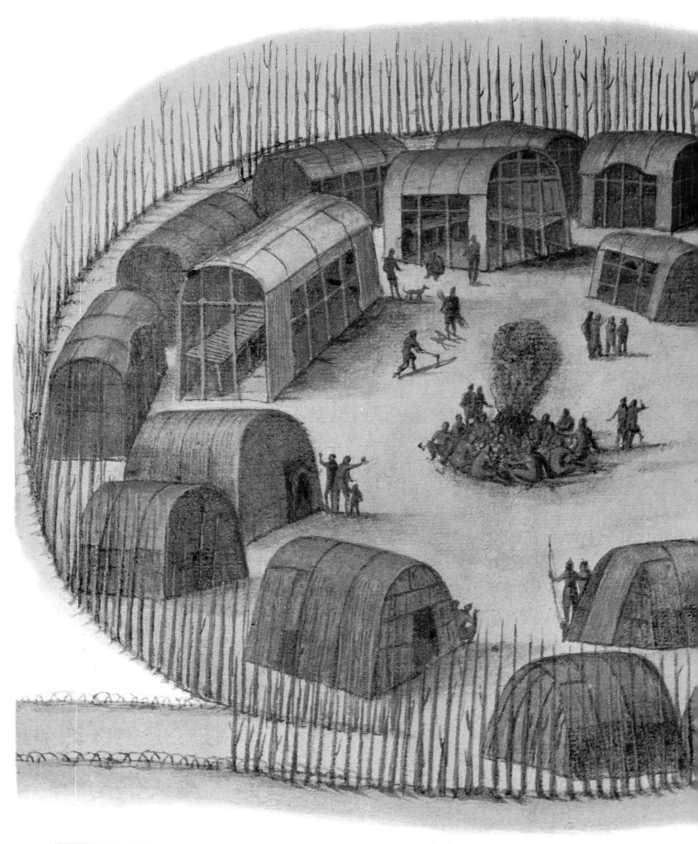

ABOVE: *Stockaded town* of the Pomeiok Indians in North Carolina depicted by John White, one of the first painters of Indian life

Hopi art and craftsmanship
RIGHT: A wall painting found in a kiva
FAR RIGHT: A sacred kachina doll; its eyes represent rain clouds, its eyelashes the rain

turn divided unequally into seven clans with inheritance reckoned through the mother. Representatives of each moiety and each clan could be found in all the villages. In marriage, one had to choose a partner outside his or her moiety as well as from a different clan.

The headmen or council of elders chose from among themselves one peace chief, one war chief and one civil, or village chief. Men achieved these positions by proving themselves good hunters and providers and by exhibiting prowess in war. But more important, they had to be recognized as possessors of exceptional power, not only by their successes, but by the aura of

wisdom they displayed.

It was during meetings of the councils that the ceremonial smoking of the pipe took place. It was considered essential to preface important events, both civil and religious, with appropriate supplication to the gods, and the pipe was the instrument through which the smoke of tobacco would convey the Indian's appeal.

Among many tribes, the pipe was a badge of high office. "Pipe Owners" were invested with authority to lead the bands when moving camp, to select the new village site, and most important, to settle quarrels among men by offering the pipe of peace and goodwill.

Wah-He-Jo-Tass-E-Neen, an Assiniboin chief, from a painting by Paul Kane. His grizzly bear-claw necklace was a sign of his bravery
Hollow Horn Bear, a chief of the Burnt Thighs Sioux
Fish Shows, a Crow Indian
Red Cloud wearing a hair-fringed shirt, the badge of an executive officer. The locks, donated by a female relative, represent the people of the tribe for whom he was responsible
Running Antelope, shown to have been a dignitary by the hair-fringed shirt and the Peace Medal
Four Horns, an Arikara, typifies the noble countenance of the Plains Indians
Two Moons, a Crow headman

Hollow Horn Bear

Wah-He-Jo-Tass-E-Neen

Fish Shows

Red Cloud

Four Horns

Running Antelope

Two Moons

Customs and costumes

ABOVE: Interior of a Mandan lodge, where animals were also stabled
RIGHT: A "dog dancer" of the Hidatsa tribe

Smoking was common throughout North America, and while pipes fashioned of stone and clay were predominant, cigarettes were used in the far Southwest. Both men and women smoked for pleasure and their pipes were unadorned, but the pipes reserved for ceremonial use were highly elaborate. Carved stems, sometimes three feet long, were decorated with porcupine-quill embroidery and the green neck feathers of mallard duck or a pendant fan of eagle feathers. The latter were referred to as "calumets" and were as reverently respected as any European monarch's scepter. The pipes, often in the shape of an inverted T or in the form of an animal or human effigy, were carved from red catlinite or black steatite and often inlaid with lead.

Young men worked hard to achieve status. On the battlefield they fought, as with the Sioux, to earn "coups," points toward their war record. Young men joined police and warrior societies, paying an initiation fee in goods. Some also took up the ways of the shamans and might become priests and keepers of the ancient lore and rituals of the Mandan.

Because the Mandans were light of complexion, possessed shorter and more aquiline noses than their neighbors, and because some of their women, even young girls, had silvery grey hair, it was long believed that they were in fact descendants of a lost Welsh colony. The theory, of course, was absurd. The fact was that a strange lack of melanin was genetically transmuted to the female.

Beasts of Burden

For the Mandan, as for most tribes, dogs were originally the only beast of burden. The Mandan villages were literally alive with them. It was not unusual for a family to own as many as 40 dogs.

During the autumn hunt, dogs were harnessed to an A-shaped frame or travois. Here a leather harness was fitted over the dogs' shoulders at the apex; the rest dragged behind on the ground. A small platform of sticks, or sometimes a hoop latticed with rawhide much like an oval snowshoe, was lashed to the travois to support the load. On this platform were piled the *parfleches*, painted leather envelopes that served as suitcases, or the bundled tepee. Sometimes miniature domed cages made of willow rods were fashioned to become a tiny playpen for small children. In the winter, dogs pulled loaded toboggans over the snow and icebound rivers.

Dogs were not only draft animals, they were an important part of Indian diet. Boiled puppy meat was a delicacy served at feasts. Dogs were treated quite harshly by their masters, beaten and screamed at for such misbehavior as stealing food. Indians were generally amazed at the white man's attitude toward dogs. As one man expressed it, "White men beat their children and pet their dogs; Indians beat their dogs and pet their children."

High Plains Horsemen

The Sioux, warlike, nomadic buffalo hunters, tepee dwelling horsemen of the High Plains,

ABOVE: The self-torture ceremony – known as the Okipa – held by the Mandans, as portrayed by George Catlin
LEFT: A Mandan brave

Art in the Wild West
RIGHT: *Buffalo Hunt*
by Carl Wimar
FAR RIGHT: Sioux
painting on hide of a
horse-stealing raid

came to symbolize all the heroism, drama and romance of the American Indian. Two factors, introduced by the Europeans, helped make for their brilliance – firearms and the horse.

Driven from their original woodland home near the head-waters of the Mississippi by over-powering, gun-carrying Crees, the Sioux migrated to the Plains. Fortuitously, they acquired the horse early in the eighteenth century, but what was more, coincidentally they began to receive firearms and ammunition from European traders. Instantly the Sioux were invincible. They had the advantage over the Indians of the West who had no arms and over those of the East who had no horses. With this advantage, the Sioux held command of the heart of the northern buffalo range to become the masters of the Plains.

The role of men among the Sioux, as was true for all Plains tribes, was that of hunter and warrior. Hunting was an arduous task. The single hunter in search of deer must be wary, know how to stay off-wind of his quarry, how to shoot his arrow with uncanny accuracy. The Indian was a skilful bowman – he shot so power-fully that his arrow could completely penetrate a buffalo; he could hit his mark at 50 yards with absolute certainty and release his arrows more rapidly than bullets could be fired from a six-shooter.

The communal hunt, as opposed to the in-dividual hunter going after game on his own time, was highly organized. Scouts were sent out from the village to seek out the location of the herd. Once sighted, the men reported the appear-ance and numbers by riding their horses zigzag at the horizon, the distance they rode indicating the size of the herd. Immediately, the police society assigned by the tribal executives or "Shirt Wearers" saw to it that no one started ahead lest the herd be frightened. Hunters who disobeyed this rule had their tepees slashed to pieces by the police.

When the signal was given by the leaders of the hunt, the riders pursued the stampeding buffalo. Seeking out a two-year old cow whose meat was tender and whose hide the proper size and thickness for robes, the hunter rode close to the left side of the fleeing beast. Here he could shoot his arrow into the heart. Some men could kill from two to three animals in this way, others were completely unsuccessful. The rightful owner claimed his animal by the painted markings on the nock of his arrow as each man had his own arrow mark. Those who did not make a kill were entitled to tie a knot in the tail of a fallen beast and thereby claim a hindquarter. Some men were "tail tiers" most of their lives, but to the competent hunter they offered an opportunity of being charitable and thereby gaining status for his generosity.

Skills at Six

Young Sioux boys were taught the skills of hunting, war and horsemanship starting in their sixth year. To become a warrior was the am-bition of every young man. As early as twelve years old, youths were taken on war parties as water boys, tending to the needs of the experi-enced warriors and watering the horses. The reasons for war among the Plains Indians were manifold – the defense of tribal territory or the expansion of it to secure better hunting, the capture of horses from an enemy tribe or retaliation for the death of a family member.

Horses were the basis of Sioux economy. With its appearance, the "holy dog" made the Sioux thoroughly mobile. Now they could hunt the buffalo much more effectively and over a much wider range. It was a well-known fact that the men with the fastest horses lived in the largest tepees. On horse-stealing expeditions, a skilful thief often tried to capture the enemy's fleetest horse – one that he might have observed on a previous war party. Horses were used as the standard of barter; shamans' families were paid in horses for effecting a cure; those who made shields and war bonnets were paid in horses. Horses were given away to those who were owed gifts as well as to the needy. An individual's wealth rose with the number of horses he was able to accumulate, but he dare not keep them. His prestige and status were judged by the number he could give away. Owning property for property's sake was unthinkable; its sole value was that it could be shared with others.

A war party, often composed of no more than ten or twelve men, might combine both the purpose of horse stealing and vengeance for the death of a warrior. A shaman versed in the ways of war – who could foresee where the enemy camp lay, who could see around hills and ridges – was invited to join as war leader. The party might travel many days and cover several hundred miles. When close to enemy territory,

**Famous portrayals
of Indian life**
FAR LEFT: Charles
Russell's *Buffalo Hunt*
FAR LEFT BELOW:
Charles Russell's
painting, *Jumped*
LEFT: Karl Bodmer's
Mandan Indians,
two warriors in full
ceremonial regalia
BELOW: Portrait by
George Catlin of the
Mandan chief Four
Bears wearing a shirt
decorated with symbols
of his exploits

Counting "coup"
A Plains Indian strikes
his defeated enemy

the men traveled under the cover of darkness, resting unseen during the daytime in the protection of the wooded bottomlands. When at last they reached the proximity of the enemy village, they sought out a vantage point, sometimes as much as ten miles distant, to spy on the encampment. Here they might spend a day observing the village, drawing maps in the dust with a stick to plan the raid, watching the movements in the village, especially to learn where the horses were pastured at night.

Paint for Battle

Before dawn on the morning of the attack, the men prepared themselves for battle. They painted themselves in special colors, marked zigzag lightning lines on their horses' legs to give them speed, partook of medicines to assure themselves power and gave some to their horses too. They dressed themselves in their finest clothes, for it was only fitting if one died on the battlefield that he be properly attired to enter the next world, "The Land of Many Tepees." Next they took up their painted buffalo-hide shields, painted by a shaman with magical protective devices received in visions from the supernatural. Those who had paid a shaman two horses for a war bonnet of golden eagle feathers put them on. The power of Wakinyan, the god of thunder and lightning, whose emissary was the eagle or thunderbird, protected one from the arrows of the enemy. When everyone was readied, the Wolf Dreamer, wearing a wolfskin over his head, performed special propitiation ceremonies. The warriors walked their horses around hoping they would urinate so that they would be able to run faster. Then they sang their death song:

Now, tremble, O enemy tribe,
I send forth a voice.
Tremble, in a sacred manner,
All sitting, tremble.

Now, in the predawn darkness, they would leave their hideout and stealthily ride toward the enemy's village. And at the moment of dawn, the warriors would charge, galloping headlong into the grazing pony herd, cutting them out and running them off, perhaps as many as 100 head.

It was customary for the Plains Indians to keep their prize horses – fast ponies with proven endurance – each picketed close outside the owner's tepee. Alerted to the loss of their horse herd, they were thereby enabled to react quickly and pursue the thieves on their fastest horses. Aware of this, the war party would frequently split up, with the war leader assigning two or three men to hurry the horses toward home while the more experienced warriors would stay to parry the enemy's attack and also to do their best to collect scalps.

The opponents might now shoot at one another with arrows, but frequently the battle ended up in hand-to-hand fighting with lance

An early map of North
America showing the
distribution of some of
the Indian tribes. It was
drawn by Herbert and
published in 1810 in
Pinkerton's World Atlas

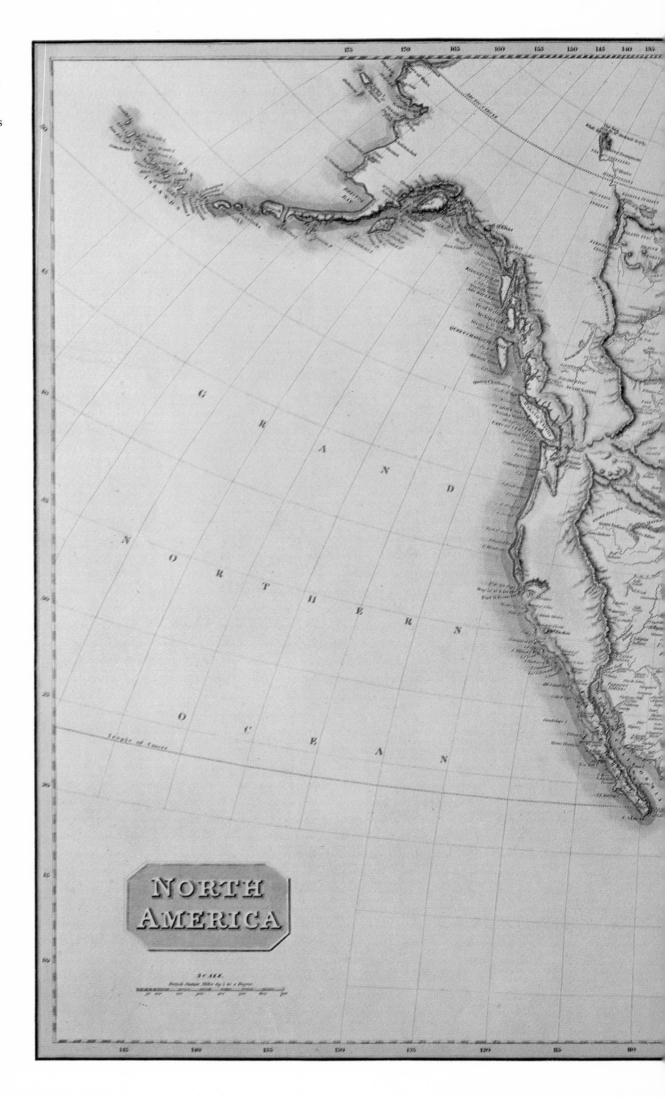

and war club. The principal object was to strike the enemy, to count "coup" and thereby earn points for one's war record. Among the Sioux, the first to strike an adversary earned four points, the second three points, and so on. A man might kill an enemy with an arrow from a distance and receive no points as such, or a fifth man might kill and scalp a victim and be entitled to nothing. In practice, however, when one killed an enemy, the victor was entitled to paint a red hand on his shirt and on his horse, but a scalp was not reckoned in this system. The scalp had another purpose.

Eagle Feathers
A man who earned a first coup was entitled to wear a golden eagle feather upright at the back of his head. Men earning second, third and fourth coups wore feathers at different angles as badges of their bravery.

If the attackers were successful in repulsing the enemy, counting coup and taking scalps, they hastily withdrew and followed after their companions with the stolen horses. If the contest were close, they might well have lost one or two of their own. Since the thieves were usually outnumbered, their compatriots' bodies could rarely be retrieved, and had to be left on the battlefield, to merciless scalping and mutilation by the enemy.

Upon reaching home, the warriors painted their faces black and rode into camp. If they had lost one of their party, four days of mourning were prescribed. Women wailed and the female relatives of any fallen warrior would cut short their hair, slash their arms and even cut off the first joint of their little finger. On the fourth day all grieving ceased, for now was the time for a victory dance, where the people celebrated, honoring in song and dance the exploits of the tribe's warriors. A scalp of one of the enemy, tied on a stick, would be given to the mother or sister of a fallen man with the words, "Here is your son. Now his spirit may join his body. Now

Braids and beads
FAR LEFT: Chief Ouray
of the Ute tribe
LEFT: A Nez Percé
woman wearing a
basket-woven hat;
otherwise her regalia
repeats many of the
chief's motifs: earrings,
braided hair and an
abundance of beads

he will be permitted to enter the 'Land of Many Lodges.' Dance with this and rejoice for your son is now one.''

The Indians believed that hair continued to grow after death and was, in truth, akin to the spirit and to life everlasting. One's own hair cuttings and fingernail pairings were buried in a secret place, lest someone find them and gain mastery of one's spirit. Throughout the Plains, scalping resulted in a vicious circle. Everyone was busy putting people together again. Any scalp would do; a woman's, even a child's served the purpose of reuniting the spirits.

Scalps as Symbols

It has been said that the Europeans introduced scalping. This is not so. It is true that the French and English paid bounties which may have increased the practice, but that is all. Among Indians, the custom of scalping was based upon a philosophical concept surrounded with ceremony and deep-rooted tradition, none of which

was so in Europe. Unlike an adversary's head presented on a platter to a king, the scalp was not a trophy, it was a symbol.

In order for a man to achieve true success in life, he had to seek a dream vision. Young men, under instruction from a shaman, "went to the hill" for several days to fast and pray, smoking a pipe to propitiate the gods. The hope was that an emissary of *Wakan Tanka*, "The Great Holy," the Bear or Wolf, the Deer or the Thunder would give him instructions, rules and, above all, "power." Power was a force emanating from the gods which enabled men to achieve things beyond the capacity of ordinary mortals. Power enabled one to be a masterful hunter, to cure sickness, to foretell the future, to see around corners, to be invincible in battle. Instructions might include how to paint protective devices on shields or directions for the preparation of a medicine bundle. Rules might forbid an individual to eat certain foods lest misfortune befall him.

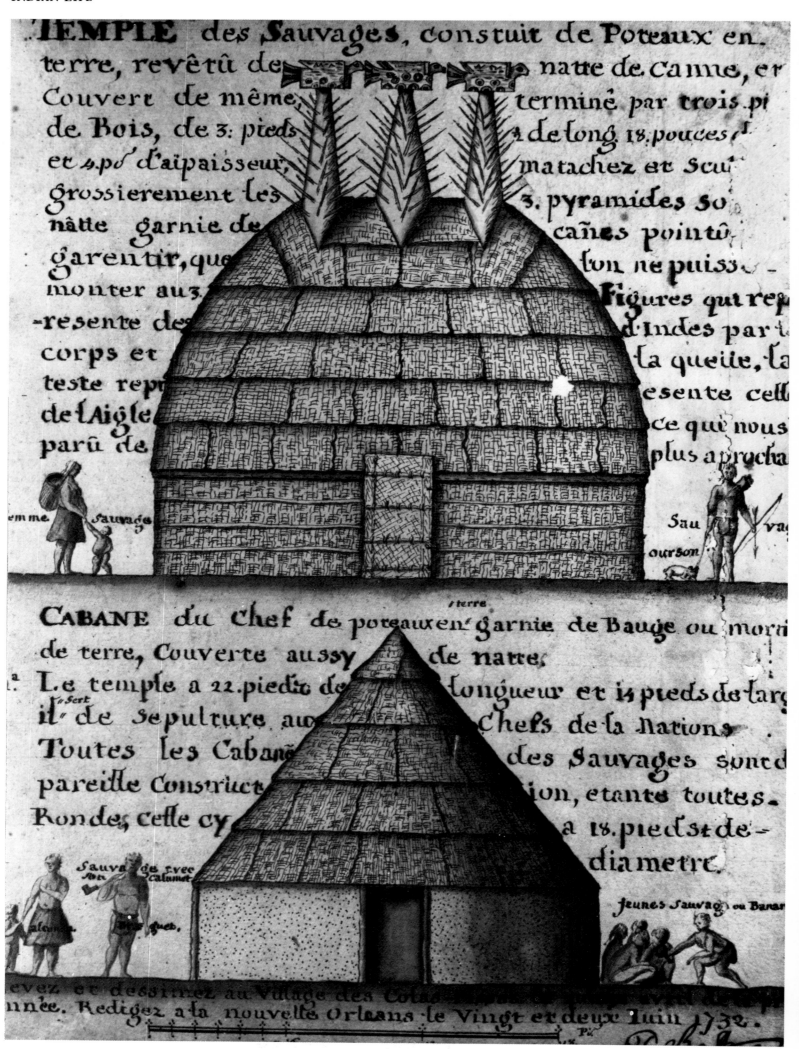

TEMPLE des Sauvages, construit de Poteaux en terre, revêtû de nate de canne, et Couvert de même termine par trois pi de Bois, de 3. pieds de long 18. pouces et 4 po d'aïpaisseur, matachez et scu grossierement les 3. pyramides so nâtte garnie de cañes pointû garentir, que ton ne puiss monter auz Figures qui rep -resente des d'Indes par corps et la queue, la teste rep esente cell de l'Aigle ce qui nous parû de plus aprocha

femme Sauvage Sau ourson

CABANE du Chef de poteaux en garnie de Bauge ou mort de terre, Couverte aussy de nate, terre Le temple a 22. pieds de longueur et 15 pieds de larg il de Sepulture au Chefs de la Nations Toutes les Caban des Sauvages sontd pareille Construct ion, etantes toutes Rondes, celle cy a 18. pieds de diametre

Sauvage avec Son Calumet jeunes Sauvag ou Banar

evez et dessines au Village des Col nnée. Redigez a la nouvelle Orléans le Vingt et deux Juin 1732.

Dreams and Cults

Men who had dreamed of the Bear were noted as specialists in curing, Wolf Dreamers specialized in warfare. Throughout the many bands, the dreamers formed themselves into little cults – the Elk Dreamers, the Deer Dreamers, and so forth. From time to time they performed before the people, testing their power against rival cults by spitting out grasshoppers which adversaries had shot at them. The *heyokas*, dreamers of the Thunder, whose speciality was finding lost articles, plunged their arms in scalding water unharmed in order to impress the people with the power of their magic.

The epitome of the vision quest was the annual Sun Dance. Here as the bands gathered for the great summer council, men who had vowed to "dance gazing at the Sun" prepared themselves for the ordeal. Like the Mandan participants in the Okipa, the volunteers were suspended from a tall pole by thongs attached to skewers thrust through their chests. Gazing at the Sun, they danced for several hours, finally to tear themselves loose. Those who completed the Sun Dance were entitled, after further instructions, to paint their hands red, a symbol of priesthood. Now they could officiate at important ceremonies, now they could speak in the secret tongue known only to the religious leaders.

Some young men, foreseeing the difficulties of the hunt and the dangers of warfare, the extremely rigorous and demanding life men must play, claimed to have dreamed that they were to assume the role of women. These transvestites, living together in tepees outside the regular camp circle, dressed as women and performed women's tasks – the tanning of hides and the embroidery with porcupine quills. Often their skills exceeded those of the women themselves. The Plains Indian tolerated the homosexual, but felt that after death his spirit, like that of the murderer, remained in limbo, never entering the Land of Many Lodges.

The Middle West

Close along the shores of the majestic and muddy Mississippi River just north of the great delta lived the elegant and highly sophisticated Natchez. Unlike the democracies of the Northeast, theirs was an autocratic theocracy of a most unusual nature. Their king or "Sun" was the absolute ruler of nine or more villages numbering over 4,000 souls and was first encountered by the French in the late seventeenth century. So revered, so esteemed was the Sun that he was waited on by a retinue of dignitaries, carried in a litter from place to place, bedecked in a feather mantle and a plumed crown.

He resided on the plaza in an especially large house set atop a ten-foot-high mound. As chief priest his residence was close by the temple. This building, too, was placed on a mound, and while similar to his, was adorned with two carved eagles perched on the roof. Here the sacred fire was kept, together with the remains of former Suns. Only the Sun himself and specially appointed priests might tend the fire and guard the bones.

Sons and Suns

It was the Sun who appointed war chiefs, as well as other dignitaries, from among his relatives. They became known as Little Suns. The Sun might not, however, appoint his children to these positions. They fell into a social class below that of the Suns and became Nobles. The Sun's word was law; he received all the worldly necessities – food, drink, attire, even huge pearls for his adornment – as a kind of tribute from his people. He could command an army of workers or warriors at will and they served him without recompense.

The female Suns, likewise, held a phenomenally high and powerful position in the Natchez society. There appears to have been a principal matriarch and it was she who selected from among her brothers or sons the Great Sun. The social structure of the Natchez was complicated. It was divided into several classes, the Suns at the peak. They were followed by the Nobles below whom were the Honored Men. Finally, at the lowest rung, were the commoners referred to as Stinkards. These poor people were considered as nothing more than mere scum, to be treated like dogs. In addition the society was divided along sexual lines with descent reckoned from the females. Thus the children of the female Suns were Suns, the children of female Nobles were Nobles, the children of female Honored Men were Honored Men. The offspring of Stinkards were obviously Stinkards. But the children of males, either Suns or Nobles or Honored Men, each dropped a class so that the child of a Sun became a Noble and so on. The Suns, whether men or women, could not intermarry. Strangely, everyone except the Stinkards had to choose a spouse from outside his class, and that class was the Stinkard!

What is almost as intriguing as the fact that such a genealogical system was devised is that the complex records were kept without benefit of pen or paper.

Throughout the Mississippi drainage area, both to the east and west, dwelt mound-building nations similar in many respects to the Natchez. Whether their social structures and kinship systems were as complicated is not really known. But such people as the Chitimacha, Biloxi and Alabama as well as the Atakapa, the Tunica

Natchez temple and the dwelling-house of a Sun

83

and the great Caddo Confederacy, though often enemies, were agriculturists who were culturally quite similar.

To the north in what is now Missouri and Arkansas lived the Osage, Siouan-speaking farmers. A powerful and warlike group, their way of life was a reflection not only of aspects of southern traits, but also those of the eastern woodlands. Reminiscent of the South, their towns were divided between the factions of War and Peace. The War people ate only meat while the Peace people were vegetarians. On the other hand, their dwellings were patterned after those of the Powhatan, though here they were covered with hides as well as mats.

The Peace people chose a chief from among their elders or "Little Old Men" as did the War people. Each of the divisions was divided into several clans – the Elk and Pumas and Bear, the Deer and Crayfish and even the Thunder. The headmen of these clans were hereditary. Children were born into the clan of their mothers and were taught to respect their affiliation with deep loyalty.

Exchange of Gifts

With the Osage, marriage was largely a matter of individual choice by the prospective partners, but their status, wealth and industriousness were subjects of concern and approval by the respective families. The young man would ask his relatives to make the overtures. Gifts were exchanged, the boy's family bringing horses, the girl's relatives offering clothing, utensils and sumptuous feasts.

Possessions – the lodge, the clothing, the utensils, the gardens, even the children – belonged to the wife. An Osage man lived, in fact, with his wife's family, for whom he was expected to be a good provider. A considerate husband might decide to marry another woman, and might even be candidly asked to do so by his first wife. A second wife could help maintain the household and garden, but more important, she allowed the first wife time to enjoy parties and other gatherings. Younger sisters were often chosen as second wives for the reason that the two wives could be expected to get along well.

Bathed and Perfumed

Osage women, like many Indians, were fastidious, bathing daily in the streams. After bathing they anointed themselves with a perfume of columbine seed, calamus root and horsemint. Girls were most often escorted to their baths by

matrons, for fear of being spied on.

At childbirth the women built a little hut for the expectant mother to which she retired. Here she was assisted by her mother and other female members of the family. The newborn was ceremonially bathed and given a name – like "The Wolf" or "The Small Beaver." Later, men might earn names from important exploits, a typical example being "The Great War Chief." Nicknames were conferred because of a physical peculiarity, as implied by the name "The Lips," or as the result of a habit or style in battle as in "The-One-Who-Crawls-on-The-Ground."

Culturally the Osage, like many of their Siouan-speaking neighbors, the Oto and Missouri, the Kansa, the Omaha, Ponca, and the Quapaw were a combination of woodland farming peoples and prairie buffalo hunters. Before the advent of the horse the Osage hunted buffalo on foot, by surrounding them. Men supplied with blankets formed a great V at the head of a gorge. While other men drove the herd of stampeding beasts toward and through the arms of the V, the men stationed along the wedge frantically waved their blankets. Yelling and hallooing, they frightened the onrushing buffalo toward the apex of the V and over the cliff. At the bottom, men with clubs beat to death those animals not already killed in the fall. Indians killed buffalo in this manner for thousands of years; it was quite an efficient method.

New Improved Method

After the appearance of horses sometime during the eighteenth century, the Osage were quick to see the advantages of this animal. By increasing their mobility the hunters could more easily surround herds of buffalo they might not otherwise reach. Moreover, they could now be assured of an even greater kill. It was after the crops had been harvested and cached that the Osage left their villages for the fall hunt. Strict rules were made to guard against the buffalo being frightened away and police were appointed to enforce the rules. Over anxious individuals were prevented from hunting on their own lest the herd should escape. Even with the fleetest of horses surprise was essential.

If the Osage were successful hunters, they were even more noted as warriors. Their reputation was recognized, especially by the Pawnee and Comanche to the southwest. War parties, sometimes consisting of no more than five or six men, were organized by a war leader.

Thatched hut village of the Caddo Indians

85

RIGHT: *Elkskin dress* worn by a Sioux girl; its yoke is of solid beading, the breastplate of bone
FAR RIGHT: *Cheedobau*, an Oto Indian, holding an eagle-wing fan and brass pipe tomahawk of European manufacture

Most Osage adventures seem to have been retaliatory in nature, such as revenge for a relative killed in battle. An enemy's scalp was evidence of recompense.

Kindness and Torture
When captives were taken, mostly women and children, they were treated with kindness, sometimes as slaves, often as adopted members of the family. If, on the contrary, an enemy warrior's life was spared, he was brought home, tied to a stake and tortured by the women and young boys until he perished.

A successful war party returned in jubilance, but should a member have been killed, the war leader had to ask permission to enter the village. It was hoped that the relatives of the fallen warrior would accept restitution in some form of property, but if their anger and grief were great, the war leader might very well be killed. For the Osage war was a serious business.

In the Great Lakes region of the Middle West were many tribes – Algonquian-speaking peoples like the Ojibwa, the Miami, the Sauk and Fox and the Illinois. To the northwest, Siouan speakers also inhabited the area – the Kickapoo and Menomini and the Winnebago. This was forest land and prairie rich in wild game – elk, deer, moose and bear. Even buffalo abounded, especially in the West.

The Sauk and Fox were a typical example of these hunting and farming tribes. Living in what is now southern Wisconsin, the Sauk and Fox had long been neighbors and were frequently thought of as one nation. They did, however, maintain their separate councils and, interestingly, their individual characters. The Sauk were recognized as straightforward and direct in their dealings, prosperous as farmers and altogether an enlightened people.

Quite the Opposite
Not so the Fox. They seemed at odds with everyone. Warlike, indolent and greedy, they were not to be trusted and were accordingly feared, resented and thoroughly disliked. What kept such opposites together is a bit mysterious. Possibly it was a symbiotic relationship whereby the Fox profited from the Sauk's productivity, while the Sauk gained a powerful ally in war. They did, indeed, join forces to drive the Illinois from their territories and took for themselves the rich farmlands the Illinois had occupied.

As a woodlands people, the Sauk and Fox lived in bark-covered lodges, fashioned their canoes of bark as well as of logs. They placed their towns close to the waterways, for the rivers and streams were the Indians' highways. The women cultivated the usual crops along the fertile riverbanks in fields as large as several hundred acres. In the spring the maple trees were tapped for syrup. It was a land rich in wild fruits and berries and according to the famous Sauk leader, Black Hawk, they never went hungry for they always had plenty. During the autumn hunt the Indians left their villages and traveled west in search of the buffalo and elk in the prairie country. Returning to their towns at the first sign of winter, they rekindled their fires to sit snug in their lodges till spring.

Time to Tell Tales
This was the time of year for storytelling, a time to recount the historical lore of the ancestors, the myths of the gods and supernatural beings.

The Sauk and Fox divided themselves into two separate divisions. Within each were several gens or clans given the names of their ancestors such as Bear or Sturgeon or Thunder and these became the totem of each family. Membership was by descent through the father's line and with it fell valuable property rights as well as important religious responsibilities.

Knowledge of the origin of the clans came through visions. Long ago when young men went alone to the wilderness seeking "power" from the supernatural, one man, for example, received instructions and rules of behavior from the Bear. These included the proper preparation of a bundle to contain items like the claw of a bear, the dried head of a special bird, and other objects considered sacred by the animal helper. If and when the instructions were adhered to precisely, the young man became possessed of superhuman qualities. Such might be the ability to foretell events, find lost objects and cure sickness by mysteriously causing the tent to shake violently as voices were heard and sparks shot about.

Bundles were handed down from father to son and the inheritor became the "keeper of the bundle," in a sense the priest head of the clan. The bundles of sacred objects were ceremonially opened during such auspicious occasions as spring planting and autumn harvest. At these times the clan members gathered to worship with song and dance, prayers and feasting, the proper delicacy being the flesh of a sacred albino dog.

Young boys were expected to seek a vision; one might receive sufficient power to become a shaman. Now he would be eligible to learn the feats of magic and to effect cures. At birth, boys were dubbed a color by their parents. Possibly the firstborn would be a black, the second white, and so forth. Throughout life they retained the designation and it determined on which side one played in competitive games.

The Southeast

Far to the south was the land of the Creek, the Choctaw and the Chickasaw. Here, in what is now Georgia, Alabama and Mississippi lived the descendants of the Temple Mound builders.

When De Soto invaded the Southeast in 1540 he observed the sacred Temple Mounds of the Creeks. This was a highly organized society which appointed from among its outstanding warriors a *mico* or king. So honored was he that he was carried around on a litter, his elaborately tattooed body the badge of his prowess in war. His council was composed of retired warriors, elders of recognized wisdom with whom he met daily. In a sense the Creeks were a confederacy composed of towns, first established in the northern part of their territory, later joined by other villages to the south. The original communities were known as "White" or "Peace" towns, the more recent ones were referred to as "Red" or "War" towns. It was from the Red town that the war chief was chosen – in reality a priest versed in the mysteries of successful battle.

Boys were taught the skill and techniques of war early, for this was the profession to which men aspired. War was waged for a variety of reasons, sometimes for conquest, sometimes to procure slaves, sometimes in retaliation for the loss of a beloved warrior. Indian attack was one of stealth, and most often at dawn. Men were usually killed, women and children taken captive. Scalps were brought home to celebrate the victory. War was a sternly cruel business and of first importance.

But all was not war and desolation. There was the necessary work of hunting and farming, there were games, and there were ceremonies associated with marriage and the new crops and death. One of the favorite games was lacrosse, which the Indians originally devised as a war training exercise. The players, often

Indians seek their rights
A delegation of the Sauk, Fox and Iowa tribes in Washington at the beginning of the twentieth century

89

representatives of different villages, were supplied with little rackets. With these they tossed a small ball, endeavoring to hit the opposing team's goalpost set up at the opposite end of the field of play. There were no boundaries and few rules. A player might run for hundreds of yards or even miles eluding his opponents to achieve a great end play. Stakes, in the form of costumes, food, in fact all manner of possessions, were offered up. For Indians gambling was as much a part of a contest as was the game itself.

Summer Celebration

In the early summer, just as the first corn was ripe, the Creeks held a most impressive ceremony. This was the time of purification and renewal. People busied themselves sweeping the village paths, destroying old clothes, breaking up their clay pots and bowls and extinguishing all fires. A new fire was set in the plaza where the men for four days were harangued by their leaders as they purified themselves with a powerful emetic. The whole affair was handsomely climaxed by a great celebration of feasting on the green corn, preening in new clothes, relighting the fires, and endless dancing with songs of rejoicing. And thus, the new year began, clean and fresh and joyous.

The Indians of Florida were a majestic people. Their kings, resplendent in their very nakedness, ruled with the power of a benevolent despot. Their queens, highly honored, were borne on litters attended by maidens in waiting. They waged war savagely, wars in which no quarter was given. By scalping, mutilating, hacking off the arms and legs of their captives, they destroyed any chance of their enemies' evil power contaminating the spirit world.

Pawns of the Spanish

In the 1500s, the Calusa were most powerful. As early as 1513 a fleet of seagoing canoes, manned by Calusa warriors, drove off the ships of Ponce de León. Parenthetically, avaricious Ponce just couldn't give up; he was hunting not only for gold, but for the mythical Fountain of Youth, both at the expense of the Indians. He never found either, but did receive a fatal poisoned dart in the back, shot from a blowgun by an Indian disturbed at his blatant trespassing.

The proud Tunicas, first encountered by the French, later became pawns of the Spanish. Like the Apalachee to the north, who were eventually crushed by the Creeks under English domination, the Tunicas were completely subdued by the mid-eighteenth century. Here in Florida began a pattern in which European contestants played natural Indian enemies one against the other to the Indians' ultimate defeat and in this instance to their total annihilation.

North of Florida, along the coastlines of the Carolinas and Virginia, English explorers, as early as 1584, first met the people of Pomeiok and later the Pamlico. Said one explorer, Captain Arthur Barlow, of them, "We found these people gentle, loving and faithful, lacking all guile and trickery. It was as if they lived in a golden age of their own."

The Eastern Seaboard

Typical of the eastern seaboard people of this time were the Algonquian-speaking Powhatans who welcomed Captain John Smith and his Jamestown colonists in 1607. Powhatan, the king, had carved himself a small empire. From his seat at the falls of the James River, now Richmond, Virginia, he controlled nearly all the tide-water country and received homage from some 200 villages. Powhatan was not only powerful, but exceedingly wealthy from the tribute he received in hides and corn and freshwater pearls. From his vassals Powhatan could muster a considerable force of warriors. With them he could conquer and plunder town after town. Following a surprise attack of flaming arrows setting fire to the mat-covered wigwams, the warriors then subdued the victims in hand-to-hand fighting with murderous war clubs.

While some of the villages were open and unprotected, the majority were stockaded. Here the fields were located beyond the palisades where the women raised several varieties of corn including dent, flint and even popcorn. They also grew squash, beans and tobacco. These they not only enjoyed freshly cooked from the gardens, but they dried and stored great quantities in underground caches against wintertime. To this diet was added all manner of dried fruits, wild vegetables and roots. Meat, too, was a staple, deer being especially favored, while fish caught in weirs were relished.

Ornaments and Ancestors

Clothing was made by the women, themselves wearing a skin apron, a string of shell beads and little more. The men's dress was much the same. Softly tanned deerskin robes and turkey-feathered mantles added warmth in winter. Powhatan himself owned a great cape of buffalo hide ornamented with shells.

Women wore their hair long over the shoulders, while the men shaved the side of the heads leaving an upright crest or roach down the center. This they embellished with feathers. Pearls, worn at the ear lobes, were especially prized as adornments, as were plates of copper suspended from the neck.

The Powhatans believed in a multiplicity of supernatural spirits called *mantoacs* and a supreme power or *Manatou* which controlled the universe. Great reverence was accorded the ancestors. The mummified remains of tribal leaders or *weroans* were preserved and guarded in a special house. Powhatan's house was in reality a temple. At the rear, in the shadows of an unlit room, sat a carved image of a man – the likeness of the gods.

All along the Atlantic seaboard, from Virginia to Maine, the Algonquian-speaking peoples held sway. In what is now New Jersey and eastern Pennsylvania, the Leni Lenapi or Delawares were dominant. Their way of life, though similar to that of the Powhatans, was far less stylized, far less formal. They had no hereditary kings, but leaders, elected in council from among the elders.

The Northeast

Sometime, almost before the memory of men, groups of Iroquois-speaking peoples, kin to the southern Cherokee and Tuscarora, began moving north. Driving a wedge through the heartland of the Algonquian-speaking Shawnee and Susquahannas, the Delawares and Mohegans to the east and the Illinois, the Erie and the Miami to the west, the invading Iroquois established their villages in what is now New York State. Here they set up a sophisticated matrilineal government. Austere sachems, nominated by the female clan mothers, formed the ruling councils of the tribes. Under the imaginative statesmanship of one Hiawatha (not to be mistaken for Longfellow's poetic protagonist) he helped form a league. Composed of the Seneca, Cayuga and Onondaga, the "Keepers of the Fire" to the west and the Oneida and Mohawks to the east, the Iroquois referred to themselves as the "Longhouse." The Senecas were known as "The Great Hill People," while the Mohawks were "The Keepers of the Eastern Door." With the arrival of the Tuscaroras from North Carolina in the eighteenth century, the Iroquois were known as the Six Nations and became the most political Indian force in Colonial America.

Their long, elm-bark-covered houses were set secure within stockades. Acres upon acres surrounded the villages. According to John Sullivan, the American general who ravaged the towns in 1779, he was amazed to observe the largest cornfields in North America.

An Experienced Spouse

The Iroquois, like many Indians, divided themselves into clans, the Bear, the Wolf, the Deer and so forth. Descent was reckoned through the mother's line and one's closest loyalties were to her family. In marriage, however, a spouse had to be sought from outside one's clan and the new husband moved in with his wife's family. The women arranged the marriages, generally choosing a young man for an older, often widowed woman and conversely an older man for a younger girl.

This system had the great advantage of assuring the young person an experienced marriage partner. It obviated the risk of two young things floundering in the mysteries of sex and marriage only to jeopardize the relationship. Furthermore, the young bride was assured the security of an experienced hunter who knew well how to provide, a successful warrior with status and position. The young groom, on the other hand, had the advantage of a partner who was wealthy in property, who owned fields of corn, beans and squash and who was knowledgeable in the ways of parenthood and housekeeping.

The role of women in Iroquois society was indeed significant. Not only did the women arrange the marriages, own the utensils, the houses and the fields, but they alone decided who should be eligible for the positions of sachem. And their authority extended further; if a clan matriarch should disapprove of a sachem's actions, she could dispose of him forthwith.

The Iroquois men were the hunters and warriors and some became shamans and priests and council members. At the "Longhouse" the elders met to decide by unanimous vote civic matters as well as those related to making war or peace.

The North

The northlands of Canada and Alaska vary not only in terrain, but in flora and fauna. Yet with

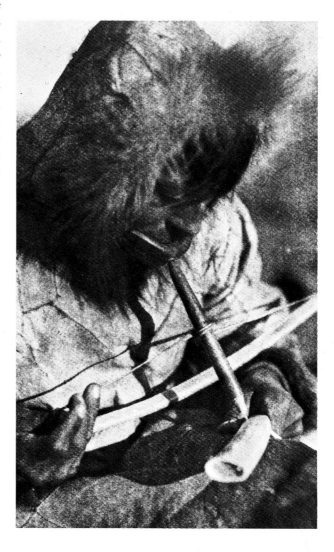

Faces from the Far North

RIGHT: Musician from Coronation Gulf, north of Hudson's Bay
FAR RIGHT: Eskimo woman bejewelled with nose ring and lip beads

deadfalls. Unlike the communal buffalo hunting of the Plains, most of the hunting was done individually. It was arduous work that required as much patience as skill. In winter men hunted on snowshoes. On these they could track a wounded moose for miles and drag home its carcass on a birchbark toboggan.

All-Purpose Birchbark

This north country was the land of the birch tree and from its paperlike bark these people fashioned their graceful canoes, box containers, even conical horns for calling moose. Instead of using hides, they covered their tepees in great sheets of birchbark.

Small boxes designed to hold valuables were often decorated by scraping away the surface of the bark to reveal a darker layer. In this manner the artist produced silhouette-like animal forms. Utilitarian containers were cut in large patterns from pieces of bark, stitched with roots and, as with the canoes, the seams were covered with pitch. Some were used as cooking vessels. When filled with water, heated stones were dropped in to make the water boil. Boiled meat and broth were favorites among all the North American tribes. Stone boiling was commonly utilized by those who made clay cooking pots as well as those who fashioned watertight baskets. The Plains Indians with neither wooden containers, clay pots nor baskets, used the paunch of a buffalo, supported on stakes, as a receptacle for boiling.

Stone boiling had one minor disadvantage. When the hot stones struck the cold water, a certain amount of flaking occurred which left tiny sandy particles in the water and in turn the broth. And this grit was especially hard on the teeth, wearing them down prematurely.

Ingenious Design

The birchbark tepee, like its skin counterpart of the Plains, was an amazingly efficient structure. With a smoke hole at the top and the fire placed directly below, the conical-shaped dwelling was uniquely functional. In the coldest of weather, the decreased volume of air at the top reduced the amount of heat required to warm the lower living space. The result was that the tepee was entirely comfortable. In a sense, the tepee-dwellers lived warm and snug in their chimneys. Interestingly, the sides of the Plains' hide tepees could be rolled up around the base in summertime, making a veritable parasol of the lodge. The tepee in no matter what region was most ingeniously designed.

Far to the northwest of the Algonquians lived the Athabascan hunters. Their fare was the moose, caribou, musk ox and hare. One tribe, the Hare, depended so heavily on the big rabbit that they were given its name. Owing to the fact that a seven-year epidemic nearly wiped out the hares, the designation was hardly a lucky one

this variation there is one thing in common – long and frigid winters. This makes for a most harsh and stark environment for all who live there. From the banks of Labrador to the Bering Sea, it was the country of moose and caribou, musk ox and polar bear, walrus and whale. Dense forests in the east stretched west to the barren tundra wastelands of Alaska. This was the land of rugged Indians. And to the far north was the most harsh of all environments, the frozen Arctic, the habitat of the Eskimo.

Algonquian-speaking tribes like the Montagnais and Naskapi occupied territory east of Hudson Bay, while to the west were the Algonquians, the Cree and Saulteaux. The Dog Ribs, Yellowknives, and Hares, the Tanaina, Taltans and Athabascans lived in the far northwestern parts of Canada and central Alaska.

Among the Algonquians, men were assigned hunting territories to which certain hunters held exclusive use. All manner of devices were employed, bows and arrows, traps, snares and

simply, a wrestling match was organized. The winner won the woman.

Clever and Cheerful

Among the world's more ingenious people, the Eskimo rates high. No man without exceeding wit and unmatchable courage could hope to survive the deep penetrating cold, the endless winter nights of the inhospitable Arctic. Unbelievably, the Eskimo did it, and did it very happily.

The Eskimo were as clever as they were cheerful. Among their inventions were the harpoon and kayak, snow goggles, the dog sled, a stone oil lamp and the dome-shaped snowhouse called an igloo. The kayak, a skin-covered canoe, was completely decked, which permitted the paddler to roll over and upright himself without fear of either sinking or even getting wet.

As hunters, the Eskimos' daring and patience were unbeaten. In great skin-covered open boats called *umiaks*, men would go to sea in search of whales and walrus. Harpooning demanded an extremely close approach to these dangerous animals. Hurling the harpoon, a spear with a detachable point, deep into the flesh required accuracy and skill. When struck, whales dived at tremendous speed. To prevent their loss, a long rawhide rope was attached to the spear point, equipped with inflated bladders. These little buoys enabled the hunters to keep track of their quarry.

Seals were caught in a similar manner, harpooned by a single hunter in his kayak. Sometimes seals could be surprised sunning themselves on an ice floor, which gave the hunter an advantage in the time it took the seals to dive into the water.

Hunting Holes

Hunting through the ice was another method. Seals made breathing holes hidden from view by the snow. The hunters often depended on their dogs to scent out the location, yet men themselves were often just as capable of discovering the holes by the same technique. Hours, indeed often several days of patient waiting might be required before a seal would turn up at a hole. When by chance it appeared, the hunter was ready to plunge his harpoon into his prey.

One of the more innovative hunting techniques was especially useful in downing a polar bear or wolf. Here the hunter rolled a strip of baleen or whalebone into a tight coil, the end of which had been sharpened to a point. This was inserted into a chunk of frozen blubber. The innocent-looking bait was then placed at a spot known to be the haunt of an animal. A wolf, later devouring the morsel, would soon fall prey to the Eskimo's deviousness. The blubber after a short time in the animal's stomach would melt, releasing the baleen spring. The sharp ends

for the Indians. With the scarcity of game, the people starved.

The Athabascan tribes were loosely divided into hunting bands, each with a prescribed territory. There were no headmen, but during times of conflict a war chief was appointed. About the only governmental controls that existed were the decisions rendered by the elders in settling quarrels in the event recompense had not been made.

As was the custom with many Indians, women were confined to a separate hut during the menstrual period as well as when giving birth. The power of women was much feared. Among the Plains tribes, for example, women might not touch a man's weapons, neither his shield nor his war bonnet lest they become contaminated and in turn ineffectual.

Polygamy was commonly practiced by these northern tribes. Several groups observed a unique method of settling disputes arising when one man coveted another man's wife. Very

Nootka and Kwakiutl
RIGHT: Interior of a
Nootka house as
depicted by John
Webber
BELOW: A Kwakiutl
chief holds a broken
copper, symbol of the
destruction of wealth
FAR RIGHT BELOW:
Chief's daughter
wearing a cedar-bark
hat ornamented with a
totemic design

would puncture the animal's insides and internal bleeding would result. Now the wily hunter had only to follow a trail of blood to his victim.

The Eskimo villages were little more than bands of hunters. There were no headmen, there was no government. People lived simply by rules of behavior established for generations, rules that demanded the utmost in cooperation and sharing. While a man might hunt alone, he carefully shared his kill with everyone. Someday he himself might be less fortunate and would welcome the generosity of a neighbor.

The Eskimos shared everything – tools, clothing, food, dog teams, even their wives. It was expected that a host would offer a visiting guest his woman for the night. This honored the woman and demonstrated the man's generosity. It is true, both he and his wife expected something in return.

Stab in the Back

Wife-sharing, however, in no way implied a looseness in the moral code. Faithfulness in marriage was expected of both sexes. On the other hand, a man enamored of another's wife might plan a tryst. More commonly, however, rather than trying to carry on an affair, he would plot the husband's murder. At the opportune moment, he would stab his victim in the back with his snow knife; Eskimos never fought face to face. Then the lover would abscond with his new woman to the safety of another village. Relatives of the murdered husband frequently planned revenge, with the result that Eskimo communities were sporadically torn by bloody feuds.

Eskimo religious beliefs were, to say the least, unstructured. They consisted essentially of a horde of busy, morbid and dangerous spirits which were to be avoided at all costs. They brought nothing but trouble, misfortune, sickness and death. Shamans, capable of such marvelous accomplishments as seeing events far away, could also diagnose sickness. Curing a patient meant removing the cause of illness. This the shaman did by ridding the body of splinters of bone or wood previously implanted either by a sorcerer or by the evil spirits themselves.

The Eskimo are a seeming paradox. Surviving most efficiently in the earth's harshest environment, comforted by the world's gloomiest religion, these northern hunters are recognized as among the happiest, most cheerful people of all mankind.

The Northwest Coast

The coasts of Alaska and British Columbia are a humid, narrow strip of pine-and-spruce-covered shorelines faced by the Pacific to the west and backed abruptly by mountains to the east. Deep blue rivers flowing through mighty fjords abound in salmon. Bear and deer and

INDIAN LIFE

RIGHT: *Fishing camp* on the Northwest coast
BELOW: *Wedding guests* arrive by boat for a Kwakiutl marriage ceremony
FAR RIGHT: *Ovick ivory figurine* from the Old Bering Sea culture, *c.* 300 B.C., probably associated with fertility rites

mountain goats were common and the ever-present raven frequented the dense forests. Whales, porpoises and seals roamed the coastal waters. And with this natural wealth, the Indians who lived there themselves became fabulously rich. Men like the Nootka and Haida, the Tlingit and the Tsimshian set their villages along the beaches, close to the source of their livelihood.

These were a warlike people; their wealth and consequent overpopulation helped to make them so. Valuable fishing sites were coveted and defended. Warriors wore armor of wooden slats and great carved wooden helmets. Some of these were fashioned as hugely grotesque faces, to awe the enemy. When captives were taken they were kept as slaves to do housework for the upper class.

Each of the many villages had its own chief, who generally inherited his position from his mother's clan. With this position went many rights and privileges. Fishing grounds, for example, belonged to the chief and among the Nootka, the renowned whalers of the Northwest Coast, it was the chief himself who threw the harpoon.

Status and wealth for these people were of paramount importance. They decorated their housefronts with monstrous paintings of their clan ancestors – the Bear, the Beaver, the Raven or perhaps the Whale. Before their planked houses they erected giant poles embellished with their family crests. Totem poles were, in fact, a genealogical record of the owner's family and advertised to all his position in the community. Nearly everything they used – carved mountain sheep horn ladles, bentwood boxes, canoes, even their paddles – was decorated with stylized representations of the mythical animal ancestors.

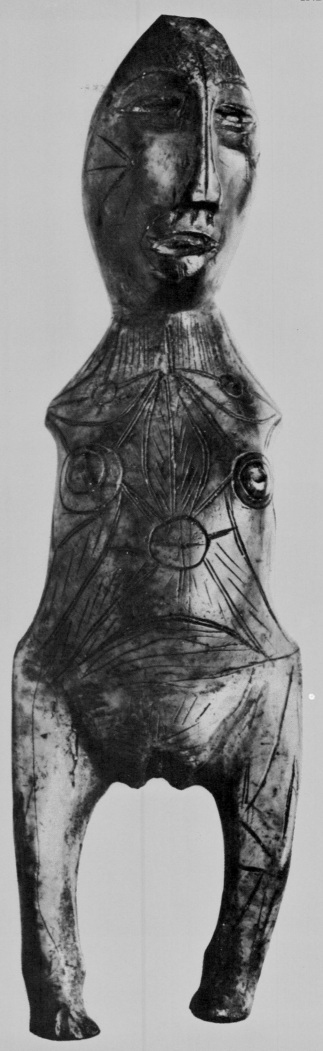

TATTANNAÆUK *Esquimaux Interpreter, named by the English in Hudson's Bay* **AUGUSTUS** *the faithful follower of Captains S.ᵗ John Franklin, & S.ᵗ Geo. Back, & D.ᵗ Richardson, in their Arctic land Expeditions in N. America.*

FAR LEFT: *Chief Sheik's house*, Fort Wrangle, Alaska; the totem pole displays frogs representing three women enslaved by the chief
FAR LEFT BELOW: *Eskimo hunter* with weapons and kayak as depicted in a painting by John Halkett

BELOW: *Carved mask*, made of wood with eyes and teeth of haliotis shell, of the Tlingit Indians of the Northwest Coast, probably early nineteenth century

Master Carvers

Aesthetically, the art of the Northwest Coast was the most elaborate and highly sophisticated of any in North America. As carvers, the men were unsurpassed. From the massive forms on the towering totem poles and grave markers to the delicate openwork on the carved handles of their little, black mountain goat horn spoons, the workmanship was masterful. Bowls were carved from a single log and decorated with incised clan motifs. These were painted in red and black and embellished with inlaid shells. Some were effigies in the form of a frog or bear, others almost life-size portraying a man on his back. These were used in the great feasts and ceremonial give-aways called Potlatches.

The art of the Northwest Coast was varied. Some was strikingly realistic as in the portrayal of the human face in certain of the dance masks. Most of it, however, was intricately stylized. Representations of animals became designs, the subject often being split down the back to form a right and left. The figure became recognizable only by familar marks – the beaver, for example, by his flat tail and immense incisor teeth.

While the men did carving, including the graceful canoes that might be as much as 50 feet in length, the women wove baskets of superior quality. They made capes and wrap-round skirts woven of shredded cedar bark. They also fashioned wide, conical basket hats whose design was perfect for shedding water in the rainy climate of the Northwest. The women at Chilkat wove blankets of mountain goat and puppy dog's hair, displaying the owner's crest in cryptic designs with muted yellows and blues outlined in black.

As is true for the majority of American Indians, the art forms of the Northwest Coast people were developed as embellishments to functional items. Even the totem poles exhibit this principle, for aesthetically handsome as they may appear, their purpose was strictly one

Life in the Northwest
FAR LEFT: Drawing by Alexander Malaspino of warrior in slat armor
CENTRE LEFT: Painting by Paul Kane of a Babine chief wearing a Chilkat blanket
BELOW: 1880's photograph of a coastal village, possibly Haida

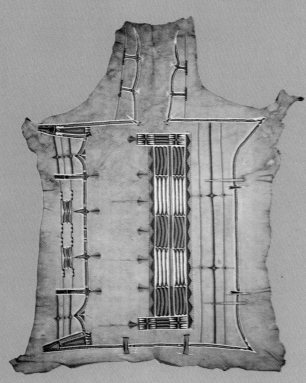

FAR LEFT ABOVE: *Sauk and Fox Indians* as depicted by Karl Bodmer
FAR LEFT: *Birch-bark box* made by members of the Cree tribe showing caribou and deer
ABOVE: *Cree chief* displaying his calumet or pipe stem in a painting by Paul Kane
LEFT: *Beaded robe* of buffalo hide worn by a Sioux woman

Decorative art in the North

RIGHT: A totemic design being painted on a cedar-bark hat
CENTRE RIGHT: Stylized totemic house post
FAR RIGHT: Painted housefronts and totem poles symbolizing the occupants' ancestry
BELOW: Forest of totems at Skidegate, Queen Charlotte Island, British Columbia

of displaying the owner's social position. The relatively recent concept of art for art's sake was unthought of by the Indian, and yet by harmoniously combining color with form to create a pleasing balance in the objects they designed for practical use, they achieved works of art. Almost as if innately, through generations of experience, uncounted years of trial and error, the object would turn out perfectly. Here was an artistic accomplishment that was not only remarkable in itself, but indisputable in its individuality.

No Two Alike

Unlike European art which to be good must be pleasing or striking to the eye, to be acceptable to the Indian, it must be correct. The Indian artist worked within rather rigid bounds determined in large part by natural resources and traditions. While, it is true, a variety of colors were found in certain areas in the form of plant dyes and earth colors, the most universally

ABOVE: *The Buffalo Hunt*, painting by Charles Russell
RIGHT: *Wolf mask* carved by a Nootka craftsman in the eighteenth century
FAR RIGHT: *Assiniboin Indians* hunting on snowshoes, as portrayed by Peter Rindishbacker

available colors were red ocher and black derived from charcoal. Thus this combination is found again and again in the earliest collected specimens of Indian art. Limitations, too, were imposed upon the craftsmen by cultural traditions. There was the proper way to carve a mask, the correct way to weave a blanket. Consequently, the forms and designs were often so distinctive that in most instances tribal identification was readily discernible. And yet with all this seeming rigidity and conformity to tribal patterns, the Indian artist was careful not to repeat, not to duplicate a finished product. Hence, no two rattles were identical, no two decorated boxes were the same. Each, on the contrary, was an expression of the individual craftsman. And it is this principle that renders the art of the American Indians enchantingly mysterious.

ABOVE: *Mythical animal ancestors* decorate a chief's housefront
CENTRE ABOVE: A *Remington painting* shows a participant in the sun dance.
FAR RIGHT ABOVE: *Bird dancers*, their great carved beaks controlled by strings
FAR RIGHT: *Potlatch gathering* of Tlingits at Sitka, Alaska

Wealth and Power

While wealth and status for the Indians of the Northwest Coast were in large measure inherited, maintaining one's high position required considerable acumen and a forthright show of power. War, of course, was one method by which a strong leader could prove his strength, but he needed also to be versatile in carrying out the Potlatch. This was the formal give-away ostensibly performed to display one's wealth and generosity, but actually to exhibit one's political clout.

The Potlatch was generally planned a year in advance, the clan chief directing his family, quite conceivably an entire village, to prepare not only enormous quantities of food, but a huge supply of blankets, boxes and all manner of useful and valuable items. When this mass of material had been accumulated, the chief would invite the headman of a rival clan and his people to the feast. Here, with everyone dressed in their finery, the host would distribute gifts to his guests – dozens of blankets and boxes and other articles he and his clan members had gathered together throughout the year. A sumptuous feast was presented with more than anyone could eat.

To climax the Potlatch, the host might take one or more of his shield-shaped coppers, valued at perhaps 100 blankets, and hurl them into the sea. The host thereby displayed to the assembled throng his utter disdain for material wealth. This ostentatious exhibition was frequently accompanied by the killing of one or more slaves, for as property, they now meant nothing at all to their owner. It was a glorious occasion, a time for receiving gifts, of feasting, of being honored by a powerful and beneficent leader.

The Potlatch Catch

There was one catch, however, to the Potlatch. The guest chief knew that within the year, all the things he had been so generously given, all the display and destruction of property, must be reciprocated, and reciprocated with lavish interest. The Potlatch was, in fact, insidious economic warfare waged with the calculated design of ruining one's rival. And it worked. Some headmen went bankrupt, others went mad and not a few ventured upon suicidal expeditions of war.

Among the upper-class Northwest Coast families, many of the rites and prerogatives and much of the wealth were inherited. Even so, those so blessed did best to seek visions. This was partly to secure more of those benefits through supernatural aid, partly to obtain membership in the secret societies. Magical ceremonies were performed by such societies as the Bears and the Cannibals. Masked dancers would impersonate the mythical ancestors in the eerie shadows of the great planked houses. Phantom figures soared down from the smoke

hole, some wearing huge beaked masks, opened by hidden strings, which clapped and banged, all to complete the ancient drama of man's mysterious past and to give meaning to his present.

Life among the Northwest Coast Indians was far from simple or relaxed. It demanded of the leaders vicious economic competition and a store of memorized knowledge about the myths and traditions, rites and ceremonies which were essential to maintaining a cohesive and progressive society. It required physical fortitude in the hunt and in war, combined with an insight akin to wisdom as an arbiter in settling disputes. And finally, it called for that sense of leadership, that charisma that on the one hand brings loyalty and respect and on the other shows benevolence and understanding. Nor was life on the lowest rung one of mere simple servitude. In addition to the menial and often arduous work, the knowledge of having been captured as a slave could be pretty frightening. To realize you might well be killed to satisfy the economic ambitions of a copper-hungry chieftain displaying his disregard for wealth at your expense hardly equates with the simple, happy life of the noble savage.

No matter how rich in tangible objects, in ceremony and religion, in the products and resources of the fields and forest, in ideas of family arrangements and systems of government some native cultures might have been, or how poverty-stricken others seemed, the individuals worked hard to achieve their way of life and fought desperately to protect it. Throughout North America, tribe after tribe gave witness to the fact that they thoroughly believed in their life-styles.

CHAPTER V
The First Cowboys

THE COWBOY AS a dashing and colorful character took shape from the ashes of that horrible conflagration – the Civil War. But long before this there were men whose job it was to tend cattle. Christopher Columbus first brought livestock to the New World on his second voyage, but it took one Gregorio de Villalobos in 1521 to bring beef on the hoof from Santa Domingo to the mainland. It is recorded that he carried seven hardy Spanish Andalusian calves, six heifers and one young bull.

As the years passed and the Spanish control of Mexico spread northward, so did the cattle. Spanish hidalgos received extensive grants of land from the coast of California through the Southwest to what is now Texas. In company with the landowners, the Franciscan friars established missions, eventually as far north as San Francisco, as far east as San Antonio. And with them the hidalgos and friars brought their livestock, sheep and goats, horses and cattle. To mind the cattle, the Spaniards taught their Indian slaves and peons to ride their tough Spanish horses.

Saddles and Spurs

By 1750, not only had these little Mexican Indians been taught to ride horses and tend cattle, but they had been invested with all the accouterments of the Spanish horseman.

Tooled leather chaparajos protected their legs against the cactus and mesquite. Wide-brimmed sombreros guarded their heads against the sun. High-pommeled and cantled saddles were patterned after a medieval predecessor. Even their cruel spurs were Spanish, though they might wear them over a pair of sandals or even with bare feet. They carried a lariat, which could be employed both as weapon and tool.

OVERLEAF:
Cowboys Roping Cattle, painting by Charles Russell

A cowboy's life
FAR LEFT ABOVE:
Guarding the Herd, painting by Frenzeny Tavernier
FAR LEFT BELOW:
Roping Longhorn steers in the 1870s
ABOVE: *Dispute over a Cattle Brand*, painting by Frederic Remington
LEFT: Driving longhorn cattle across country in the 1870s

These were the vaqueros. Their work was hard and lonely. They set their camps – crude lean-to-style shelters of sticks and rawhide – at desolate waterholes, often many miles from the hacienda. Their diet was principally corn mush and wild game.

The Southwest was a barren, desolate country of unbelievable beauty and grandeur, inhabited by the solitary stalking mountain lion, bands of vicious "javalinas" or peccaries, the prairie wolf and the stealthy "tigre" or jaguar. Even more threatening were the marauding bands of Apache, Comanche and later Kiowa Indians. But it was also a bounteous country, rich in deer and antelope, wild turkey and jack rabbits. To defend themselves, and to capture their food supply, the vaqueros had only a bow and arrow and they needed nothing more; they were experts.

While the lonesome vaquero minded his master's cattle, the hidalgo managed a small agricultural empire from his established hacienda. Some were modest adobe dwellings surrounded by crude corrals and simple sheds, others were imposing structures with handsomely carved and decorated portals, cooled by the very thickness of the pristine, white-plastered walls. Such a ranchero, living amidst the elegance of richly carved furnishing and lavish silver, was himself a striking figure. From his embroidered sombrero to his silver spurs, he was a match for any Spanish grandee.

No matter how vigilant the vaquero might be, or how loyal to his master, cows and even horses wandered and strayed. From the time Cortez first brought horses to the continent and another Spaniard introduced cows, here and there a couple of horses or a half-dozen cows

An inhospitable land
ABOVE: A cow is hauled
from the mud
FAR LEFT ABOVE:
The Outlying Camp,
with its few home
comforts, as portrayed
by Frederic Remington
FAR LEFT: An incident
during the opening up
of the cattle country

would inevitably become lost in the rugged
reaches of the Southwest. Adding to the
problem, rapacious Indians were ever lurking,
alert to capture a herd of horses or steal a beef.

The cows that were to form the basis of the
entire cowboy culture several generations later
were the descendants of these offshoots and
strays of the Andalusian cattle which the
Spanish introduced to the New World.

For Slaves and Cattle
To help insure an owner's property right, the
Spanish utilized a method which had already
been tried out on people: burning into the
flesh an indelible mark. Cortez asserted his
ownership by branding a "C" on the cheek of
his Indian slaves and his cattle he marked with
three crosses to symbolize the Father, the Son
and the Holy Ghost. God help the man who
would dare transgress this sacred sign.

Branding soon became the established method
of identification for all who tended cattle and
herded horses. In the wasteland the strays
multiplied. From the original Andalusian stock
emerged a hardy, rugged animal possessed of
great stamina, an ability to survive with little
water and sometimes on meager feed. Adjusting
to conditions, these animals acquired two unique
features – great size and tremendous horns, an
attribute which gave them their name, the
Longhorn. There has been no beast quite like
it before or since.

As the Longhorn evolved, so also did the
cow pony. Both Cortez and Coronado took
horses on their expeditions – small horses of
Arabian breeding. It is believed that strays
from these herds, as well as animals wandering
from the great Mexican haciendas, were the
progenitors of the western mustang.

A Tough Breed
These wild horses thrived, and by adapting to
the sere desert conditions of the Southwest,
they prospered. Like the Longhorns, they too
became a tough breed. But instead of attaining
size, they acquired an unparalleled stamina.
For sheer speed, orneriness, endurance and
headstrong brains, no animal could outdistance
or outsmart the mustang. It was a small, wiry,
close-coupled horse. The Indians (probably
the Comanches first, then the more northerly
tribes such as the Utes and Shoshoni, and later
the Sioux and Crow) captured and "broke"
them; and it was these Plains Indians who
earned the reputation as the world's greatest
horsemen. The vaqueros, and later the cowboys
as well, likewise captured the mustangs and
broke them to work cattle. Some became
manageable and their stamina and speed proved
them invaluable.

Challenging the Spaniards
The settling of the Southwest by the Spanish,
with missions and ranches sparsely scattered

Skill with the lariat
ABOVE: James Walker's
Vaqueros Roping a Bear
shows the Spanish
origin of the cowboy's
equipment
RIGHT and FAR RIGHT:
Cutting Out, by W. A.
Rodgers, and Charles
Russell's *Jerked Down*
both show the moments
of tough action for
which the cowboy's life
is celebrated

ABOVE: *Longhorn cattle drive* in the 1870s
FAR RIGHT ABOVE: *Cowboy at work* rounding up a stray animal
FAR RIGHT BELOW: *New Town*, Western style

here and there in the desert's vastness, had become a reality by the end of the eighteenth century. A short while afterwards the United States began to show interest in this unknown region.

In 1800 one Philip Nolan made an expedition to capture wild horses as far west as the Brazos River. It was an absolute fiasco. He was attacked by Spanish troops and killed for his efforts. In 1806 Zebulon Pike was sent on an exploring expedition to the land that was to become Texas. Though the word was probably never put in writing, his mission was a spying operation, pure and simple. By 1820, Moses Austin, a Yankee from Connecticut, was able to convince the Spanish authorities in San Antonio of an enterprising colonization scheme. Austin died before his plan materialized but his son, Stephen, carried on and in 1822 some 150 settlers had been enlisted.

The Revolution of 1821 freed Mexico from Spanish domination and the new government was at once anxious to develop its country. Settlers paid taxes, found a market for their cattle and cattle products and even scented a chance of prosperity. Individuals and families

from Kentucky and Tennessee, interested in settling farther west, were offered either 177 acres for farming or 4,428 acres for grazing. The shrewd settlers naturally accepted the grazing grants. By 1835, it was estimated that the new population had reached 35,000, and among them were the forefathers of the American cowboy, for already many of the men, rather than grub at growing cotton, were raising cattle.

Beef and Grass

It was later, after the Civil War ended, that the true cowboy evolved. The importance of beef to a burgeoning population in the East added an incentive to what had been a desultory sort of cattle gathering. It all began in Texas; then gradually the cowboy's territory spread from Kansas north to Canada and west from Arizona and Nevada to Utah and Idaho. The regions of the Great Plains, the Rocky Mountains and the Great Basin and Plateau varied in terrain and climate, but the essential and common requirement was grass.

The western parts of the Dakotas, Kansas, Oklahoma and Texas and the eastern reaches of New Mexico, Colorado, Wyoming and Montana were rich in highly nutritious grasses. These were the Plains, the area which had supported the vast herd of buffalo. By its nature, it now became ideal for grazing cattle. It was a country, however, subject to dry and searing heat in the summers and frigid, wind-swept blizzards in the winter. The undulating and unending sea of grass had a monotony that tried the spirit. It was in this treeless vastness that "a man could look farther and see less" than any place in the nation.

Survival of the Tough

The Rocky Mountains, including parts of Colorado, Wyoming and Montana, possessed lush valleys, but suffered hard winters. The majesty of the country, while handsome to behold, was harsh and cruel with unbelievably deep snows making life for the cowboy and his cows a matter of survival of the toughest.

In the Great Basin and Plateau regions of Nevada, Utah and Idaho the grass was sparse. The same was true of southwest Texas, New Mexico and much of Arizona. In the Great Plains a rancher could run a cow to every ten acres. In the far West, because of its barren and arid character, much more land was required to support one animal.

So it can be seen that a great many factors combined to produce the cowboy – but the lasting contribution of the Spanish ranchero culture shouldn't be overlooked. Many of the words, trappings and methods of handling stock owe their origin to the Spanish *caballeros* of Texas and the great Southwest. Words like "lariat" from *la reata*, "lasso" from *lazo reata*, "cavvy" from *caballado*, "pronto", "savvy" and many more are firmly established in cowboy lingo – though doubtless very few cowhands of the twentieth century ever give a thought to the wiry little vaqueros who led the way.

CHAPTER VI
Fur Traders and Frontiersmen

THE BUILDING OF the West was motivated as much by the prospect of exploitation as it was by the thought of agricultural production. In the Spanish Southwest, gold and fabulous jewels were the lure. Far to the northwest along the St. Lawrence River, fur was the magnet. The French and the English were quick to capitalize.

As early as 1668, the Hudson's Bay Company was formed to help meet the insatiable demand of the European market.

Frenchmen First

The French arrived early, establishing their principal settlements along the St. Lawrence River. Unlike the Spanish explorers who were searching for treasure, the French were seeking trade routes. Robert Cavelier, sieur de La Salle, commandant of Fort Frontenac, began building forts as far west as the Great Lakes to protect his fur-trading interests. On an expedition beginning in 1679, he took with him Father Louis Hennepin as official friar, Michel Aco, his lieutenant, and Henri de Tonti. They sailed the Great Lakes in the *Griffon*, in which they reached Green Bay, Wisconsin. Proceeding further, they came to the Illinois River where La Salle built Fort Creve Coeur.

Here La Salle split his party, sending Hennepin and Aco to explore the upper Mississippi while he returned to Fort Frontenac for supplies. Hennepin and Aco were soon captured by Sioux Indians, but did discover the Falls of St. Anthony, the site of St. Paul-Minneapolis.

Daniel Greysolon, sieur Duluth, was already in the West settling a conflict between the warring Ojibway and Sioux. At Mille Lacs, Minnesota, he claimed the upper Mississippi for France. In addition to establishing his fur-trading interests, he was searching for a northwest passage, a waterway to the Pacific. His plans, however, were temporarily interrupted by the need to rescue Father Hennepin and Michel Aco from the Sioux. In this, as was true of most of his endeavors, his diplomacy proved entirely successful. He then returned to his main ambition, seeking a northwest passage. Not finding one was a major failure for him.

Meanwhile, La Salle was making plans for an equally ambitious venture, that of finding the mouth of the Mississippi River. Unlike Duluth, who in truth was at a dead end since all the waters he faced were upstream, La Salle could reason with confidence that if he headed downstream, the Great Muddy River would surely have an outlet. Together with Tonti, La Salle set out from Mackinac Island and ended up at the Gulf of Mexico in the spring of 1682. Here he proclaimed all of Louisiana in the name of France. Some years later he undertook an expedition to the gulf by sea to consolidate France's claim more firmly. Although one of his ships was captured by the Spanish, he managed to reach shore. But he could not find the Mississippi's delta, much less the river. As he was trekking inland in a frantic search, his men finally mutinied and La Salle was mur-

dered. It was a sad end for one of France's and America's most gallant cavaliers.

Pelts for Trinkets

From Quebec and Montreal, traders set their sights on Hudson's Bay and the Great Lakes to tap the area's wealth. In return for beads and blankets, for metal tools, firearms and whiskey, the Indians gathered huge quantities of precious pelts. Fort Michilimackniac, an island at the northwest tip of Lake Huron, became the principal trading center in the latter part of the eighteenth century. Here French voyagers loaded their ninety-pound bales of furs into birchbark canoes to paddle and portage nearly two thousand miles to Montreal. With luck they could make it in less than a fortnight.

The French traders seemed to have an innate flair for living in the wilderness. Unlike the English, who considered the woods and forests as obstacles to be chopped down and the Indians as savages blocking the way to desirable land, the French discovered the forests to be a source of wealth and the Indians to be essential partners in a mutually profitable enterprise. In many instances they learned the language and often took an Indian woman as a wife. With this attitude, the French made the fur trade flourish.

The English, too, were avidly searching the country, especially for a northwest passage. Alexander Mackenzie was one of the more resolute seekers. Troubled by the expense, distance and difficulties of transporting furs from the far Northwest to his North West Fur

Company in Montreal, he determined to find a navigable passage to the Pacific. Linking the beaver trade with that of the Pacific sea otter would prove more profitable. Mackenzie had searched for the route earlier. He followed what is now the Mackenzie River to its mouth, but was poorly rewarded by reaching the Arctic Ocean. Now he would try another route. Leaving Lake Athabasca in the spring of 1793, he embarked on the Peace River in a canoe. Crossing the Continental Divide – a portage of less than a mile – he shot down the Frazer River, climbed several mountains and finally, on the Bella Cola River, reached the Pacific north of Vancouver Island. Then and there he realized the route was impracticable. His journey, however, combined with Captain James Cook's explorations, made secure the British grip on western Canada.

Stiff Competition

A wide variety of furs were in demand, especially the highly desirable mink and otter, fox and beaver. But the skins of the bear, the deer, the elk and the buffalo also sold well as robes and hides. After the treaty of 1763 when the British gained firm control of France's Canadian territories, companies like the North West, organized in 1779, spread their factories or trading posts throughout the Northwest. Scotsmen and Englishmen headquartered in Montreal hired the experienced French *coureurs de bois* to manage their western posts. They now controlled stations as far west as Vincennes Kaskaskia and Kahoka and their traders ranged from the Pawnee country throughout much of Louisiana east of the Rockies. To the north lay the territory of the Hudson's Bay Company. With profits high and competition stiff, conflict

Famous frontiersmen
FAR LEFT: *Daniel Boone Escorting Settlers Through the Cumberland Gap* by George Caleb Bingham
LEFT: Alexander Mackenzie, one of the first men to seek a Northwest passage to the sea, as portrayed by Thomas Lawrence

between the two companies was intense. Furs were stolen, Indian tribes were pitted against one another and bribes in the form of excess whiskey were commonplace. Not until 1811 was a settlement reached and finally resolved by the Hudson's Bay Company absorbing the North West.

After the revolution, the Americans determined to enter the lucrative business so long dominated by the British. Traders were licensed with provisos that no credit be extended and that no liquor be sold lest the Indians be demoralized. The idea was naive on both counts and failed brilliantly. The effective way to trade was to offer the Indians beads and tobacco, mirrors and guns, salt and ammunition and great quantities of whiskey. All these were exchanged at a high rate in return for furs at a low one. The unit of value was the highly prized skin of the castor or beaver. By disregarding the arbitrary regulations, the Americans soon began to challenge the British monopoly.

The Rise of Astor

John Jacob Astor, born in Germany in 1763, came to New York at the age of twenty. After a stint as a baker's helper, he found employment with a fur merchant. Quickly learning the fundamentals of that business, Astor set up on his own. His idea was to capitalize first on procuring furs from New York State, Canada, and by 1800, the Great Lakes Region. Trade in furs with China was now profitable. Soon Astor acquired his own ships and with this advantage was shortly counted among the wealthiest men in the United States. With the Louisiana Purchase, it occurred

Fur traders
ABOVE: *Caravan en Route* by Alfred Jacob Miller depicts the American Fur Company's traders heading for a rendezvous at the Green River
FAR RIGHT BELOW: Manuel Lisa, one of the least popular of the highly competitive businessmen in the fur trade

to him that this region would make a pleasant monopoly. In 1808 he formed the American Fur Company and later the Pacific Fur Company to handle the Far West business.

Astor planned a series of forts stretching west to the Pacific coast. To accomplish this he sent a well-named captain, Jonathon Thorn, together with a group of fur traders, around Cape Horn on the ship *Tonquin*. Their destination was the mouth of the Columbia River. Thanks to the martinet Thorn, the voyage was fraught with squabbles and quarrels. The independent traders, accustomed to the freedom of the wilderness, irked at the confinement of a ship and restive at taking orders from a pompous sea captain, spent a miserable seven months on the water.

When at last they reached the Columbia, the sea was high. One dinghy with its crew was swamped and all hands lost. Eventually the others were able to reach shore, whereupon they began erecting a small fort. They named it Astoria in honor of their employer. On June 11, the crew took the *Tonquin* along the coast to trade with the Indians. Instead of greeting them sympathetically, the Indians attacked their ship and killed most of the crew. The survivors blew up the *Tonquin* and the Indians with it. The few white men who did escape found their way, in time, back to civilization.

Hunt and Lisa

Meanwhile, Wilson Price Hunt, a young merchant from St. Louis, was directed by Astor

to proceed from there to the Yellowstone. Following that river, his party was to cross the Rockies and join forces with Thorn on the coast. But as Hunt's party moved farther up the Missouri, they became alarmed. Manuel Lisa, the fur trader, warned of the rapaciousness of the Blackfeet. Rather than travel along the Yellowstone, Hunt changed his course for one due west, traversing the Plains to the Black Hills of South Dakota. From here the men continued west, crossed the Big Horn River and once over Teton Pass reached the Snake River. Their intention was to coast down the river in canoes until they reached the mountains. But the waters in the deep canyons were roily. Canoes sank, one man was lost.

Deciding the party was so large as to be cumbersome when crossing the Cascades, Hunt divided his men into four groups. And then the troubles really began. The mountains were almost impassable, provisions dwindled, intense cold and deep snow hampered progress. Some men deserted, and some men died. Not until January, 1812, did the first party arrive at the fort. Hunt's own detachment appeared in February, the final group not until May.

News of War

No sooner had they reached the safety of Astoria than a supply ship arrived. With fresh provisions, the Astorians took on new life, but it didn't last long. Rumors of the war of 1812 reached the outpost, traders from the North

West Company appeared. Aware of their predicament, threatened by the British presence to the north and conscious of the superiority of the British sea power, the Astorians, rather than have their fort captured, sold it to the Englishmen. Within a month, the British frigate *Raccoon* appeared. After sailing halfway around the world to do battle, all they had accomplished was to capture their own godforsaken fort!

The sudden sale and capture of Fort Astoria effectively destroyed Astor's plans for a Pacific trading enterprise. But Astor was not one to be easily discouraged. He concentrated on his Great Lakes territories and soon developed a virtual monopoly. Moreover, he expanded his activities in the West. In 1834, when the American Fur Company was at its peak, John Jacob Astor retired.

Long-Term Credit

In 1809 some prominent St. Louis businessmen organized the St. Louis-Missouri Fur Company. They sent 150 of the best trappers, traders and hunters up the Missouri, establishing forts on the way. Their expedition, however, was fraught with troubles. At a fort on the Three Forks of the Missouri, Blackfeet Indians attacked and killed 25 men. Later a fire destroyed a large supply of their furs. Finally, the forts had to be abandoned. And yet, the St. Louis-Missouri Fur Company turned a profit.

As the years went by, fur companies came and went, merged and prospered. Small fortunes and

great ones were made and sometimes lost. It was a business involving considerable financial risk and dramatic physical danger, including death. While the product was purely American, the market was almost entirely European, so was operated on a credit system. A span of approximately four years existed between the time the raw furs left the American traders' hands until

BELOW: *Blackfeet Encampment* by Karl Bodmer
FAR RIGHT: *Bourgeois* at his trading post swapping guns for furs

the finished piece was sold and the credit, in the form of trade goods, finally reached the trader in the west.

Trading Posts

In the 1820s and '30s, the forts or trading posts on the Missouri were typical landmarks of the industry. They were, in fact, the beating hearts of the business. Fort Benton at the mouth of the Big Horn was established by the Missouri Fur Company as early as 1821, principally to attract trade with the Blackfeet and Assiniboine. Fort Laramie on the North Platte was erected by the partners Sublette and Campbell in 1834. Two years later they were bought out by the American Fur Company. Fort Pierre, built at the confluence of the Missouri and the Bad River, was situated, like Laramie, in the territory of the Sioux. It, too, was controlled by the American Fur Company.

The usual trading post was managed by a French *bourgeois*. He was responsible for ordering all the goods and supplies, fixing the prices, hiring the trappers and overseeing the trade with the Indians. In short, he supervised all the business. More often than not he was a partner in the company. The fact that the master of the post was referred to as the bourgeois is understandable, for the great majority of the men in the fur trade were Frenchmen. It was they who had pioneered the business in the first place, it was they who knew the wilderness almost as well as the Indians did.

Second in command was the partisan. He was in charge of all field operations including the supervision of the rendezvous when no trading post was near. To keep records, a clerk was employed. In the absence of the bourgeois, he assumed charge. Often, too, he was a stockholder in the business. Other employees included a cook, a blacksmith, a carpenter and the "pork eaters." These men, under the direction of the "camp keeper," skinned the carcasses, dressed the furs, prepared the bales and performed sundry other choice jobs such as mucking out the horse stalls.

Trappers and Indians

The key men in the fur trade, however, were the white trappers and the Indians. The trappers fell into two categories: company men and free trappers. The company men employed by the post generally left for the wilderness in the late fall to spend the winter in search of beaver. This was lonely work, for most men trapped on their own, setting their traps at remote beaver ponds.

The man's equipment included traps, a rifle, shot and powder, a hunting knife and a hatchet. His most prized possession was his horse. More often than not he took to himself an Indian woman to mind his camp and keep him warm. The hazards of the work were very real. Blizzards and bitter cold, accidents, attacks by grizzly bears were dangers enough, let alone the constant fear of an Indian assault. As a consequence, the trapper's most valued equipment was a barrelfull of raw courage. And for all his skills, his hard work, his risks for a winter's catch of furs, the company paid him a salary of about 400 dollars a year.

Of all the fur traders, none was more daring and determined than Kenneth McKenzie, who opened the first post among the dreaded Blackfeet. As factor for the American Fur Company's Fort Union, he was a taskmaster and an elegant one. Among other things, he enjoyed fine brandy, so much so that he set up a still. This bit of illegality, however, jeopardized the company and led to ruin.

The free or independent trappers lived in much the same circumstances as did the company men, except that they gambled. They took the chance that they could trap more beaver and sell the pelts at a better price than the company men. They often shopped for buyers from post to post. Sometimes they did better and sometimes they did not. They bought their own equipment, supplies, sometimes even beads and trinkets to trade with the Indians on their own. All of this was done with credit. The arrangement usually worked out very well, but not to the advantage of the free trapper. What with the trading posts discounting the value of the raw furs and jacking up the prices of blankets, tobacco, ammunition, sundry supplies and especially the price of rotgut whiskey, the free trapper was anything but free. By autumn, the time to set out on his annual expedition, the trapper was usually in debt up to his beard. The system worked advantageously for the operators of the trading posts: they could be pretty certain that the not-so-free trappers would be back in the spring to trade.

While the company men and the free trappers were important to the fur companies, the Indians were essential. The pattern had been set in the last half of the seventeenth century. Trading for

FAR LEFT: *Powder horn*, an important part of a trapper's equipment
CENTRE: *Trappers* might often live Indian style, as shown in this painting by Alfred Jacob Miller
LEFT: *Fort Laramie*, the trading post on the North Platte River, as depicted by Alfred Jacob Miller

furs in exchange for blankets and copper pots, guns and mirrors, beads and whiskey was an established commerce. Intercourse with the Indian tribes, the Iroquois and Hurons, the Ottawa and Illinois and Miami was fostered and encouraged by the French, the English and later the Americans. The Indians were the hunters *par excellence*. They could bring in great quantities of furs, buffalo, deer, elk and smaller game, too. These supplemented the beaver pelts which the white trappers secured, for the Indians preferred not to trap.

While the great bulk of trading was carried out at the posts, a pattern of rendezvous was also developed. This was true of the mountainous regions of western Wyoming and eastern Utah, an area where there were no forts. Here, once a year, traders bringing caravans of goods from the East would meet with free trappers and Indians from various nations. In one great and colorful binge of bartering, competing in games and contests of skill, they would drown themselves in drink. The merriment might go on for several weeks, until the last pelt had been bartered for the last bead. Then the eastern traders, their pack mules and horses laden with furs, would head for St. Louis, and the Indians and trappers disperse again into the wilderness.

Jim Bridger, Mountain Man

The character of the trapper and mountain man is typified in the life of James Bridger. Born in Virginia in 1804, he moved to St. Louis where he worked as a blacksmith. One day in 1822 he noticed an advertisement in the *Missouri Republican* for a hundred enterprising young men

wanted to head up the Missouri River, there to be employed for one, two or three years. To Jim this sounded attractive and he promptly hired on, exchanging the heat of the forge for the cold of the trail.

The idea had originated with two men named William Ashley and Andrew Henry. Rather than tie up large sums of money in constructing trading posts with the attendant cost of manning them and paying the *engagés*, Ashley would take free trappers to the wilderness, to meet them later at a predetermined rendezvous where he would pay them off for their catch. This he would do either in goods or in cash, paying about half the amount he would expect to receive in St. Louis. Ashley was gambling on the spirit of free enterprise. Judging by the number of men who answered the advertisement, the plan was manifestly workable. Not only did Jim Bridger respond to the opportunity, but other men who were later to become famous joined up. Thomas Fitzpatrick, William Sublette, Hugh Glass and Louis Vasquez were among them.

Jim Bridger's first claim to a niche in history was hardly to his credit. During one of Andrew Henry's expeditions to the Yellowstone, the brash and daring Hugh Glass was savagely gored by a grizzly bear. So serious were his wounds that he was left to die. Henry offered to pay two volunteers to guard the dying man, give him a decent burial or, in the event of his recovery, bring him along west. John Fitzgerald and Jim Bridger volunteered. After a while, thinking Glass dead or tiring of their vigil, Bridger and Fitzgerald abandoned the trapper. They were careful to take his rifle.

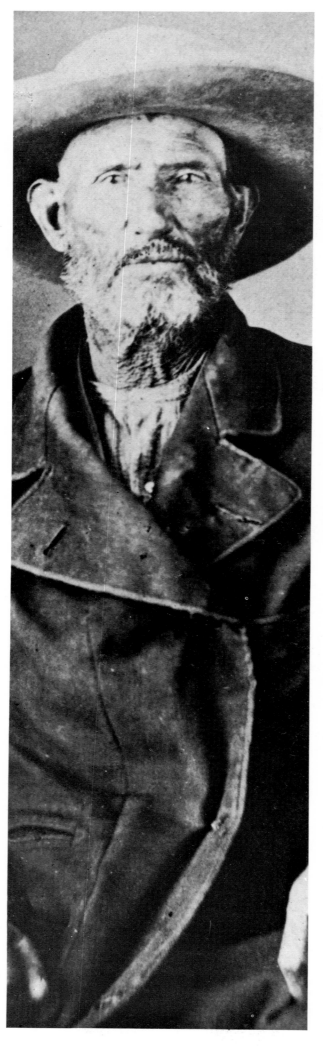

Left for Dead

But Glass was not dead. Weakly he dragged himself to a nearby spring which, by good fortune, was surrounded by wild cherry and buffalo berry bushes. For over a week he recouped here, and then with only his razor for weapon, he lurched in an easterly direction toward Fort Kiowa on the Missouri. Along the way he came upon the carcass of a young buffalo being devoured by wolves. Frightening them by setting fire to the prairie grass, he gorged himself. Once revived, he plodded on again for some 200 miles until finally, half-starved, he reached Fort Kiowa.

Glass's immediate aim was to find his faithless companions, and he made straight for the Yellowstone and the Bighorn River where he heard Henry was building a fort. Jim Bridger was understandably dismayed on learning of the resurrected Glass's impending arrival, so he was more than somewhat relieved when Glass did appear and, to the amazement of everyone, forgave him.

Relentless Pursuit

Glass hadn't yet forgiven Fitzgerald, who by this time was long gone. Relentlessly Glass pursued him, running him down at Fort Atkinson on the Missouri River and giving him a tongue lashing to the effect that from now on Fitzgerald must live with himself and his conscience. Glass also got his gun back.

Ten years later, Glass was again on the Yellowstone. This time his luck ran out. He and two companions were caught by the Arikara Indians and scalped. Such was the fiber – and the fate – of many a mountain man.

Jim Bridger fared better, his character and reputation undamaged by the Glass incident. In 1835, in partnership with Milton Sublette and Thomas Fitzpatrick, Bridger bought Fort Laramie, soon thereafter to be absorbed by the American Fur Company. Two years later he led a large party to the rendezvous on the Popo Agie.

Bridger was a big man, some six feet tall, powerfully built with a bull neck, altogether astonishingly athletic and sinewy. Yet for all his respected recognition as a mountain man, he could neither read nor write. But he was imaginative; in later years he became a teller of tall tales. One of them concerned a river composed of ice on the surface and boiling water beneath, another told of a glass mountain strewn about with the corpses of animals and birds that had run into it headlong. There was a third one about a boiling geyser that shot a spout of water three hundred feet into the air; another of a petrified forest with petrified birds singing petrified songs.

Jim's favorite story was of leading a large party of men through the mountains. Suddenly they

were surprised by Indians. The whites began to flee, the Indians pursued. As the trappers' horses tired, the men ran for the protection of a wooded canyon. The Indians finally killed all the whites save Jim. Trying to escape, he progressed deeper into the canyon, only to find his way blocked by a waterfall bounded by rocky cliffs a hundred feet high.

At this point Bridger would stop, close his eyes in deep reflection. His listeners, anxious to hear the outcome, would urge with a "What happened, what happened?"

"Well," Jim would reply with a sigh, "well, they shot me and buried me by the falls."

The Chouteau Family
Among the important family enterprises in the fur trade, the Chouteaus were phenomenal. In 1763, fourteen-year-old Auguste Chouteau accompanied his stepfather Pierre Laclède from New Orleans to establish a fort on the Mississippi. In the years following, the two of them built a post at the mouth of the Missouri, a site that was later to become the city of St. Louis.

In time, Jean Pierre Chouteau also came to St. Louis and entered the family business. He soon commenced trade with the Osage Indians, a monopoly he enjoyed for over 30 years. When finally he lost it, he simply moved his operations farther west to what is now Salina, Oklahoma. The Osage obligingly moved their villages west as well.

It was in 1809 that Jean accompanied a party up the Missouri, partly to oversee the safe return of the celebrated She-he-ke to his Mandan village. This headman had agreed to

135

Wilson Hunt, leader of Astor's overland party. And it was he who effectively discouraged Hunt from proceeding into the Blackfeet country of Montana, recommending instead that he cross country. Lisa wanted the territory for himself. And when Jean Chouteau was endeavoring to return the Mandan She-he-ke to his people, it was rumored that it was Lisa who turned the Arikara against him, thereby reserving the northern reaches of the Missouri watershed for his own plans. At any rate, Lisa reached the confluence of the Yellowstone and Bighorn rivers. With the gates now securely shut behind him, he erected Fort Raymond, naming it in honor of his son.

Lisa had the reputation of being hated by his *engagés* and thoroughly disliked by his competitors so it is surprising that Chouteau should have agreed to a business deal with him. Nonetheless, together with others, they formed the Missouri Fur Company. Lisa was to be the leader of expeditions. His influence with the tribes of the upper Missouri was extraordinary, so much so that during the war of 1812 he successfully retained their allegiance for the United States.

The Wilderness Life
When Lewis and Clark reached the Mandan villages on their return home, John Colter, a member of the party, requested a discharge. Manuel Lisa had offered him a job. The proposition was for Colter to act as guide for Lisa's planned post at the headwaters of the Missouri. Colter accepted, trading the chance to see civilization again for a life in the wilderness. After reaching the mouth of the Bighorn where Lisa built his Fort Raymond, Colter was sent on to the land of the Crow Indians. Traveling farther along on foot, he reached the Wind River Mountains and the Grand Teton range. Returning, he was seriously wounded in a battle between the Crow and Blackfeet Indians.

While Colter survived this foray with a bad leg wound, he was later captured by the Blackfeet. This time he was stripped and his partner riddled with arrows.

The Indians debated as to the manner of torture they would put him through before killing him, and decided to make him run for his life. Giving him a head start they pursued. When the leading Indian finally threw his lance, Colter grabbed it, turned on his pursuer and ran him through. With the other warriors in hot pursuit, it is said that Colter dived into a pond and hid in a beaver's lodge. After the Indians gave up the chase, Colter staggered naked to Lisa's fort. It took him seven days.

Among the renowned mountain men, none was more respected than little five-foot-four-inch Kit Carson. As an orphan, he worked as a

visit Washington at Lewis and Clark's behest. The hostile Arikaras, however, were not about to allow a chief of the enemy to pass north through their territory and they attacked the party in strength, eventually forcing the traders to retreat downstream. It wasn't until two years later, with a military escort of a 120 men and 200 trapper-traders, that they succeeded in cowing the Arikara and She-he-ke finally got home.

Manuel Lisa Again
It was during this expedition that Chouteau apparently worked out arrangements for a business deal with the inimitable and wily Manuel Lisa. Lisa, born in New Orleans, appeared early in St. Louis. Like the Chouteaus, he traded with the Osage. Learning of the discoveries of Lewis and Clark, Lisa led a party up the Missouri beyond the Arikara villages. It was near here that he caught up with

saddler at the eastern terminus of the Santa Fe trail. At the seasoned age of seventeen he quit and ran away. A wagon train headed for Santa Fe offered him his escape.

When Carson got to Santa Fe, he continued northward to the fabled town of Taos. The life of the hunter fascinated him so he took up hunting and became most proficient. He proved his mettle at the rendezvous of 1835 when a hulking drunken bully of a trapper named Shunar threatened to eat any Yankee he could find. Carson, already with the reputation of being a wildcat, cheerfully challenged the thug, and outdrew him, shot him in the hand and brought him down to size. The browbeater was soon begging for his life. In later years Carson became an important scout and guide and ended his career in 1867 as commanding general of Fort Garland, Colorado.

Daniel Boone

It was not only greed for profits in furs, or the simple lust for adventure, that sent men westward into the wilderness. There was also the growing nation's need for more living space which some frontier adventurers could clearly see coming.

One of the most resolute of these frontiersmen was Daniel Boone, a Pennsylvanian by birth, who first moved his family south to a little valley in North Carolina called Yadkin.

Daniel Boone was a small man, standing only five feet six inches, but well and powerfully built. Blue-eyed and black-haired, he was regarded by some as good-looking. As was customary with most frontiers-men, he wore Indian buckskins and often a coon-skin cap. While illiterate, at best barely able to write his name, he was bold and wise in the ways of the Indians and the forests. During one of his forays, he was captured by the Shawnee. Instead of being put to torture and killed, he was adopted into the tribe, though kept well under guard.

Boone never made much of a record as a farmer, but kept his wife and children supplied with meat from his continual hunting trips. The buckskins he brought home could be converted into cash. They were worth a dollar a hide, which accounts for the term "buck," long part of the American vernacular. But Boone was hunting for more than game.

At that time, colonists were already making determined efforts to occupy land to the west, to carve out tiny farms, to establish small settlements in the fertile valleys of the unending forest lands. Moving from the coastal regions, they reached the foot of the Appalachian Mountains from the Carolinas north to Pennsylvania.

The Pioneers

Englishmen and Germans and Orangemen from the north of Ireland, colloquially referred

FAR LEFT: *Indians Returning to Fort Berthold* by Rudolf Kurz
LEFT: *The Trapper's Last Shot*, painting by William Ranney
BELOW: *Judge Richard Henderson*, who speculated in land, made an illegal treaty with the Cherokee and finally lost his shirt

to as "Scotch Irish," were among the most intrepid of the pioneers. These were hard men who had little to lose. For the most part they were independent to the point of fanaticism. They relied upon the eastern cities for such commodities as copper pots, knives and axes, firearms, powder and lead for making balls, and maybe a book or two; otherwise they were amazingly self-sufficient. Their chief crops were corn, wheat, rye and oats, surpluses of which they shipped East. Most of the pioneers supplemented their agricultural labors with hunting. The meat they fed their families, the hides they used to make clothing or sold for cash. They were famous for their marksmanship, and it was the invention of the rifled barrel that made the Kentucky rifle so superior a weapon.

Under the policy of the colonial governments, East Coast investors were permitted to speculate in large tracts of western land. They could get rich selling acreage to potential settlers. Many of the frontiersmen, however, having already staked out holdings for themselves in advance of the land grants, hoped to hold their claims by a sort of squatter's right. They gambled on being able to pay for a proper title when the time came.

The squatters reasoned that since they had cleared the land and tilled the fields, they were putting the land to use. Thereby they had a prior right. The speculators argued differently.

In most cases the Eastern interests prevailed. The settlers forfeited their shaky claims, picked up their belongings and moved west again.

Burning Trees

Daniel Boone, aware of this problem, marked out likely farmlands on his hunting trips by

Boone became something of a hero. In 1773 he led his first party of anxious settlers across the mountains to the beautiful valleys of Kentucky. The beautiful valleys, however, belonged to the Cherokee Indians and the treaty of 1763 had specified a boundary beyond which no white man might pass. If Boone failed to recognize the line, the Indians didn't. They promptly drove Daniel and his followers off, killing Boone's oldest son in the skirmish.

Boone was more popular with the Shawnees who took him to the British-held fort of Detroit. Here he pleaded the British cause and they offered to buy him for $100, but the Shawnee, who regarded him highly, refused to sell and took him back with them. Despite the Indians' precautions, he eventually made his escape. After an incredible four day trip through the wilderness sustained by only one meal, he returned safely to his family. Once there, he warned the residents of an impending attack, a raid which, thanks to his foresight, ultimately failed.

It was Boone who urged Judge Henderson to lay claim to the Western lands before someone else did. And Henderson acted. He formed the Transylvania Company, raised $10,000 to invest in trinkets, traded goods and firearms and forthwith made a treaty with the Cherokee. Without any trouble at all, he bought the better part of Kentucky and Tennessee. While it was absolutely illegal for an individual to treat with the Indians for land, this didn't seem to bother Henderson. He immediately set Boone to carving out a trail through the mountains, the Wilderness Road as it came to be called, a rough and rugged highway to Transylvania. When the original trail was completed, Boone established a small fort near what is now Lexington, Kentucky. He named it Boonesboro. In March, 1775, Boone, like a conquering hero, led his people to the land of hope. They were buying the land, of course, from Henderson.

Losing His Shirt

But once the settlers got to Transylvania, they wouldn't pay for the land. Henderson was losing his shirt. It came to him that North Carolina and Virginia might bail him out. Adding a country to one of the colonies for an agreed sum would certainly help defray expenses. But the governors were furious at his high-handedness and would not recognize his claim.

Henderson tried another tack. The colonies were just now proclaiming their independence at Philadelphia. Henderson sent an emissary to the newly formed Continental Congress with the proposition that Transylvania be incorporated as another state. He really had little to offer save some wilderness and a dream. The new Congress fumbled for months and then

blazing the trees. But he did more than that. He cozied up to Judge Richard Henderson, a Westerner of questionable ethics, who speculated in land. Henderson financed Boone to make a survey of the West. And what Boone saw impressed him deeply. Here was an abundance of wildlife, salt licks and lush valleys. And while working for Henderson, Boone marked out desirable tracts for himself, feeling assured that what he had selected would be honored by the judge.

When Boone returned, his tales whetted the appetites of the settlers. Already angered by the attitude of the Governor who favored the Eastern financial interests at their expense, they were quick to follow Boone to his newfound paradise.

at last made a definite decision by tabling the whole matter. The upshot was that Henderson lost all claim to Transylvania. Years later he was granted a measly tract of land in compensation for his expenditures. The exquisite little valley was insignificant and moreover was miles and miles beyond the farthest reaches of Western settlements. Judge Henderson, scoundrel though he was, had been had. And Boone's extensive land claims were found to be defective. He lost them all in land suits. Angered, he moved to the Spanish territory of Louisiana and in 1799 was granted a large tract of land. With the Louisiana Purchase, his title was again found to be worthless.

Only through the intervention of Congress was some of it restored. Living with his sons, Boone saved money enough to pay off his debts. But the urge to move was still strong in him. In 1814, at the age of eighty, he made a hunting trip to the Yellowstone River. Upon his return he decided to move again, declaring he felt hemmed in by the growing numbers of settlers. Death, however, intervened. Daniel Boone died in September of 1820, having lived eighty-six remarkable years.

Lewis and Clark

In the first years of the new century, Thomas Jefferson, third President of the United States, was well aware of the pressures upon the nation for expansion. British domination of the territories north and west of the Great Lakes and Spanish control of that vast and unknown region west of the Mississippi called Louisiana posed a threat to a struggling nation, a nation that was bursting at the seams.

Whether the thought of military conquest of Louisiana ever entered Jefferson's mind will probably never be known. He did, however, in 1803, enlist the services of young Meriwether Lewis to make an exploratory expedition to Louisiana with the object of ascertaining Spanish strength in the area and of discovering a practical water route to the Pacific. The President, furthermore, got Congress to appropriate funds for the ostensible purpose of extending United States commerce.

FAR LEFT: *Trapper*, richly dressed and well armed
ABOVE: *Fort Laramie*, a sketch of the interior by Alfred Jacob Miller

RIGHT: Mandan village
on the banks of the
Missouri where Lewis
and Clark spent their
first winter
FAR RIGHT ABOVE: *Fur
trader* negotiating with
Indians
FAR RIGHT BELOW:
Fort Union, the
American Fur
Company's base on the
Missouri

Captain Lewis recruited Captain William Clark to be his lieutenant and then promptly began making preparations for the journey. At the time, it was planned as little more than an outright spying mission. But then, fortuitously, a major upset in world events took place.

Napoleon Bonaparte, who had accepted Louisiana from Spain in a treaty of 1800, found himself in dire financial difficulties. His warlike ambitions were costing France more than she could afford. Alert to this situation, Jefferson boldly sent emissaries to France with an offer of $10,000 to purchase New Orleans and Florida. New Orleans was an area vital to American trade on the Mississippi and one which the Spaniards as toll collectors had always made a bottleneck.

When the American diplomats arrived in France and made their proposal to the French, they were startled out of their lace shirts by the negotiator's counter offer – $15,000,000 for the whole of Louisiana. Hastily the Americans sent for instructions.

When James Monroe arrived as Jefferson's new envoy, he risked the bargain and bought nearly 10,000 square miles of wilderness. At four cents an acre, the "Louisiana Purchase" was a dazzling buy.

Flags and Medals

Lewis and Clark's preparations had proceeded with dispatch. A notable addition to their equipment now, however, was a supply of American flags and silver Peace Medals with which to impress the Indians as they entered the newly-acquired territory. Now they would come as official representatives of the United States. This was assuredly better than skulking around like a couple of spies.

On May 14, 1804, leaving Kahoka near St. Louis, with a party of 30 frontiersmen and hardened army men recruited from Western posts, they started up the Missouri River in a 55-foot keelboat fitted with a sail and two wooden canoes. Laboriously they worried their way up the river. The sail proved to be mostly for appearance as they poled and towed their way.

As they progressed, the officers conferred

with Indian tribes they met along the route. Lewis and Clark were careful to inform them that their allegiance from now on was to be to the United States. To confirm that relationship, they doled out beads and ribbons and Peace Medals. All went well until they encountered the Sioux near the Bad River. The Indians were more than delighted with the gifts, but soon became surly and overbearing. The Sioux had no intention of permitting white men to open trade negotiations with their Indian enemies farther upriver. The Sioux feigned drunkenness, would not leave the boat and at one point one headman boisterously insulted Lewis with such lewd and suggestive gestures that the captain was, in his own words, "forced to draw my sword."

Among the Mandans

By November the party had reached the Mandan villages perched high on the banks of the Missouri. Here Lewis and Clark decided to set up winter camp and train their men and refurbish their equipment. It was here also that they persuaded Charbonneau, the trader, to serve as an interpreter and to bring with him his young Shoshoni wife, Sacagawea. Having earlier been captured by the Hidatsa, she knew her way back to the Rocky Mountains.

By April 7 the explorers were ready. Again

they rowed and poled and tugged their over-laden canoes and pirogues against the current of the river. After a portage at the Great Falls of the Missouri, a decision had to be reached. It was now necessary to determine which of three rivers – the Jefferson, the Gallatin or the Madison – offered the best passage to the West. It turned out that the Jefferson was the one. Sacagawea reassured the party by recognizing the scenery.

Proceeding up the Beaverhead River, they

Lewis and Clark

RIGHT ABOVE: *Into the Unknown*, by J. K. Ralston, shows the two explorers meeting the Shoshoni Indians
RIGHT BELOW: A Blackfeet Indian chief, painting by Karl Bodmer. Lewis and Clark clashed with Blackfeet on their return journey
FAR RIGHT ABOVE: Contemporary portraits of Lewis, Jefferson and Clark
FAR RIGHT BELOW: *Indians Bartering*, painting by Coke Smith

was arduous and especially telling. While Lewis and Clark were well aware of the mountains' existence, they had no idea whatsoever of their extent. Instead of one range, there were many. And between them were vast stretches of barren and inhospitable plateau land.

When at last the expedition reached the Clearwater River, they abandoned their horses. After making new canoes, they were rushed down the surging torrents of the Clearwater, Snake and Columbia rivers until they were poured out into the Pacific. Arriving on November 7, 1805, they made plans to build a small fort in the vicinity. They named the place Clatsop and there they spent a very wet and miserable winter, much like bedraggled muskrats in an overflooded pond. An annual average rainfall of over 120 inches is something to put up with. The Lewis and Clark party just had to put up with it.

Over the Cascades

After some five months of re-equipping themselves, of preparing notes and establishing a claim to the region for the United States, the explorers set out on the return journey. They followed their original route over the hazardous Cascade Mountains until they reached the Nez Percé villages, where they picked up their horses. At the forks of the Bitterroot they split their forces, Lewis heading east over the Lewis and Clark Pass. Near Great Falls he explored the Marias River, hoping to find a western waterway. There was none. On his return to rendezvous with Clark, who had turned south

crossed the Continental Divide and traversed the mountains by the Lemhi Pass to the land of the Shoshoni. It was here the explorers hoped to obtain horses. Without these animals their trek to the Pacific would be almost impossible. The first meeting with a band of Shoshoni was an edgy confrontation, but everything was soon happily resolved when it transpired that the Shoshoni chief was in fact the brother of Sacagawea. With that bit of good fortune, the group was provided with horses and the expedition continued.

The trip through the Rocky Mountain region

Meriwether Lewis *Thomas Jefferson* *William Clark*

and east to follow the Yellowstone River to its junction with the Missouri, Lewis was confronted by Blackfeet Indians. Parleying, the Indians insisted on making camp with the party. While Lewis slept, the Blackfeet tried to steal his gun and his horses. Awakening, the explorers pursued the Indians, killed two and then hastily retreated down the river to safety. Lewis and his men were badly outnumbered and could easily have been massacred. Sleeping with the enemy in camp was one of the few mistakes Lewis committed and he was lucky it cost him no dearer.

Lewis joined Clark below the forks of the Yellowstone on August 12, 1806. Together they reached the Mandan villages on the fifteenth and were welcomed in St. Louis a month later. Their mission had been a complete success. They had failed to find a Northwest Passage, it is true. There wasn't one. They had dispelled that myth. But they had established the United States' claim to the Northwest, they had informed the Indians and the fur traders that henceforth their allegiance was to be to the new nation, and finally they had compiled copious and valuable information about the nation's vast new territory, Louisiana.

The Pioneer Spirit
The pioneer spirit exhibited by such men, along with the need for elbow room and hope for a better life in greener pastures lured Americans westward in greater and greater numbers. Indian borders were continually being pushed back as they were violated. By 1830 the line of settlement approximated the Mississippi River.

And it was about this time – specifically in 1834 – that a change in men's hat fashions was seen in Europe. For more years than men could remember, hats had been made of beaver felt.

Now there were dandies sporting hats made of – silk! The style spread and as more and more men chose silk hats, fewer bought felt. And this little whim, this shift in style, within a few years was bringing the fur trade to an utter and irretrievable collapse. In any case the companies, in their competitive struggle to stay in business, had by this date pretty well trapped out the beaver. Men whose only way of life was that of exploitation now found they had hit the bottom of the barrel. In their avarice, they had shortsightedly destroyed the very basis of their existence. The change in fashion from beaver to silk added a nasty insult to a fatal injury.

Though the fur-trapping days were numbered, the real Western story was just beginning. It was through the fortitude of such men as Boone, Carson, Lewis and Clark and those before them that the building of the West was made possible, for it was they who opened the vistas and unveiled the mysteries of a fabulous new empire.

CHAPTER VII

White Man Against Red Man

OVERLEAF:
Custer's Last Stand,
painting by Otto
Becker

BELOW: *Kutchin men*
sketched by Alexander
Murray in the middle
of the nineteenth
century

FAR RIGHT: *Penn's
Treaty with the
Delawares* by Benjamin
West records the
signing of one of the
few agreements
honored by whites

WHEN THE FIRST English colonists landed in 1607 at what was to become Jamestown, Virginia, there was no real conflict between the natives and the newcomers. At first the natives even welcomed the white men, to the extent of bringing them life-sustaining foods when the colonists' crops failed and famine was imminent. And a fragile alliance was formed when an Englishman was married to an Indian princess.

She was Pocahontas, the daughter of the powerful chief of the Powhatan Indians, who was himself called Powhatan. His own position was at the outset favorable to the colonists but he ran into opposition within the tribe. Several *weroans*, particularly one *weroanqua*, or queen, and Powhatan's own brother, Opechancanough, were strongly opposed to the white man's encroachment in Indian territory. At one point a colonist, John Smith, was captured and brought before Powhatan. Smith's life was saved by the intervention of the chief's daughter, who, legend records, threw her body over the English captive. Later, she herself was captured and held hostage by the governor at Jamestown on the pretense of keeping the peace.

Presented at Court

Pocahontas was christened and married at the age of seventeen to one John Rolfe. It was generally agreed that by her various acts of conciliation she was instrumental in maintaining the transitory peace. Pocahontas was taken to London where she was feted; because her father, Powhatan, was the only foreign personage ever to be accorded sovereignty by England, she was treated as nobility. Eligible for an audience with the queen, she was received by Elizabeth, while John Rolfe, a commoner, stayed in the wings.

Pocahontas bore John Rolfe one son, and died of smallpox in England at the early age of 21.

After her death and that of her father shortly after, her uncle, Opechancanough, assumed power among the Powhatans. Much bloodshed followed and in 1622 the English colony was reduced to a mere 350 souls. And yet, over a period of 40 years, the white man prevailed. In a series of retaliatory attacks, the Indians were decisively overcome. By 1650 the Powhatans were crushed, dispersed and impoverished. The Englishman's foothold in the New World would now be secure.

The First Thanksgiving

As with the Jamestown colonists, so it was with the Massachusetts settlers. Landing at Plymouth Rock in 1620, they, too, were welcomed by the Indians. The following year the struggling Pilgrims, who had been instructed in the planting of crops, celebrated with neighboring Indians their first Thanksgiving. With a harvest they had raised, added to what the Indians contributed, they also feasted on four wild turkeys. But as this and other English colonies prospered throughout New England, friction developed. Fearing an attack, Miles Standish marched against the Indians as early as 1623. Peace was made with Massasoit, chief of the Wampanoag, which lasted 50 years, but that was most unusual. The Indians and the colonists clashed again and again. The result was that the Indians were gradually driven from their lands. The pattern for America's westward expansion was already being set.

During both the drawn-out French and Indian wars as well as the American Revolution, the frontier was awash with blood. The French and the English each made alliances with the Indians, much to the alarm of the struggling farmers. A vicious raid by the French against the little town of Deerfield in 1704 nearly destroyed the village. Led by Hutel de Rouville, 50 Frenchmen and 200 Abenaki and Christian Indians ravished the town, killing 53 men, women and children. They marched over 100 others into captivity in Canada.

John Butler with a party of Indians and Tories perpetrated a similar massacre on the Wyoming Valley settlements in Pennsylvania in 1778.

Breaking the Iroquois

The Iroquois had been waging war long before the white man presented himself as a potential

enemy. They fought for conquest and domination – the Hurons to the northwest were nearly annihilated in 1649, while the Delawares fell under the Iroquois yoke a little later.

The Six Nations, jealous of the trading advantages of their neighbors, for a time controlled the entire fur market by their military victories. During the French and Indian wars, while they remained more or less neutral, they did serve as a buffer for the British settlements against the French in Canada. During the American Revolution, with the exception of the Oneida and Tuscarora, they sided with the British.

Under the leadership of Joseph Brant, the Iroquois ravaged the American settlements, burning, capturing, torturing and pillaging. Finally, so incensed at the massacres did the Americans become that in the spring of 1779 General George Washington ordered an expedition under the command of General John Sullivan to eradicate the Indian menace. Sullivan led a large army of Continentals to the Iroquois villages, and by summer's end he had completely destroyed them. With this conquest, the power of the Iroquois was forever broken.

At the end of the Revolution, such young states as Georgia, the Carolinas, Virginia and Pennsylvania, all of which possessed western national borders, were finding it especially difficult to restrain the westward migration of their citizens.

In the Greenville Treaty of 1795 with such tribes as the Wyandot and Shawnee, the Piankeshaw and Delaware, a line was drawn beyond which the white man might not go. But arbitrary and imaginary lines agreed upon by far-off diplomats were meaningless to rude and hardy frontiersmen. They argued that the Indians didn't use the land except for hunting, besides which, as a treacherous menace, they should really be eliminated anyway. To a lone settler in the wilderness, the best Indian was a dead Indian.

With that theory for support, the Westerners disregarded the treaty and breached the line. As squatters, they boldly cleared the forests and set up their little farms. This drew the wrath of the Indians, who retaliated by burning their cabins and scalping the trespassers. It was a conflict that was to last for a century and a half.

The Color of Treachery

No sense of honor seems to have hampered the white man in his dealings with the red man, at least in the majority of cases.

OVERLEAF:
The Horse Thieves, painting by Charles Russell

Indians fight back
ABOVE: *The Murder of David Tulley's Family*, painting by Peter Rindishbacker
FAR RIGHT: Artist's highly caricatured impression of an Indian massacre in 1813

One exception was William Penn, the man for whom the state of Pennsylvania was named. Penn negotiated a deal with Lapowinsa, a Delaware Indian leader. This was the so-called "Walking Purchase" of 1686, for as much land as a man could cover on foot in a day and a half. For over 50 years Lapowinsa kept his word and so did Penn. Then, in 1737, unscrupulous land-hungry men, wanting more territory, convinced the Delawares to negotiate another such treaty. This time, however, instead of one man walking three men ran, covering some 60 miles to the Pocono Mountains. Cheated, the Delaware had to acquiesce, and sadly gave up their lands.

And so it was all along the eastern seaboard from New York to Massachusetts. The Manhatts, a subtribe of the Delawares, were euchred out of Manhattan Island by the Dutch for a mere 24 dollars. Seventeen years later, the Wappinger Indians, of which the Manhatts were probably a part, sought refuge from marauding Mohawks in New Amsterdam, now New York City. The Indians were at first given protection by the Dutch governor, but after a few days were suddenly ambushed at night by their very protectors. The Dutch brought eight trophy heads of men, women and children to the fort together with other captives. Here one Indian was brutally tortured and mutilated, much to the amusement of the pantalooned Governor himself. The Europeans were showing their color – white – and white was now equated with treachery and evil.

A Tribe Decimated

In Massachusetts the Wampanoags, or rather their remnants, first met the Pilgrims in 1620.

They had been a populous nation, numbering some 10,000 souls, only to be decimated by a plague of smallpox introduced earlier by white traders. By now there were a mere 1,000 left. At first they naively aided the colonists, teaching them the techniques of growing corn. They were unaware that as they helped, the Christian Puritans were praising the Lord for the disease that had cleared out the savages.

Not all New England tribes welcomed the Europeans. The Pequots in particular had reason to resent the English. While the Pequots were warlike and powerful, had conquered over 25 villages and posed a threat, they had never attacked an English settlement. They themselves were raided in 1636 by a force of Puritans on the trumped-up charge of harboring the murderer of a drunken trader. The raid was inconclusive. The following year the English, allied with over 1,000 Narrangansets, waged a war of extermination, completely destroying the Pequot nation.

As the colonists prospered, so did their ambitions hampered only by the presence of the Indians. By 1671 the proud Wampanoags, threatened by outright war, yielded to the English yoke. Metacom, their chief, agreed to pay £100 annual tribute. But Metacom, known as King Philip, was biding his time. By 1675 his diplomacy had won the great Narrangansets to his side and war burst upon the surprised New England settlements like a blood bath in a slaughterhouse.

The Puritans reacted in kind, butchering women and children and gloating over the rout of the savage heathens. In the summer of 1676 King Philip was killed and his severed head displayed at Plymouth before the very eyes of his captive widow. Outnumbered, outgunned, their leaders gone, the Indians' resistance collapsed. The white man's policy of extermination had prevailed again.

Sizable Giveaway

As was so often the case when the Indians first met the Europeans, the Creek Indians of the Southeast welcomed them – in fact they did more than that. In 1732, in high hopes of obtaining great rewards in goods and education and the wisdom of the whites, several of their leaders trekked for 25 days to meet with Governor James Oglethorpe of Georgia. In exchange for little more than a conversation with Oglethorpe, they literally gave him a sizable piece of their territory to start his new colony.

At first, relations between the English and the Creeks were mutually profitable and Creek culture appeared to flourish. But as time passed unscrupulous traders, politicians, land speculators and squatters had created such tensions, now within the Creek nation itself, that in 1812 actual civil war broke out. Taking full advantage of the conflict the then General Andrew Jackson

used the old European ploy of arranging for Indians to fight Indians. With a force of militia, 600 Cherokees, Yuchi and allied Creeks, he utterly defeated the Creek dissidents and ended Creek power in the Southeast forever. Jackson became a national hero and his victory served as a springboard for his election as President. Then in 1830 he rammed through the Indian Removal Act.

Indian Territory

Very simply, this bill meant that eastern Indians would be forcibly evicted from their homelands and in turn given space in a newly carved-out piece of worthless country west of the Mississippi River, to be known as Indian Territory. Here the Indians might govern themselves, protected against land speculators, whiskey purveyors, unscrupulous traders. It

was all very neat and tidy, somewhat like sending a naughty boy to boarding school and forgetting about him.

People from the Southeast, Cherokee, Choctaw, Chicasaw and Creek were physically removed from their homelands and militarily escorted to the Indian Territory in a trek which the Cherokee sadly called "The Trail of Tears."

Not all the Cherokees acquiesced; many hid in the vastness of the rugged Carolina mountains they loved. Nor did all the Creeks accept Jackson's fiat. The Seminoles, affiliates of the Creeks, escaped to the Florida everglades. After losing 1,500 men in five years, the army finally gave up. The Seminole are still in Florida.

Many Enemies

The Plains Indians waged incessant warfare among themselves, and, with the encroachment

OVERLEAF:
Custer's Last Stand
A scene from the famous battle as depicted by William Dunton, a white artist who was not present during the action. In the INSET is a representation of the events by Kicking Bear, an Indian eyewitness; his work might even be classified as reportage

W. Herbert Dunton.

Geronimo

General George Custer

of the white man, another enemy was added. Valiantly they fought to defend their lands. Kiowa and Comanche raided Texas settlements, continually pillaged caravans of freight and cargo along the Santa Fe Trail and even waged a pitched battle against the whites at the Adobe Walls. The Sioux and Cheyenne long made travel on the Oregon and Bozeman trails hazardous.

Angered at the construction of military forts on their lands, at the railroads cutting the buffalo ranges, the influx of miners scratching for gold in their sacred Black Hills, the Sioux retaliated. Sometimes with assaults on the wagon trains, other times with attacks on the United States Cavalry assigned to protect the trails, the Sioux, under the leadership of Red Cloud, waged war. Outraged, too, at the duplicity of the Washington commissioners who broke treaties before the ink was dry, at the unscrupulous traders rich with graft from short-changing on rations and rot-gut whiskey, the Indians' attitude was anything but friendly. Men of the United States not only forced treaties upon these Indians, but systematically killed off the buffalo. With the basis of their existence destroyed, the Indians were quite simply starved into submission.

Ominous Prophecy

Some Sioux leaders, like Sitting Bull and Crazy Horse, no longer able to endure seeing their people suffer the confinement and shoddy rations of the reservations, defied the authorities and left, so they could hunt in freedom.

Early in the summer of 1876 a large encampment of Sioux, as well as some Cheyenne and Arapaho, 10,000 to 12,000 strong, had set their tepees along the west bank of Little Big Horn River in Montana. Sitting Bull, the highly respected headman and powerful shaman, reported having seen in a vision "many soldiers falling into camp." And within a very few days his prophecy came true.

In the early afternoon of 25 June, the Sioux in the Hunkpapa village at the north end of the great camp suddenly found themselves being attacked by a cavalry charge of some 140 "bluecoats." The Sioux were quick to respond. Warriors by the hundreds grabbed their weapons, donned their war bonnets and mounted their ponies to repulse the invaders. They were marvelously successful. In charge was a Major Reno, whom the Indians did not know; he and his troops were soundly beaten. The major led a gallant retreat across the river and up the cliffs to a craterlike position which he hoped to defend, but he had little chance. He was completely outnumbered. His orders from his commander, the willful and arrogant General George Armstrong Custer, were simply, "Charge after them, you'll be supported by the whole outfit" – but the support failed to materialize.

The adversaries
FAR LEFT: Geronimo, valiant fighter for his people
LEFT: General Custer, whose decisions led to the destruction of his troops
BELOW: Fanciful depiction of the battle by Frederic Remington, who put sabres in the painting although they were not actually used in the battle

Custer's Stand

No sooner was Reno defeated than the Sioux at the north end of the encampment sighted fresh troops. About three miles or more from the point of Reno's initial attack, cavalrymen were riding along the ridge to the east. At first, a group of five or six valiant Sioux crossed the river hoping to stall the bluecoats' approach, hoping to protect the great camp, the women and children.

Within minutes, not tens, not hundreds, but thousands of Indians came to the defense of the brave five or six defenders. More and more soldiers appeared along the ridge – 215 of them, it is guessed – as Crazy Horse, Gall and others surged up the hill to surround the troops under General Custer.

Authorized to help wipe out the Sioux recalcitrants, Custer had undertaken his job with glee. Now he took matters into his own hands, foiling any hope of a pincer movement of General Terry's troops coming from the North and General Crook's advance from the South. Crook's forces, however, had already been beaten by a Sioux force. Eight days before after the Battle of the Rosebud, Crook had returned to the safety of Goose Creek like a whipped dog with its tail between its legs.

Custer, in splitting his command, monumentally failed in his promise to reinforce Reno. And poor Reno spent the rest of his life feebly defending his reputation. He was the scapegoat for Custer's impetuousness.

Enough of Killing

The Sioux, Cheyenne and Arapaho, outnumbering Custer's troops by as much as twenty to one, were quick to press their advantage. Black Medicine, or Coffee, a nephew of Crazy Horse, having been wounded in the knee in the Battle of the Rosebud, rode up to observe the fight. "It wasn't much to see. Too much smoke and dust. It all ended about the time it takes a man to smoke a pipe," he reported later. When it was over, when the last man of Custer's troops had been killed, the Sioux harassed Reno's stronghold and they would have destroyed him save for Sitting Bull's forebearance. "There has been enough of killing," Sitting Bull decreed.

The Indians scalped most of Custer's soldiers, stripping them of their uniforms, the women mutilating their bodies to prevent their spirits from haunting the world. Custer, nicknamed "Long Hair" by the Indians, had had a haircut in accordance with Army regulations just before the campaign. His body was found stripped but unmolested, and his scalp was not taken. To the Sioux, the scalp of a suicide was useless, for the spirit of those who committed self-destruction hung forever in limbo, like those of murderers and hermaphrodites. Custer's body was found with a bullet hole in the chest and one in the temple.

The Sioux Crushed

It was a magnificent and symbolic victory for the Indians, but it was short-lived. In less than a year Crazy Horse and his 1,100 followers surrendered. Sitting Bull escaped to Canada, but gave himself up in 1881. The power of the Sioux was crushed.

In 1890, having been inspired by Wovoka, a Piute visionary, the Sioux, like other Plains tribes, embraced the "Ghost Dance" religion as a last hope. By strict adherence to the rituals and with the aid of the ancestors, it was believed the

buffalo would return and the white men would just disappear. Government authorities, seeing the Indians assembled, grew uneasy and suspicious. Troops from the 7th Cavalry, Custer's old command, surrounded a group of Sioux with rapid-firing cannons. Arguments ensued and a shot was fired. Immediately, the cavalrymen commenced a barrage. Sioux men, women and children fought, some with guns, some with knives, some barehanded. Before it all ended, 29 soldiers were killed. Except for a few who may have escaped, all the Sioux perished. The

killing of whites, under Custer, had been matched by this massacre of red men, at Wounded Knee.

In the Pioneers' Path

The lands of the northern Plateau Indians lay directly in the path of American expansion. In the mid-nineteenth century pioneers sought new lives in the Oregon Territory, miners grubbed and dug and panned for quick riches in gold and the United States Cavalry were ever present to protect the interests of these white intruders.

Osage Scalp Dance, painting by John Mix Stanley

ABOVE: *Battle scene* from the Sioux wars FAR RIGHT: *Chief Washaki* of the Shoshoni, famous for his eloquent advocacy of the Indians' cause

More treaties were made in which the Indians relinquished their lands. These were frequently broken by the white, but never by the Indians.

In 1877 Chief Joseph, of the Nez Percé, refused to renegotiate the terms of the unconscionable treaty of 1863. Moreover, he withdrew, firmly convinced justice would not be done. Taking many members of his tribe, Joseph led a retreat north toward Canada, outmaneuvering and outfighting pursuing troops.

At the Yellowstone River in Montana, however, Joseph miscalculated and was cornered by General Miles. Here he surrendered and was promptly imprisoned at Fort Leavenworth, Kansas. Later released, Chief Joseph returned to his people. He had earned not only their love, but the respect of the United States' military leaders as one of America's outstanding strategists.

As with all Indians, the Plateau people regretfully ceded their lands. Their sorrow was eloquently expressed to the Governor of Wyoming by Chief Washaki of the Shoshonis in a piece of oratory which became famous.

Familiar Fate

The fate of the Midwest farming tribes after contact with the white men paralleled that of the eastern Indians. The Natchez at first were co-operative with the French. By 1722 the intruders had established plantations in the Indians' realm, built towns and a capital, New Orleans, in their domain.

Inevitably, frictions occurred. A French sergeant shot an aged Natchez in the back in an argument over a debt. Men from the Natchez town of White Apple retaliated in kind. Angered, the French Governor sent an expedition bent on destroying several of the Natchez towns, but when it reached them, the people had fled. The Governor thereupon demanded the head of Old Hair, a town leader and, in fact, a Sun. And the war leader, Tattooed Serpent, brother of the Great Sun, acquiesced in order to keep the peace.

Death of Tattooed Serpent

Matters, however, worsened, not only with the death of the Tattooed Serpent in 1725 and that of his brother, the Great Sun, in 1729, but with the arrival of a new French Governor, who proved to be a most evil and rapacious tyrant. Demanding for his own plantation the young Great Sun's very town, he managed at last to exhaust the patience of the Indians. Enlisting the neighboring Choctaws as allies, the Natchez rose. Attacking the French settlement, they killed over 200 men, and captured even more women and children. The Governor himself was clubbed to death by one of the Stinkards.

But the end for the Natchez was near. Their allies, the Choctaws, had tongues like snakes and sided with the French. This finished the Natchez and after only a few months of warfare, the Great Sun surrendered. Many escaped and sought refuge among the Chicasaws and Creeks, but the Great Sun and his family were sold into slavery at Santo Domingo. The French had got their way – the destruction of an Indian nation which had thwarted their imperialistic ambitions.

Anguish and Death

The fate of the more northerly tribes along the Mississippi and its tributaries, though by no means so quick and so final, was nevertheless one of anguish, cultural destruction and physical death. As early as 1804, land-hungry Americans were eyeing the fertile valleys of the Sauk and Fox. The United States' relentless expansion knew no bounds. Nor was there anything subtle about their determination. With audacious blatancy the American commissioners forced through an inequitable treaty under threat of military destruction. In fear and ignorance, the Sauk and Fox, as did so many tribes, naively signed away their lands and with them their very way of life.

Forced to move west of the Mississippi, one Sauk group under the intrepid leadership of Black Hawk refused to accept the terms of the treaty. Instead, Black Hawk endeavored to enlist the aid of other tribes – the Osage, the Winnebago, the Cherokees and the Creeks. He and his son pleaded for help to resist white encroachment.

Skirmishes flared here and there and in 1832, with 500 warriors, Black Hawk and his band returned to their homelands. But his allies fell away and he attempted to surrender. His peace emissaries were cold-bloodedly shot down, and he attacked the white forces with some success, and retreated north. Here he was pursued by the militia and a party of Sioux. Cornered, Black Hawk surrendered under a white flag. This overture was ignored. Instead, his band was mercilessly slaughtered, men, women and children. Black Hawk himself escaped, only to be captured and imprisoned. Finally, in 1833, was released to return to the forlorn remnants of his people in Iowa.

The Indian threat, the Indian obstacle to American destiny east of the Mississippi was shattered.

The Pueblo Revolt

In the Southwest a kind of resigned acceptance of European domination prevailed, except for one massive attempt to overcome the invader who had made slaves of the Indians, extracting tribute – euphemistically called taxes – and throwing them into prison for recalcitrance. The Spaniards had also imposed their insistent Christian friars on the villages. But through it all the Pueblos retained their Indian ways – their economy, their family life and, to the consternation of the Franciscans, their native religious ceremonies.

Nearly a century of subjugation had passed when an Indian named Popé was released from jail at the colonial capital of Santa Fe. So incensed, so bitter was this man of the San Juan Pueblo that he brooded and schemed and then devised a brilliant plan. By organizing each Pueblo to concerted action, he believed the Indians could drive out the invaders and rid the land of a veritable plague. It was no simple matter to win unanimity among divergent peoples, but Popé's enthusiasm prevailed. The Pueblos arose in unison. They killed the friars and burned the churches and drove before them the 2,000 Spanish settlers. They rousted the Spanish Governor from his adobe palace at Sante Fe and killed about 500 palefaces.

The revolt was a complete success, but a short one. In 1692, only twelve years after the uprising, the indomitable Spaniards returned. Within four years they had re-established their oppressive domination.

Adapting Religions

As the years passed and the Spanish settlements became ever more firmly established, the Pueblos overtly accepted the tenets of Catholicism while still practicing the ancient tribal ceremonies not only secretly in their subterranean kivas, but

OVERLEAF:
Faith soon to be broken
Ceremonial signing of a treaty with the Shoshoni Indians depicted by C. C. Nahl. Of some 370 treaties made with Indian tribes, all to the advantage of the whites, nearly all were broken by the whites, none by the Indians

Wounded Knee
The scene after the massacre as depicted by Mary Irvin Wright

openly in their town plazas. And the friars finally had wit enough to see that the Indians were very smart – that they could readily add Christian precepts to their own native beliefs. If one set of gods were effective, what harm in adding the Father, Son and Holy Ghost? The Spaniards, by conquering them, had demonstrated that they had powerful gods. Surely the Pueblos could use all the help they could get.

It wasn't until 1848 when the United States acquired New Mexico and Arizona from Mexico that the balance of power changed in the Southwest. Up until this time the Apaches had been raiding the Pueblos and Spanish settlements. Nor were the Navahos opposed to pilfering sheep and horses and goats. But they were a little more inclined to make friends than the Apaches. They had even harbored Pueblo people during the period of Spanish plundering and from them learned many skills. Not so the Apaches. They had suffered too much from the ruthlessness of the Spaniards and were ever resentful of the callous white man. Now they must contend with the white men from the East.

Starved Into Surrendering

In 1863 Colonel Kit Carson was ordered to bring the Navahos to peace and this he did most expeditiously. Rather than trying to overcome them militarily, he and his troops systematically killed their flocks of sheep, destroyed their crops of corn and peaches. Within a year the Navahos, starved to the point of surrender, flocked to Fort Defiance some 8,000 strong. For four long years they were kept prisoner at Fort Sumner along the Pecos River of New Mexico. And then by the Treaty of 1868, in return for a promise never to defy the authority of the United States, they were returned to their homeland. Here they were given sheep in replacement for those destroyed, supplied with tools and clothes and schools for their children. While over a century has elapsed, the Navahos have not forgotten the horrible sadness of "Fort."

the region. When he finally surrendered to General Nelson Miles in 1886, he and his people were shipped to Florida and confined in the bastions of the ancient Spanish fort at St. Augustine. Later removed to Oklahoma, their imprisonment did not end until 1913.

The demise of the California tribes was the same sad story as elsewhere throughout the nation. What the Franciscans and their missions didn't destroy psychologically, the settlers and miners did physically. The Indians were in the way. By 1850, it is estimated that there were barely 17,000 Indians in California.

The northern village tribes, the Mandan and Hidatsa and the Arikara, as well as their relatives to the south, the Pawnee, had relatively minor conflicts with the whites. The Pawnee realized the power of the white men and decided to join them militarily as scouts against their enemies.

The Mandans were destroyed without a fight in a most insidious and tragic manner. Smallpox struck their villages in the late eighteenth century. Epidemic followed epidemic. When Lewis and Clark, the hardy explorers of the United States' new Louisiana purchase, wintered at the Mandan villages in 1804, the Mandans reported that formerly they did not fear the Sioux, but that now their force of warriors was so decimated that they could barely defend themselves. Plague after plague fell upon them. And so, by the middle of the nineteenth century, there were a mere 39 ragged souls left in two dilapidated villages.

Cost of Killing

During the long years of the new nation's expansion westward, many were the battles between the white man's armed force and the Indians – the Fetterman and Wagon Box, the Sand Creek, Beecher Island and Rosebud, to name a few. Some were decisive victories for the army. Many more were standoffs and a few were utter disasters. In this last category, Custer's of course capped the record.

The life of an Indian fighting trooper was a combination of absolute boredom and great danger. All sorts of men joined up. The pay was enticing – $13 a month for enlisted men, $117.50 for officers. With good army food, comfortable lodgings and a clothing allowance, the risk of an arrow in the back seemed well worth taking.

Actually, throughout all the Indian wars, most battles were short and casualties were small. This fact, of course, was little consolation to the victims, either Indian or soldier. Nonetheless, the government funneled vast sums of money to the army, partly to ensure the safety of travelers, but indisputably, as well, intended to effect the complete subjugation of the Indians. A student of arithmetic once calculated that it cost the nation $1,000,000 for every Indian killed.

The marauding Apaches were like wary wolf packs, harassing settlers, miners and travelers with a canny slyness. Led by men like Cochise, they were hard to find, hard to shoot and hard to kill. Only at the conclusion of the Civil War in 1865 did the United States make a concerted effort to control their resistance. And only after costly campaigns aimed at their complete annihilation were the Apaches partly subdued, eventually to be placed on reservations throughout Arizona and New Mexico.

Humiliation and Hunger

Their treatment under government jurisdiction was at first pitiful. Forced onto reservations in areas they said they did not like, existing on short-change rations on which unscrupulous suppliers got rich, the Apaches suffered humiliation and absolute hunger. In the mid-1870s their resentment flared. Geronimo, a wily and artful warrior, assumed leadership of a small band of Chiricahua and raised terror throughout

CHAPTER VIII

The Drive Westward

THE COLONIZING of the continent proceeded for 200 years, from the time when the Dutch reached the mouth of the Hudson River in 1624, and a year later named their settlement New Amsterdam. Farther south along the shores of the Delaware, the Swedes set their towns. Penn's Pennsylvania and Oglethorpe's Georgia lured men and women to the opportunities of the New World.

From England and Germany, from France and Northern Ireland, colonists arrived on the east coast and pressed inland. They sought their fortunes as coopers and blacksmiths, as millers and farmers. Within a century the feebly struggling settlements at Jamestown and Plymouth had grown into established cities. Savannah, in Georgia, New Bern in North Carolina, and Williamsburg in Virginia, all became important urban centers. By 1730 Philadelphia was the largest colonial capital with a population of 40,000, while Baltimore, New York, Providence and Boston were also thriving towns.

In large measure the prospering of these cities as centers of commerce was thanks to the growing agricultural economy of the colonies. By the mid-eighteenth century, German immigrants had well-secured farming communities north along the Hudson River. Germans and men from the north of Ireland, referred to as "Scotch-Irish," had already pushed into western Pennsylvania and down the Cumberland valley, hard against the barrier of the Appalachian Mountains. Englishmen from Virginia were also hewing their way west, chopping out little clearings. Like the New Yorkers of the Hudson River and Pennsylvanians of Lancaster County, theirs was a life of mere existence, of felling trees, of building rude log cabins, of grubbing a few acres for a crop of corn and potatoes and beans.

In a sense, these pioneers were people with their backs against a wall. Their very desperation demanded a courage and industriousness which in reality saved them. In addition to the arduous work for sheer survival, they had to contend with the ever-present threat of attack by Indians.

The eastern parts of the New World were becoming more and more densely settled; the stage was now set for the greatest American drama of all – the opening of the West.

Frontier Fever

By 1830, ten years after the death of Daniel Boone, the settlements had reached the Mississippi River, and the frontier fever had attacked a Boston schoolteacher named Hall J. Kelly.

The thought of making tracks for Oregon was a dream Kelly could not dispel. Depressed by the loss of Fort Astoria to the English, and inspired by the potentialities of Oregon, he read and studied everything he could lay his hands on about the territory. So enthusiastic did he become that he gave talks and wrote articles about

the wonders of Oregon. Kelly had never been West, but by 1833 he had so convinced himself and a few reluctant others of the wonderful prospects in Oregon that he led a small party as far as New Orleans. Here the loyal followers threw in the sponge.

The inconveniences of the trip were surpassed only by Kelly's bumbling and the immigrants went home. But Kelly was a determined man. He made his way alone from Vera Cruz across Mexico, where the Mexicans promptly confiscated his property and supplies. To recoup his losses, Kelly rounded up some cattle with the plan of driving them to Vancouver in the hope of selling them to John McLoughlin of the Hudson's Bay. But McLoughlin, although renowned for his hospitality, took Kelly for a cattle thief and treated him rather shabbily. On top of this, Kelly contracted malaria and almost died. Finally, hard-luck Kelly was put on a ship and eventually arrived back in Boston in 1836. His dream had become a nightmare.

Dream to Reality

Kelly's dream, however, became reality for others. Not only was colonization being promoted, but Christianizing the Indians was also

a popular goal. As early as 1835, Marcus Whitman and Samuel Park spent some time in the Green River region proselytizing the heathens. Convinced that more and more money was needed to do an effective job in bringing the true religion to the Indians, Whitman decided to go back East for help.

There he gathered more funds from the Presbyterians and Congregationalists. He also gathered himself a wife, Narcissa Prentis, who proved as inspired a missionary as her groom. In the spring of 1836, the Whitmans and another newly-married couple named Spaulding headed West on what turned out to be one of the longest honeymoons on record.

A Fatal Misunderstanding
The men provided wagons so their brides might ride, but after reaching what is now Boise, Idaho, they found conditions so hard that the women had to walk. They made it to Oregon despite the hardships, and there the Whitmans set up a mission among the Cayuse Indians, in a region where there were a few scattered colonists. Here the missionaries ministered to the Indians' needs and extolled the advantages of the Christian faith.

Things went well for several years until a plague broke out among the natives; when Whitman could not cure them the Indians accused the good missionary of having caused the illness. He had been observed giving a patient medicine from a bottle. The Indians concluded that the contents contained the source of the epidemic and forthwith destroyed the mission and killed Whitman and his wife.

The Oregon Trail
The migration to Oregon began on a small scale in the late 1830s. Then in 1842, 130 pioneers set out under the leadership of Elijah White, with eighteen wagons to haul their belongings. Shortly afterwards one group of a 1,000 immigrants headed West.

It was John Fremont's expedition of 1843 that focused public attention on the marvels of Oregon and the possibilities of practical settlement. Fremont had already commanded an exploring party to the Rocky Mountains in 1842, his guide being the inimitable Kit Carson. This latest Oregon trip, again led by Carson, took them through Nevada, across the Sierras and into California.

It was Fremont's lengthy, detailed and glow-

Attack on the Emigrant Trail, painting by Carl Wimar

Travellers and Settlers

RIGHT: The trek across the plains by "prairie schooner"

FAR RIGHT: After the new homestead, a sod house, had been built, the family posed for a photographer

ing report of the region that gave the real impetus to the great migration that followed. Congress came alert and ordered that a 100,000 copies of it be printed. Everyone wanted to read about the dashing "Pathfinder," as Fremont was universally dubbed, as well as about the wonders he described.

Between the years 1845 and 1847 from 3,000 to 5,000 opportunists hit the trail for Oregon.

Most of the caravans were assembled at such towns as Independence, St. Joseph, or Westport, now Kansas City, along the Missouri River. The majority of pioneers were Missouri and Iowa farmers. Disgruntled at the poor prices they had received for the crops following the depression of 1837, and feeling hemmed in, they decided to make a new start to their lives in the Promised Land.

Saddled with all their worldly possessions, pots and pans, guns and ammunition, chairs and tables, beds and chests, even cows and chickens, they must also buy supplies for the trek. Flour and sugar, beans and bacon were the staples. They might also buy a wagon, and mules and oxen to pull it. A few of the wagons were Conestogas, those sturdily built "Prairie Schooners" designed for the rough roads of the East. Many more were box wagons fitted with high, curved ribs over which canvas was stretched to form a protective cover against both the searing sunrays and the drenching rains. The hope was that even with all their belongings inside there would be space enough for at least the women and children to enjoy some sleep and find privacy.

When the Grass Was High

The usual plan was that the caravans should leave as soon as the grass was tall enough to provide forage for the livestock. When the party was almost ready, a guide, usually a retired trapper and mountain man who knew the route, would be employed. In addition, a member of the party would be elected as captain or wagon master. Frequently this selection was not made until several days after the wagon train had departed, by which time everyone would be better acquainted and able to make a sounder choice.

The day began punctually at dawn with the sounding of a bugle. After breakfast, the mules and oxen were hitched up and by seven the procession was on its way. Shortly before noon the wagons were halted for the animals to graze and the people to prepare a midday meal.

Not until about three in the afternoon did the caravan start up again. The women and children rode in the wagons, if there was room. The men and boys, walking alongside, or riding a horse, had the job of herding the livestock. At dusk they would halt for the night, the wagons drawn up in a circle, the tongue of each wagon being pushed under the rear of the next as a defense against Indian attack. The livestock were often corralled inside as an additional precaution.

Fifteen Miles a Day

Well-organized caravans had a definite route and schedule. About fifteen miles a day was what they needed to cover if they were to reach the Cascade Mountains before the October

Facing appalling hazards
William Ranney's painting entitled *Prairie Fire*

snows. Trying to cross the mountains in winter would be sheer disaster. Leaving the Missouri, the route cut northwest over the rolling prairies of eastern Kansas until it reached Fort Kearney on the Platte River. From there it followed the river past Chimney Rock and the impressive stone ridges known as Council Bluffs. About 45 days after leaving the Missouri River, the pioneers should have reached Fort Laramie, a welcome resting place. The men repaired the wagons, fitting new iron tires when necessary, shoed the oxen, mules and horses. The women washed the clothes. This was the last stop where they could refit and obtain supplies.

Northwest from Laramie

From Fort Laramie the trail led northwest, still along the Platte, past Independence Rock, the granite landmark on which many carved their initials and the date as mementoes of their progress. At the confluence of the Sweetwater River the trail headed due west through the gentle South Pass at the foot of the Wind River Mountains. By now they had been 50 to 55 days on the trail and were nearly 950 miles from their starting place.

It was not unusual that at this point tensions mounted, quarrels exploded and dissension led to ugly brawls. Blame for conditions was generally directed at the wagon master. Sometimes he would be displaced by someone else who the group felt had stronger qualities. It was here that laggards were often left behind to fend for themselves; some gave up and turned around to head for home.

Following tributaries of the Green River and

then the Green itself, the course dropped in a southwesterly direction to Fort Bridger. From there it turned north along the Bear River to Fort Hall in Idaho.

End of the Trail

Now the trekkers' real troubles began. Along the Snake River west toward Fort Boise and on toward the Whitman Mission in Oregon was barren country with good water in scarce supply. High-growing sagebrush clogged the wagon trails. River crossings were as difficult as they were hazardous. The draft animals were worn and tired. To relieve the strain, dispensable luxuries such as stoves and trunks were often cast out to litter the trail.

It was a troublesome trip over the Blue Mountains and down the Columbia River from the mouth of the Umatilla River. Here the Oregon Trail officially ended and the wagons had to be abandoned. All the goods and belongings were then stacked on rafts or sometimes in canoes for the trip down the Columbia River. A few foolhardy souls lashed their wagons to rafts and in some cases were lucky. More often the raft would capsize with its top-heavy load and everything would be lost including a few pioneers. Altogether the trip to Fort Vancouver and the ocean, over 2,000 miles from Independence, was an ordeal which would take about five months.

California-Bound

To those for whom California was the goal, the route split at the Snake River west of Fort Hall, with the travelers dropping south along the

Staking a claim
Would-be homesteaders
race to sign up for land

Raft River and past the strange natural formations called the City of Rocks. Progressing further, they would reach the Humboldt River. Here the going was made easier by an abundance of grass and good water, but traveling westward through the Humboldt Sink was a nightmare. Progress was slow and precarious through marshes and saltwater bogs. Beyond the sink lay an arid desert backed by the almost impenetrable Sierra Nevada Mountains. The Truckee, a turbulent, boulder-strewn river, led up to Donner Pass, and then the trail led to the California valleys of the Sacramento and San Joaquin.

While the Oregon and California trails were the principal routes west, others were tried, but generally given up as too difficult. The hardship endured on these trips was often acute. The livestock might die for want of good grazing and water, and sickness and death overtook many of the pioneers themselves. Cholera was especially feared. Tragedy appeared in the form of accidents like drownings, and small children falling out of wagons to be crushed under the wheels. Danger of Indian attack was ever present, though the very numbers of wagons and people served as a deterrent to the warriors. Actually very few engagements occurred.

Short cuts were sometimes plotted which might save many miles, but were often so hazardous as to be barely worth the time saved. An example was the Sublette cutoff on the Oregon Trail – 50 miles without a drop of water from the Green River west to the Bear.

Marked for Tragedy
Small, independent parties were subject to the greatest danger. Often they were composed of a few determined individuals who believed they could make it without benefit of a scout.

One such group marked for grisly tragedy was the Donner Party. These were a group of emigrants from Iowa and Illinois, led by the Donner and Reed families. To save time, since they were running late, they foolishly decided to take a short cut. Known as the Hastings cutoff, the path ran from Fort Bridger south around the Great Salt Lake. It turned out to be a hellish ordeal over endless salt flats. Arguments flared over the choice of route. Reed knew nothing of the terrain. Donner was old and knew less.

When the group reached what is now Donner Lake, high in the Sierras, they stopped to recoup their strength. By now it was mid-October and to stop at this time was disastrous; suddenly a great blizzard engulfed them.

Short of supplies and fuel, they tried to dig in, building little cabins to ward off the wintry gales. By December, one group of seventeen could stand it no longer. Risking the deep snows, they tried to make it down the mountain enduring untold suffering during their trek. It took them over 30 days before they reached the low-

lands. The trip had cost the lives of six men and a boy, and the 60 or so others who remained behind were by this time slowly starving. Those who did not die from want of food were freezing to death. Frantic from the pangs of hunger, they began to devour their dead companions. By the time they were finally rescued, there were less than half the original party of 87 surviving.

A New Religion
The Mormon migration to the West had its origins in central New York State in the 1820s

in a somewhat eccentric family named Smith. The grandfather, called "Old Crooked Neck" Smith, suffered fits from time to time. His grandson Joseph, like other members of the family, delved into the occult; Joseph wore a little stone in his hat which he claimed enabled him to find gold hidden in the earth.

In 1827, according to his own account, Joseph had a mystical vision which revealed to him the whereabouts of some fabulous golden tablets. Although nearly illiterate, he translated the inscriptions, it is recorded, by means of a pair of magic glasses, and was astonished to learn that the tablets contained certain missing books of the Bible. The translation became known as the *Book of the Mormon*. It referred to the lost tribes of Israel, two of which, amazingly, had found their way to America. One was the good Nephites, the other the cruel Lamanites. The Lamanites, who were reputedly the Indians, totally annihilated the Nephites, all except one named Mormon. His sacred mission, as Smith interpreted these revelations, was to conquer the Lamanites.

Smith published the book, but at $1.75 a copy, a price revealed by God, it didn't sell very well; so God reduced the price to $1.25. Sales picked up. After many people had studied this new-

found gospel, Smith believed he had sufficient followers to form the Church of Jesus Christ of the Latter-Day Saints. Neighbors' ridicule of the Saints soon drove the converts to Kirtland, Ohio. Here in 1831, Smith organized a command colony; from there he sent out missionaries. So successful was their proselytizing that 1,000 new converts were recruited. A particularly zealous missionary, one of the newer converts, was a man named Brigham Young.

Spiritual Banker

Smith, besides being spiritual leader of the Church, was also the banker. As such, he amassed considerable wealth in land and small industry. In his divine capacity, he received revelations which banned such earthly pleasures as smoking and the use of alcohol. Somehow, the revelation concerning abstinence excluded Smith himself, who drank and smoked as he pleased.

Again the neighbors gave trouble. Apprehensive of the strength of the Saints' communal economy, skeptical of their being true Christians, and shocked by rumors that they indulged in polygamy, the good people of Ohio showed their distaste by giving Smith a good tar-and-feathering. With that, Smith promptly received a revelation that Independence, Missouri, was the new Promised Land.

At Independence, the Mormons built a temple, worked hard and prospered. But here again they antagonized their non-Mormon neighbors. Pitched battles erupted and yet again the Mormons pulled up stakes. Offered a haven in Illinois, they began life again in a town named Nauvoo. Their industriousness was phenomenal. By 1840 Nauvoo was one of the most flourishing communities in Illinois, numbering 10,000 people and growing daily.

Twelve Wives for a Saint

Smith was a willful man. He demanded complete autonomy for his Mormon "state" – his own courts, his own militia, his own monetary system. In 1843 he announced a new revelation that sanctioned polygamy, whereupon he took to himself twelve wives, a situation his first wife, Emma, was enjoined to accept without complaint. Not long after this, Smith managed to run for the presidency of the United States. But this only increased already existent animosities. By 1844 Smith and his brother Hyrum had so angered the surrounding communities that they were arrested and charged with treason. The two were imprisoned in Carthage, Illinois, though not very securely, for they were murdered by a mob which stormed the jail.

A New Leader

With Smith's death, the Saints were left without a leader. Several candidates tried to fill the

Above A consciously posed work gang, with relatives, on the framework of a barn. Co-operation was the key to survival on the frontier

On the Mormon Tra

Brigham Young

Joseph Smith

New homes in new lands
ABOVE: A work gang –
plus their relations –
pose proudly on the
framework of a barn on
the frontier, where
co-operation was
essential for survival
BELOW: The Mormons,
who hit the trail not
once but repeatedly

vacancy, but it was Brigham Young, largely responsible for maintaining a measure of unity in the wake of the assassination, who was finally elected to succeed Smith. In a very short time Young proved himself to be an able and strong leader, one who was more concerned with sound organization than the erratic Smith had been.

But the ill feelings aroused in Illinois did not disappear with Smith's death. Rather, they increased, finally becoming active religious persecution. Matters grew so tense that Young decided there was no choice but to abandon Nauvoo. Again the Saints left their homes, their shops, their industries and their beloved temple. Almost aimlessly they moved westward, with no fixed destination in mind.

To the Great Salt Lake

Young was familiar with Fremont's journals. It occurred to him from descriptions he had read of the Great Basin and Salt Lake that this might be a region remote enough for the Mormons to carry on their way of life there unmolested. And so the decision was made.

The Saints set out boldly across the Plains, their spirits sustained by a little brass marching band. When the advance party eventually worked its way through South Pass, they happened upon Jim Bridger. Young learned more about the Great Basin from Bridger, and

concluded that the land east of Salt Lake might be habitable. The party continued on, dropping south from Fort Bridger toward Salt Lake. Finally, after a most toilsome trip, someone spied the great shining body of water.

The Mormons were quick to choose this as the site for their new home. They had to be. It was now the end of July, and crops needed to be planted if the people were to survive the winter. The earth was sunbaked to the hardness of a brick, but they diverted a stream, plowed the moistened soil and hurriedly planted corn, beans and potatoes.

That was 1847. In succeeding years other Mormons flocked to the new Salt Lake City. One group, lacking wagons and draft animals, pushed and pulled handcarts over the long trail. The next year Young led nearly 3,000 Saints to their new home. No sooner had they arrived than disaster threatened. A plague of grasshoppers descended over the fields, menacing all the crops. Starvation seemed to be imminent. And then, almost as though from nowhere, a great flock of gulls appeared in what was claimed as a beneficent act of God. The birds devoured the insects and the crops were saved.

The Santa Fe Trail

Not all trails west were trod by pioneers, and the Santa Fe Trail was one. It was begun exclusively for trade with Mexican settlements in and about Santa Fe. Until the Mexican Revolution in 1821, the Spanish Southwest was sealed against the Americans. But with the lifting of restrictions, a lively commerce was begun.

Freighters generally collected their wares at Independence, Missouri, and loaded them into Conestoga or sturdy Pittsburgh wagons. These were drawn by as many as twelve oxen or mules. Mirrors, woolen shawls, yard goods of silk and cotton, tools and hardware accounted for the bulk of the 3,000 to 5,000 pounds of merchandise that would make up the cargo.

From Independence, the freighters headed west, each leaving separately in the spring as soon as ready. At Council Grove, Kansas, they waited for one another until all had assembled, enough to form a great caravan. From here on, the danger of Indian attack, especially by the Kiowas and Comanches, was constant. Strength in numbers was an essential consideration. Here the trip was organized, captains chosen, night guards assigned to duty, cooks elected.

From Council Grove the trail led southwest to the Big Bend of the Arkansas and on along that river for some 120 miles. There the trail split. The main route continued along the river to Bent's Fort and then south to Santa Fe. The short cut dropped southwest in a direct line to the old Spanish capital. The short cut was quicker, but was fraught with a nasty hazard, the Cimarron Desert.

In Santa Fe the traders sold their goods. They sold over $1,750,000 worth in 1846. Some of this money was spent on mules and horses, pelts and bars of gold. These they took back with them on the return trip and sold at a handsome profit. The Santa Fe Trail, for those who dared risk it, yielded no mean jackpot.

The New Texans

The colonizing of Texas differed from that in most other regions in that the enemy to be over-

FAR LEFT: *Emigrants Attacked by Indians*, painting by John S. Davies
BELOW: *Ruthless in victory*, the Mexican General Santa Anna captures the Alamo, and *Sam Houston*, whose troops retook the Alamo and assured Texan independence

Missouri steamboat De Smet tied up at Fort Benton, Montana, in about 1870

come was not Indians but the Spanish.

In 1820, a Yankee from Connecticut named Moses Austin proposed to the Spaniards a grandiose scheme of colonization. The Spanish agreed but Austin died suddenly and didn't get to see his plan fulfilled.

Austin's son Stephen inherited his father's enthusiasm. He completed the transaction with dispatch and by 1822 had enlisted 150 settlers. Each man was to receive 640 acres, each wife 320, and each child 60. For this they were to pay twelve and a half cents per acre.

The Mexican Revolution of 1821 sent Austin rushing to Mexico City to validate his rights. Not only did he secure them, but he was granted 354 acres of farming land and 66,000 grazing acres on the understanding that he would bring 200 families enticed by the prospect of each acquiring either 177 acres for farming or 4,428 acres for grazing.

Austin was successful in his recruiting. The American settlers were for the most part from Kentucky and Tennessee, shrewd Germans and Irishmen. They were quick to take the 4,000-acre grazing grants. By 1827 it was estimated that there were 10,000 Americans in Texas and by 1835 over three times that many.

As time passed, the Mexican government began imposing restrictions upon the colonists – custom fees, military posts and the closing of the borders to further American immigration. The Americans, as might be expected, resented any curtailment of their imagined freedoms. Talk of Texas as an independent nation or as a territory of the United States spread as bickering with Mexican authorities increased. It was during this period of tension that Sam Houston, a lawyer and former congressman, as well as a former governor of Tennessee, wandered onto the scene. As a politician, he thought he knew a good thing when he saw it. He believed that the best interests of Texas lay in becoming part of the United States. He even wrote President Andrew Jackson to that effect.

Loyal to Mexico

Stephen Austin thought not. He went so far as to urge his fellow Texans to remain loyal to Mexico and to work harmoniously with the Mexicans for a smoothly running country.

The Texans did not take kindly to the plans which General Santa Anna, the Mexican military dictator, had for them. He took even less kindly to rumblings of a revolution. Backed by 6,000 troops, he was fully capable of quashing it.

In October 1835 the Texans hastily met in convention to prepare for the dictator's invasion. They elected Henry Smith provisional head of the government and Sam Houston military commander. While the title sounded impressive, Houston didn't have much to command. His forces were divided and widely dispersed. There

were 150 men at San Antonio, 100 at St. Patricia; at Goliad there were 400, while Houston had 350 men at Gonzales.

At word of the Mexican advance, the Texans determined to defend San Antonio. Having already destroyed the 150 men at St. Patricia, Santa Anna attacked. Outnumbered, the Texans were forced to retire to a small fortified chapel called the Alamo. They resolved to hold it against the Mexican army at all costs. While there were only 184 men for the defense, they were daring and independent, and they were superior marksmen. Among them were renowned frontiersmen James Bowie and Davy Crockett.

Santa Anna was confident of his superiority and demanded surrender. The Texans refused and on February 24, 1836, the siege began. For over a week the defenders held out against hopeless odds. Not until March 6, in a bitter hand-to-hand struggle within the very walls, did Santa Anna take the fort. His men did not leave a single Texan alive.

Remember The Alamo

While Santa Anna enjoyed a resounding military victory, the fall of the Alamo gave the Texans

a moral cause. Everywhere the settlers rallied to the cry, "Remember the Alamo." Volunteers joined Houston in increasing numbers until soon he had some 1,500 recruits under his command.

Because of the Mexicans' greater numbers, however, Houston was compelled to take delaying actions and the armies did not meet until April. At San Jacinto Ferry Santa Anna, sure of his strength, relaxed his vigil. This was his mistake. On the afternoon of April 21, the Texans charged.

Inspired by the cry, "Remember the Alamo,"

they completely surprised the Mexicans. The encounter was brief, and while shots were being exchanged, the Mexicans broke ranks and fled. The next day Santa Anna himself was captured. The victory was complete; Texas was no longer under the Mexican yoke.

Mule Skinners

The increasing number of pioneers, freighters and, later, miners and railroad builders were under perpetual threat of Indian attack. To the Kiowas and Comanches, the freighters on

the Santa Fe trail posed not only the danger of further inroads into their own territories, but were also on occasion a plum to be picked. It was not until 1829, however, that protection in the form of a military escort was provided. Unfortunately, the infantrymen trudging along beside the wagons were only partially effective as guards. Better protection was needed for the rich cargoes and the "mule skinners," or wagoners, who drove the teams. In 1833 ten companies of dragoons were assigned for the sole purpose of patrolling the Southwest. Under Colonel Stephen Kearny, they rode around the southern Plains with a show of arms intended to intimidate the Indians. Not much happened, but at least there were no fights.

To the north along the Platte River, the Oregon Trail ran through the southern territories of the Sioux. While at first the Indians allowed the wagon trains to pass unmolested, the immigrants were nonetheless in constant fear. To afford them protection, mounted troops were garrisoned at Fort Laramie. Recently purchased by the government, from the American Fur Company, it served as a base for later forts along the Bozeman Trail leading to the Montana mining towns.

One Wandering Cow

The first real trouble with the Sioux came as the result of a worn-out cow. It was mid-August, 1854, and a group of immigrating Mormons were approaching Fort Laramie. As they passed near some Sioux villages a few miles east of the fort, a footsore cow somehow escaped the caravan. Before its owner could catch it, a young Miniconjou warrior playfully shot at it and butchered it on the spot. When the Mormons reached Fort Laramie, the owner reported his loss to the commandant, Lieutenant Hugh Fleming, in the hope of restitution. Fleming didn't give the matter much attention. Even when Conquering Bear, chief of the Brule Sioux, with whom the Miniconjous were camped, came to the fort to try to settle the matter, Fleming treated the affair casually and nothing was settled.

Among the officers under Fleming's command was a brash shavetail lieutenant named James Gratten. The next day he was able to convince his superior that he should take a force of 29 men and two howitzers to bring the Miniconjou culprit to justice. Fleming naively agreed.

Gratten knew nothing about Indians. Foolhardily, he marched his troop straight toward the Sioux villages where close to 5,000 Indians camped. It is estimated that over 1,000 of them were fighting men – Oglalas, Brules and Miniconjous. Past the Oglala camps and on to the Brule he went. Confronting Conquering Bear, he demanded the Miniconjou. The chief

"WESTWARD THE COURSE OF EMPIRE TAKES ITS WAY" WITH McCORMICK REAPERS IN THE VAN.

could not produce him. Instead, he offered two of his horses. Gratten grew impatient. Suddenly he quit conferring and willfully commanded his men to shoot toward the Indians. Conquering Bear ordered his warriors to hold their fire, but when Gratten had the cannons fired, the Indians could no longer be restrained. In a matter of minutes, swarms of angered Sioux warriors surrounded the troops, wiping them out all but one man. Conquering Bear was mortally wounded, Gratten was the first to be killed.

The sole surviving trooper escaped to hide at a nearby trading post, but died of his wounds two days later. And so, with the loss of one dumb cow, the Sioux wars began; they were not to end for over 35 years.

Treks by Water

In the opening up of the West, one of the earliest, most common, most dependable and least expensive modes of transportation was the river traffic. The French *coureurs de bois* were quick to adopt the Indians' canoe. This was a conveyance for transporting furs from the Northwest to Montreal. Using both birch-bark and dugout, voyageurs could traverse the 5,000 miles of waterways carrying up to eight tons of goods within 100 days. Lewis and Clark made their journey as far as the mouth of the Marias in a bateau equipped with 22 oars, a sail and two piragnes. They could make about fifteen miles a day upstream, more often than not tugging it with ropes along the shore.

Flatboats were in common use. They were, in reality, mere 40-foot-long boxes with a twelve-foot beam and eight foot depth, and drew practically no water at all. Usually equipped with four 30-foot oars, a 50-foot tiller and often a sail, they were great for downstream navigation. The keelboat, slightly less cumbersome than the bargelike flatboat, was 50 feet long and twelve feet wide with a tapering prow and keel.

Advertising made full use of the contemporary spirit of pioneering adventure to promote, in these examples, clothing and reaping machines

Ghost town
Cattle grazing near the deserted settlement at Bodie, California

These boats carried oars and a sail, and were fitted with a platform at the gunwale. A man standing on this plunged one end of a long pole into the river bottom and walked forward pushing the pole, followed by another doing the same, and thus they propelled the boat: when the last man on the platform reached the forward position, he removed his pole and returned to the aft position and again began his walk. Keelboats could carry up to 40 tons of freight and every man who pushed a pole could guarantee it.

West of the Mississippi two other types of boats were popular. The "Mackinaw" was a 50-foot rowboat with a five-foot bow and stern and a three-foot mid-section where the cargo was stored. At the forward section were four oarsmen, while a helmsman guided the craft with an oar from the aft deck. Most unwieldy was the "bullboat," originally used by the Missouri River Indians. This was composed of a series of bent willow rods lashed together to form a dome, over which were stretched buffalo hides. Sewn together, the seams were caulked with tallow. These huge tubs were sometimes 30 feet in diameter and ten to twelve feet in depth. Usually two men with paddles and oars tried to maneuver the ungainly craft. In fast currents and eddies it would spin crazily and was more often out of control than not.

Wood-burning Steamboats

As early as 1817, the steamboat *Pike* had reached St. Louis and three years later the *Western Engineer* churned up the muddy waters of the Missouri as far as Council Bluffs. The *Yellowstone* reached Fort Union in 1832, and in 1860 the *Key West* and *Chippewa* docked at Fort Benton, the head of navigation. While the *Yellowstone* was a side wheeler, most boats plying the Missouri and its tributaries were stern wheelers.

The advantages of river travel were that great amounts of cargo and a sizable number of passengers could be transported inexpensively. But there were also dangers – snags to puncture the hulls, shifting currents causing hidden sandbars upon which the boats became grounded. All the boats were wood-burning and were often overstocked to get a higher head of steam. Greater speed, however, often meant burst boilers and fires. These accidents could destroy the cargo and ruin the consignor, and spoil the trip completely for the passengers if it didn't blow them to bits.

The drive westward, which had been a gradually accelerating process for two centuries, suddenly exploded after a discovery at a place called Sutter's Mill, in California, in 1849.

Johann August Sutter, born in Germany of Swiss parents in 1803, arrived in America at the

age of 31. Reaching St. Louis, he had an urge to go farther, so taking the Santa Fe Trail he proceeded to California. Here he was soon successful in developing extensive trading interests along the coast and out into the Pacific as far as Hawaii. Later he established a community which he named New Helvetia and his own mills, livestock and agricultural holdings made him a wealthy and powerful man. And then, on January 19, 1849, Sutter's whole world changed.

J. W. Marshall, a partner in a sawmill project,

found traces of gold in the millrace. Promptly reporting his find to Sutter, they together verified its genuineness. Sutter decided it was best to keep the whole matter a secret, but word got out and rumors spread. Almost overnight, shopkeepers left their stores, farmers dropped their plows and headed west. News soon reached the East. Early in 1849, booklets were printed describing how to mine and how to get to California.

Gold fever struck the nation. The "forty-niners" began their greedy rush to get rich.

The Gold Rush

There were several routes to California. The safest and most convenient was to take a sailing ship around Cape Horn. Aside from the mono-tony and poor food, the chief disadvantage of going by water was that it took so long – six boring months. A shorter way was to go by sea to Panama, across the isthmus, and take another ship to California. Port cities of Colon and Panama were filthy and the jungle was ridden with cholera and fever. So it was both more inconvenient and dangerous.

The two principal overland routes were the Santa Fe and Oregon trails. Here the travelers faced all the hardships of their predecessors and more. In their frantic haste to start mining gold they often didn't prepare themselves; they went ill-equipped and physically soft. Unlike the pioneers before them who were already hardened to frontier life, many of the forty-niners were city people unaccustomed to the rigors of outdoor living. This inexperience cost many lives.

Boom Town

San Francisco suddenly became a booming port. Not only did prospectors arriving by ship jam the city, but the gold seekers from overland congregated to refurbish their supplies. Sailors abandoning their ships in favor of seeking gold swelled the ranks. Lodgings were in short supply. A bunk in a tent might cost as much as $20 a week, a room in a lodging house $250 a month. Food, too, was high: sugar, for example, brought three dollars a pound. Most purchases were made in gold dust and all shopkeepers had assayer's scales for weighing it.

The chance of easy riches attracted not only the prospectors, but others who hoped to find wealth from the miners themselves. Glittering saloons and dance halls flourished, and any gold these failed to drain from the miners' purses the gambling halls did. The city became a haven for the professional gambler, the best-dressed man in town.

Harlots, too, unabashedly plied their trade and houses of ill repute were common. Except for the dance hall girls, who were not usually prostitutes, the ladies of pleasure were about the only women in town. Crime ran high in San Francisco and murders were commonplace.

Matters became so critical for the respectable element that a vigilante committee was formed. The committee, however, decided that crime paid and itself became an organizer of the criminal element. Not until 1851 was a new committee formed. It still took five years and another 1,000 murders before the city was cleaned up.

Joaquin the Terrible

While San Francisco had its problems with crime, the countryside also had its share. The name Joaquin Murieta brought terror to ranchers, store owners, saloon-keepers and stagecoach passengers alike, for Joaquin was the leader of a gang of ruthless Mexican bandits, one of whom was known by the descriptive name 'Three-Fingered Jack. So much of a threat was Joaquin that in 1853 the Governor of California put a reward of $1,500 for him dead or alive.

The gang was hard to find, added to which

there happened to be not one, but five Joaquins, a problem easily resolved in the event by the pursuing rangers. They simply captured the first gang they came upon. One of the members was Three-Fingered Jack. The rangers chopped off this hand and, assuming him to be their man, removed his head. Both these trophies were pickled in jars of alcohol and exhibited in Sacramento as Joaquin's head and Three-Fingered Jack's hand. Years later Joseph E. Badger, Jr. wrote a dime novel entitled *Joaquin the Terrible* which made the bandit out to be a sort of Robin Hood. The book sold well, but could hardly be accused of sticking to the facts.

Nuggets and Dust

Early gold mining was something of a simpleton's task requiring a considerable amount of extremely hard work. Essential tools were a large pan, a pick and a shovel. Gold was found as pure nuggets by merely digging in the earth and along the stream banks or as dust in the stream beds themselves. In either case the sand and earth that was dug out was placed in the pan over which water was sloshed. In this manner the mud was cleared from the pan while the sand and gold, being heavier, remained in the bottom. When this combination was dried, the sand was simply blown away leaving pure gold.

Other devices were developed using this same principle. A rocker, a kind of box with a screen, took three men to operate, one to pour in the dirt, one to pour the water and one to operate the rocker. Later, hydraulic systems were designed utilizing sluices to carry the water. No matter what method was employed, all meant hard work and sore muscles.

At first most of the mining was done in and about the American and Sacramento rivers for it was in this area that men made the richest finds. It was on the American River that Sutter's Mill was located. Sutter's land was trampled and dug up, and his stock killed to a point where he faced financial ruin. Powerless to hold back the flood of miners, he finally went so far as to ask Congress for compensation, but the request was turned down by the Supreme

The quest for gold
FAR LEFT: Panning for gold by hand in a California stream
BELOW: A dipper gold dredge in operation in central California during the 1890s

Court. Sutter left California in 1873 and moved to Pennsylvania, utterly wiped out.

Getting Rich Slow

In 1849 it was estimated that $250,000 worth of gold was mined, four years later over $81,000,000 worth was extracted. Yet it is interesting to note that few individuals attained great wealth. It has been reported that two men found $17,000 worth of gold in a week, but that was unusual. The average California gold miner dug up only four dollars' worth a day; this was scarcely a way of getting rich quick.

As gold became harder to find, the miners moved on to richer fields. News of a good discovery spread quickly and men swarmed to it hoping for better luck. They would form camps, composed mostly of tents and rude shacks. Then they set up rules, especially with respect to the size of individual claims, theft and claim jumping. Claims varied in size depending on the character of the land, but the largest was usually no more than 100 feet square; even ten feet by ten was not uncommon.

By 1857 the easy pickings had begun to peter out. Surface mining in California became less and less profitable for the independent

miner. Only well-financed groups with large investments in expensive equipment could afford to continue. Now, however, men were searching all over the Rocky Mountain regions of the West for new finds. In Nevada a strike was made in 1855 and the miners flocked there. Farther east other discoveries were made in Idaho and later in Montana. By 1863, Virginia City was prominent and a year later Last Chance Gulch was an established mecca.

Another Gold Rush

One of the greatest discoveries occurred in Colorado. In 1858 one William Green Russell made a strike on Little Dry Creek, a tributary of Cherry Creek some 40 miles south of what is now Denver, 35 miles north of towering Pikes Peak. And with Russell's find, the gold rush began all over again.

As a result of the panic of '57, many Easterners were only too eager to grab at the chance of easy riches. This time the cry was "Pikes Peak or bust." Here, as in California, the miners at first merely grubbed the surface, hunting only for pure gold in the form of nuggets and dust.

By now, however, most men were aware that the gold they found was only particles washed down from a hidden "mother lode," in the mountains. As more and more strikes were made in such places as Central City and Black Hawk, new and improved techniques were utilized. Fewer and fewer men were content simply to pick around on the surface. Soon shafts were dug to reach the rich veins. Stamping mills and smelters were constructed to extract the gold from the rocky quartz. Men were employed in the mines and a true industry boomed. Here was a bonanza, first in gold, then in silver, and some men grew fabulously wealthy.

Overnight Wealth

Men like James G. Fair, John L. Routt, Bert Carlton and Nathaniel P. Hill became rich men almost over the weekend. Among them H. A. W. Tabor stands out as one of the more colorful.

Tabor was a Vermont stonecutter who went West in the 1860s. Cutting was hard work, but he succeeded in landing an easy job as postmaster in Leadville, Colorado. He also worked in and about the mines there for many years. And then in 1875 two miners asked Tabor for seventeen dollars for a grub-stake – seventeen dollars' worth of hope. Tabor complied.

In a few years his stake was worth enough for Tabor to sell it for $1,000,000. With this money he bought the Matchless Mine and other property. The Matchless brought him in some $11,000,000. For a time everything Tabor touched seemed to turn to silver. His wife, appropriately named Augusta, was prim, proper and penny-wise, and bored Tabor stiff. He divorced her for a young lady who looked, it was said, exactly like a kowpie doll.

Everyone called this young lady "Baby Doe," and anything Baby Doe wanted, Tabor bought for her. Even when she didn't need it, Tabor bought it for her – matched teams of horses, for instance, to go with her attire of the day.

Tabor's influence grew along with his wealth and in 1883 he was appointed to fill the unexpired term of a United States Senator.

He and Baby Doe flew high. Tabor was flamboyantly generous. He gave both Leadville and Denver fabulous opera houses; the Denver one considered by many to be the most elegant opera house of its day. And then all the splendor, the ostentatious lavishness to which he and Baby Doe had become accustomed, disintegrated in less time than it takes gold dust to settle in a pan. The Depression of 1893 rendered Tabor practically penniless. He lost nearly everything he owned. His political friends took pity on him and bailed him out to some extent with an appointment as postmaster of Denver; this was one of the most undemanding government jobs ever conceived.

The Death of Baby Doe

On Tabor's deathbed he implored Baby Doe to "hold onto the Matchless." This she did.

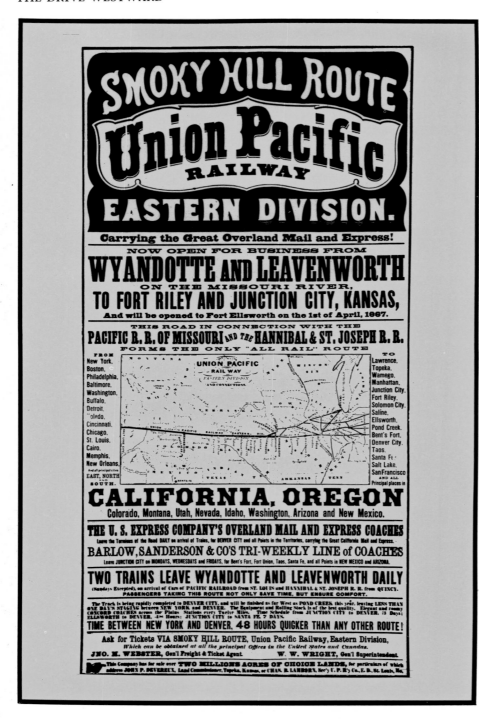

ABOVE: *The Smoky Hill Route*, opened in April 1867, represented one more step towards the transcontinent link, finished two years later
CENTRE: *Logging train*; the transcontinent link, needed large supplies for ties and bridges
FAR RIGHT: *Breaking a log jam*; timber supplies seemed limitless, and sadly no attempts at reafforestation were made

Although the mine never produced enough silver to buy a postage stamp, Baby Doe faithfully held on there, guarding her empty dream in a rickety shack for 36 years. There, in 1935, she was found, in rags, frozen to death.

This story has been made, appropriately, into an opera called *The Ballad of Baby Doe*.

Paltry Return

Besides the paltry return for time and energy spent, and the possibility of going completely broke, mining offered other hazardous surprises. Lone prospectors were sometimes attacked and killed by Indians; others fell down shafts or were crushed to death by cave-ins. One fate, however, that few miners figured on was devised by an Alfred E. Packer while prospecting in the mountains of Colorado with five friends. The party became stranded in a

blizzard. Food ran out and the chance of rescue was nil. Alfred got hungry, so he butchered his pals and ate them up one by one.

Don't Eat Democrats

Later, when the remains of Packer's repast were discovered, he was apprehended and brought to trial. It has been said that in pronouncing sentence the judge, who was a Democrat, not only chastised Packer for committing a heinous mass murder, but deplored the fact that in a country with only seven Democrats he had had the audacity to consume five of them. There is a bronze plaque at the site to Packer's victims; Alfred's name does not appear.

Gold was not the only resource which the Westerners sought. Timber was another rich target. Loggers were already cutting Wisconsin trees by the 1830s. Minnesota and later Washington, Oregon and California were seemingly inexhaustible forest sources.

While domestic demands were large, foreign markets for ships' timbers were equally great. The lumberjack's work was hard and dangerous, but the rewards were worth the risks. As it had been with the fur traders, no one dreamed that the resource could become depleted – that within half a century the forests could be cut to the point of devastation.

Tracks Across the Nation

As the Western mining towns' wealth grew, the dream of a transcontinental railroad increasingly

"Westward the course of empire takes its way"
RIGHT: *The Rocky Mountains, Emigrants Crossing the Plains*, a romantic print evoking the appeal of the West
FAR RIGHT: *Conestoga Wagon* by Thomas Birch shows "prairie schooners" heading West

excited the imagination of the nation. By 1861, the vision was becoming a reality.

In California, four big money men, Mark Hopkins, Collis P. Huntington, Charles Crocker and Leland Stanford, sank $8,500,000 in the dream. Together they formed the Central Pacific Railroad, and a year later Congress granted them a charter. At the same time, the legislature appropriated money for the Union Pacific in the East. With the terminus at Omaha, the Union Pacific was to receive $16,000 a mile for laying tracks. The Central Pacific could count on as much as $48,000 for putting down rails through some parts of the rough, mountainous stretches.

The founders of the two railroad companies hedged against losses by forming contracting companies to receive the money and complete the work. Crocker and Company, later the Contract and Finance Company, was the front for the Central Pacific. Stanford and his colleagues conveniently awarded themselves the contract. For the Union Pacific, the Credit Mobilier was set up, and it feathered the nest of the Eastern financiers in a similar manner.

At first progress was slow. By 1863 only 40 miles had been completed. After the Civil War, however, the tracks began to stretch out from both West and East.

Chinese and Irish

Labor was a problem at the start, but this was solved by the Central Pacific's employment of hundreds of Chinese coolies. The Union Pacific hired an equal number of Irishmen. Tent cities sprang up all along the way.

Every ten miles or so the grimy, bawdy rail towns with shacks for trollops and tents for saloons thrived on booze and gambling until the tracks had been laid for another stretch. Then the claptrap towns were dismantled, only to be ·re-established farther along the line. Some,

like Cheyenne, became established and later served as centers of local commerce and trade. Others fell apart from dry rot, blown away by the winds of the high plains and rugged mountains.

In the early spring of 1869, six years after the first spikes had been driven, the two lines were fast approaching one another. Oddly, no one had given much thought as to where they would connect. And yet, not oddly at all. The backers of both companies were in the construction business. They were making fortunes in building railroads, not running them. Actually, few of the backers had any intention of operating the lines. That was a fool's gamble. Rather, they intended to sell out to the highest bidder.

casions, Congress acted positively. It decided the railroads should meet and moreover connect, at a specific place named Promontory Point in Utah.

The historic link-up, the Union and Pacific Railroads join at Promontory, Utah, on 10 May 1869

The Golden Spike

On May 10, 1869, the two companies joined rails. Prayers were offered, speeches were made and the locomotive engineers shook hands. President Stanford of the Central Pacific and President Dillon of the Union joined forces in driving in the "Golden Spike," thus tying the nation together in one grand symbolic gesture. Stanford raised his sledge and with a masterful stroke aimed for the spike. Brilliantly he flubbed it. His next stroke found him placing the head of the sledge gently on the spike, and Dillon struck it neat and clean. With this earth-shaking ceremony, the nation was joined, tied together with two ribbons of steel.

Before the advent of rail travel, communication between the East and West was sporadic, haphazard and extremely difficult. In fact, it was all but nonexistent. Letters and newspapers were carried West by immigrants and freighters. Letters were often mailed in cabins and even in the crotches of trees. It was better to have a letter publicized and get there than not reach its destination at all. Probably only half the letters mailed ever got through.

The first regular mail to reach San Francisco came by the Pacific Mail Steamship Company's boat on February 22, 1849. This coincided neatly with the gold rush, so neatly that every last sailor jumped ship. The company finally got sailing again with bimonthly deliveries at 50 cents a letter.

Explored and Exploited

And so the West was won. By 1850 it had been thoroughly explored and to a degree exploited. The fur trade had pretty well destroyed the beaver population, and gold miners were beginning to demolish the landscape in their lust for the precious metal.

The countryside east of the Mississippi was already filled with people, and farmers as far west as Iowa were feeling cramped. California and Oregon were now the meccas. While it would be another quarter of a century before the Indians would be subdued or the railroads and telegraph really tie the nation together, the pattern was firmly set. Nothing could stop this crusade of national expansion, for the new Americans felt increasingly challenged by the chance to conquer the difficult.

Hard work, frugality and faith in God were the keys to economic security, social recognition and quite possibly safe passage through the pearly gates. And with that spirit, the Americans made the hard seem easy and the impossible merely hard.

So, to keep the money rolling in, the two lines didn't connect but passed each other. Appallingly, each continued running parallel to the other for a considerable distance. Congress, as usual bogged down in its self-congratulatory rhetoric confined chiefly to representing each politician's own self-interests, was somehow jarred into reality. On one of its historic oc-

CHAPTER IX

The Wild West: Myths and Realities

OVERLEAF:
The Cowboys shows what the Wild West means to most people via Hollywood's red-tinted glasses. In fact, the cowboy's lot was hard and his days long and more often than not monotonous

Cows and cowtowns
RIGHT: A town on the Plains
BELOW: *Trail Drive*, painting by W. H. D. Koerner
FAR RIGHT: Map showing the trails along which cattle were driven to the railheads

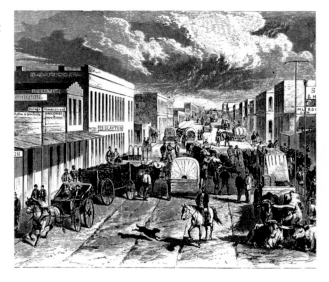

IN 1848, THERE were, according to tax records, over 350,000 head of cattle in Texas and by 1855 there were over 1,000,000, not counting the wild ones. A way had to be found to get all this beef to market, and that way was the cattle drive.

Appetite for Beef
As early as 1846, Edward Piper, anxious to find buyers for his cows, drove a herd to Ohio, where he sold them at a profit. During the '49 gold rush, another man, W. H. Snyder, lured not by gold but by the thought that he could get rich from the goldminers' appetite for beef, drove a herd from Texas to San Francisco. It took him and his men two years. Unfortunately, he kept no records, so no one will ever know how he made out financially. It is known that he didn't make a second trip West.

In 1855 some enterprising cowboys drove a herd of semi-wild Longhorns all the way to New York City. Unfortunately, like Snyder, they filed no report.

At the conclusion of the costly Civil War, the South was an economic shambles and Texas was no exception. Returning soldiers found their farms in ruins, their livestock strayed. The far-seeing among them realized there would be a growing demand for meat in the burgeoning Northwest which could prove an economic boon. Railroad tycoons were boldly stretching their tracks toward the great plains, which with newly-developing meat-packing houses were instrumental in getting beef to the eastern urban centers. These factors, combined with the introduction of ice-packed box-cars and the invention of the "airtight" or tin can, gave impetus to the entire industry.

There was no such thing as a typical cattle drive – no two were just alike, as to weather conditions, number of cows, caliber and experience of the drovers, the ever-present threat of Indian attack, even the market price of cattle at the end of the trail. Such were the determinants of success or failure.

COWBOY
COUNTRY
showing trails
leading to railheads

**Charles Russell,
cowboy artist**
RIGHT: *Broken Rope*
FAR RIGHT ABOVE:
*A Tight Dally and a
Loose Latigo*
FAR RIGHT BELOW:
Bronc in a Riding Camp

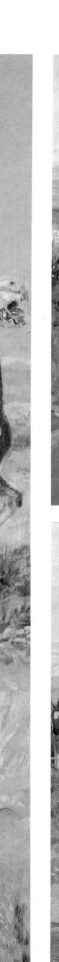

ABOVE: *Mounted men* patrol a trail of cattle
FAR RIGHT ABOVE:
A Cowboy's Holiday, an engraving showing the cowboy's pursuits when visiting town
FAR RIGHT BELOW:
Emigrants Attacked by Comanches depicts one of the hazards of the Santa Fe trail

Ike Pryor, an ardent organizer and drover, figured that an efficient drive involved about 3,000 head of Longhorns, one trail boss or "ramrod," nine men, a cook and between 60 and 66 horses. He expected to pay his trail boss $100 a month; his cook $50 at most, plus all he could eat, and nine cowboys $30 per month apiece. His provisions would cost $300, based on a three-month drive. Another way of calculating his expenses was to reckon a cost of about a dollar per head per mile to drive cattle. He figured out that by paying $8 per head, selling at the railhead (perhaps Abilene or Dodge City) for $20, and by subtracting his expenses and losses through deaths, straying and theft of stock, he could realize a profit of $30,000. A drover could get rich on a single drive if he didn't lose everything in a stampede, a flooding river, a blizzard or a dried-up market at the railhead.

Into Indian Territory
Nature was perhaps the single element most likely to make life difficult for the cattleman; thunderstorms, droughts and blizzards could spell ruin. And a stampede, which was a constant threat could be almost as bad. But the tempers

of the cows and vagaries of the elements were not the only matters which brought grief to the cattlemen. When the herds had crossed the Red River, they entered Indian Territory, a vast stretch of land that was later to become Oklahoma. This was land set aside by the government for many eastern tribes: the Cherokee, Choctaw, Chickasaw, Creeks and others. These Indians were farming people who had crops and livestock of their own, and they were dismayed and angered at the thousands of trampling hooves damaging their pastures and destroying their property. A highly sophisticated group, they were quick to demand tolls from the drovers – sometimes as much as ten cents a head, sometimes payment in cattle. The Texas drovers bitterly resented this blackmail, but were powerless to prevent it, for the Indians appeared in great numbers backed by firearms to prove their point.

As if this weren't enough, when the herds finally reached the Kansas border, they were confronted by an even more belligerent barrier – the "grangers" and the Kansas Jay Hawkers.

The grangers were the small farmers who had been lured to the West by cheap land. Self-

reliant Yankees, they earned their living raising crops and keeping dairy herds, and they were terrified by the thought that the Texas Long-horns, which carried the dread Texas tick fever, might infect their herds. Consequently, they formed armed bands and posses of vigilantes to ward off the Texas herds.

Preyed On By Jay Hawkers

The Jay Hawkers were a bunch of self-appointed ne'er-do-well bandits sometimes enlisted by the grangers. They pillaged and robbed and were happy to hold up the Texans, demand-ing ransom, running off a herd and even killing the cowboys to prove their invincibility. As a result more than one Jay Hawker was left un-buried on the prairie, killed by a stubborn cowboy.

Due to this situation, many herds became stalled below the Kansas border, often at great loss to the drovers. Good grazing land would soon wear out and the cattle waste away. Speculators, some in cahoots with the Jay Hawkers, made unconscionable deals which many Texans had no alternative but to accept.

In 1886 a man named Nelson Story purchased 1,000 Longhorns in Fort Worth with the idea of selling them in the North. Then like so many

ABOVE: *Cowgirls* were rare; this photograph shows the Becker sisters of Alamosa, Colorado, branding their cattle in the 1880s
BELOW: *Bronco Busting*, one of Charles Russell's many paintings of Western life
FAR RIGHT ABOVE AND BELOW: *Cowboy Camp during the Roundup* and *Smoke of a .45*, both by Charles Russell

others, he found himself bottled up south of Baxter Springs, Kansas, by the grangers and Jay Hawkers. Story had an idea — risky, he decided, but worthwhile. He had been a freighter on the Oregon Trail, had struck it rich in a Montana gold field and knew that there were about 10,000 hungry miners in the region of Virginia City. And that's where his bride was.

Moving his cattle west past the Kansas border guard, Story circled his herd north to Fort Leavenworth. Here he outfitted a wagon train with oxen and 27 men armed with new Remington breech-loading rifles. Setting out with his herd and men, he pushed west along the Oregon Trail to Fort Laramie. The Bozeman Trail to the north swarmed with hostile Sioux

Indians. Near Fort Reno, the Sioux attacked, wounding two of Story's men with arrows and running off some of his cattle. Story and his men pursued the Indians, shot them up and retrieved every last cow.

When Story reached Fort Kearny, the frightened commandant, Colonel Henry Carrington, refused him passage, convinced that Indian attack was imminent.

Story the Unstoppable

Story would not be stopped. Under cover of darkness, he and his men drove the cattle on. Now they traveled by night and grazed by day. One man, scouting ahead, was captured by Indians, scalped and pinned to the prairie with arrows before Story could rescue him. Two other Sioux attacks were parried, the Remington rifles being too hot for the Indians. And then, on December 9, 1866, with no further incidents, Story drove his herd triumphantly into Virginia City, there to be welcomed by his wife who had ridden out to meet him.

Nelson Story was a truly courageous man, and so were Charles Goodnight and Oliver Loving.

Goodnight got the idea that in the Southwest where 7,000 Navaho Indians were held captive near Fort Sumner, New Mexico, there might be a good market for beef cattle. The government had to feed these hungry souls and Goodnight believed he could make money filling this need.

Goodnight was an experienced bushwhacker who knew the Southwest. He met, by chance, one Oliver Loving, recognized as a topnotch cattle drover. Loving had once led a herd as far as Quincy, Illinois, and had also moved 1,000

head of cows to Denver City to tap the market of the Colorado gold miners.

These two men agreed to try to reach Fort Sumner by a route no one in his right mind would think of taking: south over the Staked Plain of Texas, where the chance of attack by marauding Comanches would be somewhat reduced, but crossing 96 miles from the Middle Conco to the Pecos River, where there was absolutely no water at all.

With these obstacles well understood, Goodnight and Loving acquired 2,000 head of cattle – cows, bulls, steers, even calves. Goodnight also designed what is now thought to have been the first chuck wagon. This was to be drawn by ten oxen.

The Scent of Water

Problems appeared early in the drive. The calves could not keep up with the herd. At first the newborn were placed in the chuck wagon, but this didn't work at all and the decision was reluctantly made that the "little fellas" had to be killed. Though the men experienced no trouble from the Comanches, they got their share of misery from the 96 waterless miles.

The cows were at first stopped for a rest during the night, but instead of resting, they milled the entire time. It was decided that since the cattle were going to be moving, they might as well be moving in the right direction, so the stops were cancelled. By the third day dehydration had shrunk the animals so badly that those which could move looked like dried hides stretched over a picket fence. Those that sank down from thirst and exhaustion never rose again.

Men and horses were not much better off. The water, stored in large barrels in the new chuck wagon, ran out. And then, on the morning of the fourth day, the animals scented water. With what little energy they could muster, they weakly stampeded nearly twelve miles to the Pecos River. When they reached it, they were so dazed that they plunged clear across the river to the far bank before turning to drink.

Despite the 96 miles of hell they had endured, only 300 head perished.

Goodnight and Loving rested the herd, letting them fatten on the grassy banks and enjoy the life-giving water which flowed down the Pecos. Then they drove on to Fort Sumner to the starving Navaho. They sold their beef steers to the government at eight cents a pound live weight – a real killing on the market!

Loving drove the remainder of the 1,700-head herd – cows, calves and bulls – north to

Hard Winter, painting
by W. H. D. Koerner

Denver City where he made a good profit.
Goodnight rode east from Fort Sumner to
make arrangements for buying another herd to
trail them west again. Some determined men
just aren't easy to stop; Charlie Goodnight and
Oliver Loving were perfect examples.

The Abilene Brainstorm

While Story, Loving and Goodnight bypassed
the Kansas border, many more drovers worried
their way direct to the railheads through the
grangers and Jay Hawkers. Tensions grew and
animosities boiled, sometimes to the point
where buyers and sellers could barely do
business. And then, the whole matter was
resolved, thanks to the ingenuity of a young
Illinois cattle dealer, Joseph McCoy. In a
flash of brainwork, he brilliantly solved the
puzzle and put the pieces together.

After many cold shoulders from railroad men
and town fathers, McCoy finally convinced the
skeptical directors of the Kansas Pacific Railroad and the enthusiastic business leaders of
the little town of Abilene that the combination
of a salesyard and railhead would prove profitable
to all concerned. Here buyers could meet with
Texas drovers to purchase the huge herds
without interference by grangers, Jay Hawkers
or unco-operative townsfolk.

McCoy proposed to build the great holding
pens himself and take only a small commission
on the shipments. He sent an agent to the
Texas drovers who gladly turned their herds
westward. Almost overnight Abilene became a
boom town. It took a little longer for McCoy to
go bankrupt.

Trails to Railheads

Abilene had become the marketplace where a
man made his profit or lost his shirt. Here was
the reward for all the work, the loneliness, the
danger – the end of the trail.

From southern Texas several trails led to the
Kansas railheads. One of the earliest was the
Shawnee, which terminated in Sedalia, Missouri
and St. Louis. As the railroads pushed farther
west, other trails were developed. The famous
Chisholm Trail led to Abilene and Ellsworth,
Kansas and later the Western Trail to Dodge
City.

The cow town of the 1860s and 1870s was a
steaming brew. Opportunistic men from the
East, anxious to cash in as the number of
grangers grew, became bankers and merchants
overnight. Then with the coming of the Texans,
glittering saloons, ornate gambling houses,
hotels and gaudy brothels sprang up like
mushrooms after a spring rain.

The grangers, mostly solid Scottish Presbyterians, resented the trespassing Texans with
their disease-ridden cattle. The bankers and
merchants had mixed feelings – the new money

was welcome, but the gambling, drinking and whoring were unfortunate. For the saloon proprietors, the madams, the gamblers and the hotelkeepers, the cattle drives were of course a bonanza.

Quick on the Draw

The survivors of a cattle drive, the cowboys who hit the cow town, were anything but God-fearing types. These were men who had already ridden through the shadow of the valley of death. Abilene, Ellsworth and Dodge City were the pearly gates.

To control the pent-up exuberance of the cowboys and maintain a semblance of order in the community, the town fathers were generally pretty quick to employ the services of a "lawman." Almost without exception, these characters were as quick on the draw as they were short on the law; life was cheap, men shot first and asked questions later, and even the sheriffs themselves operated on that basis.

Wild Bill Hickok, who was taken on to keep the peace in Abilene, had already caused the deaths of 70 men. He was definitely the real thing among Western gunslingers.

A homespun code of honor was in operation, and it worked, after a fashion. Cheating at cards was unpardonable; drawing one's six-shooter on an unarmed man was a disgrace. Either offense could mean sudden death for the offender at the hands of the victim or the victim's friends. Arguments and brawls were commonplace and shootings were the usual outcome.

The constant sounds of gunfire so upset the good citizens of Abilene that in February, 1872, they signed a manifesto to the effect that the Texans were not to bring their cattle to Abilene any longer.

Stagecoach days
LEFT: A concord wagon about to start the day's run across country in the 1880s
FAR LEFT BELOW: H. W. Hansen's painting entitled *Indians Attacking a Stage*
BELOW: Overland House, Idaho, a welcome resting place for stagecoach passengers on the Overland Trail

Stagecoach banditry
RIGHT: The stages of the Wells Fargo Company were popular targets for holdup men
FAR RIGHT: The rhyming robber, "Black Bart" (his real name was C. E. Bolton), examples of whose verse are reproduced on this poster offering a reward for his arrest

$250 REWARD!

A REWARD OF $250 WILL be paid by Wells, Fargo & Co. for the arrest and conviction of each of the parties who attempted to rob our TREASURE BOX,

And shot at the driver, on Pit River Hill, on the night of Oct. 19th, 1875.

JOHN J. VALENTINE,

Genl. Supt. Wells, Fargo & Co.

Reading, Oct. 20th, 1875.

The Texans obliged, but not entirely for unselfish motives. The railroads had moved farther west, and new towns, like Ellsworth, offered better services, so quitting Abilene suited the cowboys just fine. The citizens of Abilene, realizing that they might have cut their own life-line, hastily sent a second proclamation reversing the first, but it was too late. As a result, Abilene's boom burst like a circus balloon and the town's economy hit the skids. Abilene's slide produced Ellsworth's boom. But soon, as the railroad pushed west, Ellsworth died too, and Dodge City blossomed into the new Cowboy Capital.

Like its predecessors, those glittering dens of iniquity, Dodge City too was doomed to wither, though for a different reason. It was the cruel killing blizzard of 1886 that left the entire cattle industry a financial shambles.

This worst example of nature's wrath began on the last day of December, 1885. The autumn had been a gentle one with an "Indian Summer" that went on and on, until the afternoon of December 31. Then, from the north came a mild drizzle; slowly the temperature fell and soft white flakes drifted quietly in the air. It was the start of the greatest blizzard cattlemen had ever seen. For three days the white death surged in from the North, driving before it all the cattle in its path. From the Dakotas to Texas the animals moved, halted only by the drift fences or in cuts and coulees beyond which they could not pass.

Many cowboys, fearful of the imminent tragedy, rode after their herds in what proved a hopeless attempt at rescue. Many of the men themselves froze, their remains to be found later near their dead ponies and cattle in the shelter of some gulch.

The blizzard of '86 was disaster. Cattle carcasses by the tens of thousands were found, often hundreds of miles from their home ranches. Losses were astronomical. The OS Ranch in Kansas lost nearly 11,000 head, while the Circle M's losses were over 5,000. With similar tolls in the Dakotas, Nebraska, parts of Arizona and Colorado, the destruction was appalling.

Another Bad Year
The following summer was cursed by drought, and cattle that had survived the blizzard found pickings sparse. By fall, the cows were walking rib-cages with hides stretched taut. Winter came early that year. The first snow fell in October. While there were no raging blizzards, the snows fell and fell and covered the grasslands so the cattle couldn't graze. Horses will paw through snow to reach the grass, while cows go to the low country where the grass grows tallest. If the grass is deeply covered, cattle just stand there with their backs humped up and starve to death. The heavy storms of the winter of '86–'87 were to the west of those of the previous year, so herds that had been spared the previous year were now destroyed. When spring came and stockmen counted up their

☛Agents of W., F. & Co. will **not** post this circular, but place them in the hands of your local and county officers, and reliable citizens in your region. Officers and citizens receiving them are respectfully requested to preserve them for future reference.

Agents WILL PRESERVE a copy on file in their office.

$800.00 Reward!

ARREST STAGE ROBBER!

1.

On the 3d of August, 1877, the stage from Fort Ross to Russian River was stopped by one man, who took from the Express box about $300, coin, and a check for $305.52, on Grangers' Bank of San Francisco, in favor of Fisk Bros. The Mail was also robbed. On one of the Way Bills left with the box the Robber wrote as follows:—

> "I've labored long and hard for bread—
> For honor and for riches—
> But on my corns too long you've trod,
> You fine haired sons of bitches.
>   BLACK BART, the P o 8.

Driver, give my respects to our friend, the other driver; but I really had a notion to hang my old disguise hat on his weather eye." (*fac simile.*)

Respectfully
B. B.

It is believed that he went to the Town of Guerneville about daylight next morning.

2.

About one year after above robbery, July 25th, 1878, the Stage from Quincy to Oroville was stopped by one man, and W., F. & Co's box robbed of $379, coin, one Diamond Ring, (said to be worth $200) one Silver Watch, valued at $25. The Mail was also robbed. In the box, when found next day, was the following, (*fac simile*):—

here I lay me down to sleep
to wait the coming morrow,
perhaps success perhaps defeat
And everlasting sorrow
I've labored long and hard for bread
for honor and for riches
But on my corns too long youve trod
You fine haired sons of bitches
let come what will I'll try it on
My condition cant be worse
And if there's money in that Box
Tis munny in my purse
*   Black Bart*
*   the. Po 8*

RIGHT: *Lawman or outlaws*, these men all dispensed the rough justice of the West: from left to right, Wild Bill Hickok, Wyatt Earp, Bat Masterson, Doc Holliday
BELOW: *Statue* commemorating the Pony Express

losses a great many just quit. Among them were the Swan Land and Cattle Company which lost 5,400 steers and folded. The Worksham Cattle Company didn't even bother to reckon the ruin.

When the losses were reckoned, Dodge City melted down like a snowball on a pot-bellied stove. Thus an end to the era of the fabulous Texas Longhorn drives and the legendary cow towns was brought on not by sin, but by an over-supply of pretty white snowflakes.

The Stagecoach Trail

Long before railroad tracks spanned the country, as the California mining communities grew, so did the necessity of getting gold and letters of credit to banks, which in turn increased the demand for improved transportation.

In 1852, Alvin Adams formed the Adams and Company Express to meet just that need in California. Henry Wells and William Fargo knew a good thing when they saw it and they founded a competing company, the Wells Fargo.

The Santa Fe trade had already proved feasible. Now pack trains and freighters went on from Santa Fe to El Paso and then north to California. The Oregon Trail was also used, now dropping south to Salt Lake City and over the Sierras. The trip was an interminably long and slow one, and in some instances dangerous. It took the mule teams 30 days from Salt Lake to California. Slow as it was, it was big business. The Butterfield freighting operation involved over 6,000 wagons and 75,000 oxen.

Despite the Westerners' demands for mail service, it was not until 1857 that the Postmaster General, back East, called for bids. John Butterfield of the American Express Company and William Fargo of Wells Fargo Express, together with four other men, founded the Butterfield Overland Stage and received the mail contract.

In 1858 the stages began running. From St. Louis to Little Rock, south to Preston and El Paso, the route continued to Yuma and on to San Francisco. It was a distance of 2,750 miles and the stages made it in twenty days.

Jostled and Soused

The stagecoaches, wagons made in Concord, New Hampshire, were pulled by a team of six horses for ten-mile hauls to "swing stations," where worn-out horses were exchanged for fresh ones, and the jostled passengers could stretch their legs. The stages traveled day and night with periodic stopovers at "home stations." Here the herds of horses were corralled, and food, such as rancid bacon, stale bread and bitter coffee, was served to the travelers. They had paid a $200 fare, but such tasty meals might be expected.

The roads were sometimes so rough as to be almost impassable. Sleep was a matter of cat-naps, though if there was no excess baggage, ladies might sleep on the stagecoach floor. No food or water was served between home stations. Passengers were permitted to bring their own snacks and whiskey, which most did. There was also the threat of bandits, a growing menace. After twenty days of being jostled in a swinging, swerving coach, either drenched by rain, or smothered in dust, possibly robbed, eating poor food and drinking bad whiskey, the survivors of such a trip would be a pretty haggard, bedraggled and often soused group of travelers.

There were two good things about it: the stage often got through and the scenery was lovely.

While the Butterfield Stage ran the southern route, Russell, Majors and Waddell traveled a central road. This ran along the Platte to Julesburg and on west. Like the Butterfield,

their coaches were drawn by four to six horses. Drivers sat atop the stage. These "ribbon handlers" were men of skill, strength and courage. Often they were accompanied by a guard "riding shotgun" on the lookout for attack by Indians or "road agents." These were bandits who took great pleasure in commandeering the "box," a chest containing money and valuables, as well as relieving the passengers of any precious belongings they might have on their persons.

Black Bart the Bandit

One of the more imaginative holdup men was Black Bart. Armed with a shotgun and wearing a white duster and a hood fashioned from a flour sack, he carried out at least 28 stagecoach holdups. Black Bart had a flair for writing poetry which he would sometimes leave at the scene as a kind of trademark. One of his better efforts went as follows:

> I've labored long and hard for bread,
> For honor and for riches.
> But on my corns too long you've tred,
> You fine-haired sons-of-bitches.
>
> Black Bart The P O 8

The Wells Fargo Company, victim of too many of his robberies and fed up with his doggerel as well, finally offered an $800 reward for his capture. Bart, committing his crimes, also committed a small oversight. Near the scene of one of his holdups he left a couple of bags of stale crackers, three dirty linen cuffs and a

Major Frank Wolcott   Red Angus   Billy the Kid

Rogues' Gallery

ABOVE: This collection of western characters includes some pillars of society and some of society's greatest enemies

RIGHT: Four handcuffed bank robbers, who made the mistake of trying to rob two banks at once

FAR RIGHT: Steve Young, an outlaw hanged by vigilantes at Laramie, Wyoming, in October 1868

crumpled handkerchief. The handkerchief contained a telltale laundry mark: FX07.

Supplied with this clue, detective J. B. Hume, a gumshoe for Wells Fargo, went to work. After doggedly spot-checking over 90 laundries in San Francisco, he finally found that the mark was assigned to a prosperous and well-dressed miner named C. E. Bolton. The game was up. Mr. Bolton was charged and convicted and for several years enjoyed fresh crackers at the taxpayers' expense in San Quentin penitentiary.

Even with the stagecoaches rushing back and forth as fast as they could, the Californians still clamored for faster mail service. Senator Gwin of that state is credited with the bright idea that a relay of horsemen could carry the mail through in a good deal less time than the horse-drawn Concords. Russell, Majors and Waddell were quick to buy the idea and promptly received a contract to execute it.

The Pony Express

The service, dubbed the "Pony Express," quickly proved efficient, and it became one of the more ingenious contributions to the making of the West. As many as 190 way stations were set up ten miles apart on the nearly 2,000 mile run from St. Joseph, Missouri, to Placerville, California. To reduce the weight, only small men and boys were selected as riders. To lighten the burden further, they were permitted to carry as arms only a pair of Colt revolvers, even though parts of the route traversed hostile Indian

country. Generally between 40 and 90 letters were carried wrapped in oiled silk and stuffed into leather saddlebags. The cost for mailing was five dollars per ounce.

Riders changed mounts every ten miles and each rider covered between 70 and a 100 miles before he was relieved. In the case of a rider's sickness or injury, another man might have to take a double turn. William Cody once rode continuously for twenty hours to cover 320 miles. His record was broken by "Pony Bob," who covered 380 miles non stop. Riders were as courageous as they were calloused, and for the pounding they took were well paid.

By Wire and Rail

The first run was made on April 3, 1860. The riders made it from Missouri to California in

Pat Garrett   *John Tunstall*   *John Chisum*

ten and a half days, just half the time it took the stagecoaches. The venture was a complete success and hailed as a milestone in the conquest of the West.

In October, 1861, came another milestone: telegraph lines sent their first message ticking across the nation. And within a year and a half of its beginning, the glamorous Pony Express became as useless as a dead horse; the founders, Russell, Majors and Waddell, promptly went bankrupt.

Much competition existed between the big stage freighting companies and their promoters. The panic of 1855 ruined Alvan Adams, and Wells Fargo took over.

An uneducated opportunist named Ben Holliday bought out Russell, Majors and Waddell when they went broke in 1862, their contract not having been renewed. By 1866, Holliday controlled 5,000 miles of stage lines from Utah to Montana and all the country between. He apparently never tried to acquire his chief competitor, Wells Fargo, possibly because so many of their boxes got stolen. Instead, sensing the imminence of the Pacific Railroad's destruction of his own business, he sold his holdings to Wells Fargo.

The most important milestone of all, the linkup of the railroads, came about in Utah in 1869, and a new era began. With the country joined, commerce could flourish. Farmers and ranchers could get their produce to urban centers more quickly and cheaply. The West would now fill up with people and towns. Prosperity would abound and law and order would prevail. The theory sounded fine and indeed it worked. All, that is, except for law and order.

Lawlessness and Disorder

To say that law in the West was rudimentary would be a gross overstatement. Cattle rustlers, horse thieves, stagecoach robbers were commonplace. Banks and trains were prey to the outlaws' greed. Criminals ran rampant. Courts were insufficient and those that did exist were often poorly served by ill-trained judges. Skill in politics was always more valuable than a knowledge of jurisprudence. The cowtown pattern prevailed, in which men took the law into their own hands. To shoot first and ask

questions later was a common practice, and the popular name "peacemaker" for the six-shooting revolver had a certain warped logic.

While the cowtowns were wild, the mining towns were roaring. Tombstone, Arizona, was as rough as any. Big and wealthy, it attracted many miners as well as the usual crop of unsavory characters. It was here that Wyatt Earp made the OK Corral historic in just about one minute. Together with Doc Holliday and his own brothers Virgil, who was marshal, and Morgan he blasted to smithereens three cattle-rustling cowboys who threatened them. The victims died with their boots on and "Boot Hill" became their resting-place under the frying sun.

The list of the more infamous criminals is a long one. Books and biographical sketches fill library shelves. Many are highly romanticized and purport to make the outlaws some kind of heroes. Legion are the tales of urchins bullied into self-defense, good boys turned sour, courageous thieves robbing the rich to pay off a destitute widow's mortgage and save her starving children. In the 1880s and '90s, dime novels luridly portrayed the life and times of these desperadoes. The populace avidly absorbed

the blood and thunder, the aggressive violence these cheap books purveyed. Schoolboys were caught reading these ghastly tales in haylofts and attics. And after they were confiscated, fathers read them at night in the comfort of their Boston rocking chairs.

Bad Was Bad

The fact of the matter is, the bad men of the West were no good. Even for evening an old score, it isn't reasonable to kill 37 men, as did John Wesley Hardin, to avenge a single beating once administered by one bully. There is no record of outlaws rescuing beleaguered widows. Rather, the road agents and the bank robbers spent the money they stole, on themselves — for whiskey, women and for the fun of gambling.

While many of their exploits are legendary, the outlaws themselves were real enough. Frank and Jesse James teamed up with the Younger brothers, Bob, Jim and Cole, to rob trains and banks. Billy the Kid, Sam Bass and Hardin were erstwhile cowboys specializing in murder. Doc Holliday was a cavernous consumptive, deputized by the Earps. His specialities were pulling teeth, playing cards and shooting men

FAR LEFT: *Fight* in a
western town
LEFT: *Lily Langtry*,
loved from afar by the
bar-tending judge

who accused him of cheating. Grat, Bob and Emmett Dalton were masterly train robbers. However, when they tried their hand at robbing two banks at the same time, the irate citizens of Coffeeville, Kansas, sent Grat and Bob to see their Maker and Emmett to the state penitentiary for life.

Butch Cassidy's Bunch

And then there was the "Wild Bunch" led by "Butch" Cassidy. The gang held up banks and trains and stole cattle at will. Safe in the "Hole in the Wall," their hideaway in the mountains of Wyoming, Butch and the "Sun Dance Kid," the "Tall Texan," "Kid Curry" and others counted their loot.

In one way or another justice nearly always prevailed. If the outlaws didn't kill one another in vendettas, the posses and the sheriffs managed it. Lynchings by outraged citizens often ended in hangings, "necktie parties" that drew crowds of spectators. Sentences were stiff and in the case of a murderer or horse thief the pronouncement was likely to be "hung by the neck until dead, dead, dead."

One of the severest judges was the dignified, over-bearing, bible-reading Isaac C. Parker. His Honor sternly sentenced to hanging 88 men during his term of office, some in lots of four or five at a time. This sort of thing earned him the name of the "Hanging Judge."

The Bar-tending Judge

Judge Roy Bean was a different sort. Fat, uneducated and as genteel as a hog in a wallow, Bean moved west with the railroads. He finally stopped at a town called Langtry. (He was a great fan of Lillie Langtry, the darling of the English stage.) Here he set up a saloon, got himself elected judge and held court in his bar-room.

The judge had three loves: convicting crim-

*Row in a Cattle Town
Saloon* from a painting
by Frederic Remington

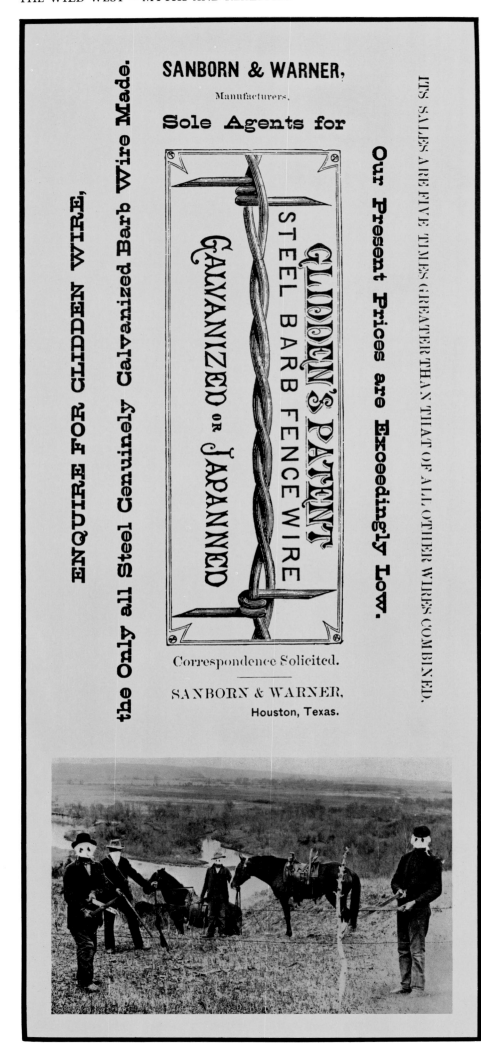

inals, whiskey and Lillie. He confused himself with God, and manipulated the law to suit his fancy. He went so far as to fine a corpse for carrying a gun, the amount being the sum of money found on the body. A convenient tree which stood by his court served as an excellent gallows. But the best thing about Bean's trials was that the jurors could buy drinks at the bar before the case was heard.

The judge's first two passions were adequately satisfied. But the lovely Lillie Langtry, who was persuaded to visit the place that bore her name, didn't arrive in town until eight months after the judge had died.

While the courts maintained, at best, a rough sort of justice, lawmen and detectives did likewise. Wyatt Earp, Bat Masterson and Pat Garrett were among them. In 1870 Abilene hired Tom Smith to keep the peace for $150 a month. Smith promptly ordered all firearms banned in town and knocked down a ruffian named Hank when Hank defied the ruling. When one "Wyoming Frank" wanted to keep his guns, he was pushed into a bar by Smith, who then disarmed him while he was down. The citizens of Abilene forthwith raised Smith's pay by $75.

Wild Bill Becomes Sheriff

After Smith was murdered by a vicious settler named McConnell who chopped off his head to end a quarrel, "Wild Bill" Hickok became sheriff. He already had a considerable reputation as a gunman. He once modestly admitted to having killed over 100 men.

In Abilene Hickok spent most of his time gambling in a saloon and keeping the peace at a distance. After less than a year of this, Hickok's contract was allowed to lapse. He drifted about the country and ended up in the mining town of Deadwood, South Dakota, where as he was playing cards, he was shot in the back by a man named Jack McCall for no better reason than that McCall wanted to wipe out a famous gunman. It was August 2, 1876, and Hickok was 49 years old, a ripe age for a lawman in those days.

The Cattle Barons

Free grass and water rights were the factors responsible for the creation in this period of enormous ranches, and a new phenomenon: the "cattle kings," who controlled these holdings. Moneyed interests in the East (and even as far away as Great Britain) made investments in cattle and valuable water rights in Colorado, New Mexico, Wyoming and Montana. By the late 1870s great spreads were being built and the power of the cattle barons was becoming formidable. One man, John Iliff, acquired over 30 miles of Platte River frontage in Colorado and ranged his cattle for 100 miles along the

CATTLE KINGS.

At war with the cattle barons
FAR LEFT ABOVE: Advertisement for Glidden's patent barbed wire, which nesters used to enclose their homesteads
FAR LEFT BELOW: A gang cutting the wire
LEFT: Some of the men who ruled the ranches

ABOVE: *In Without Knocking*, painting by Charles Russell
RIGHT: *Sheepman, sheep and sheepdog,* as unpopular as cattle thieves in the eyes of ranchers
FAR RIGHT: *Bucking bronc* as depicted in an engraving by Frederic Remington

Platte, with Julesburg as the center of his operations.

The men who controlled the water were permitted, or usurped the right, to range their cows as far as they could go and still get water.

As ever greater numbers of cattle filled the northern grazing lands, more cowboys were needed to tend the herds. With this pattern, the cowboy's role gradually changed from that of drover to herdsman.

A ranch of 1,000 square miles was by no means unusual, and although borders were vague, they were agreed upon in a general way by the neighboring owners. Cattle that drifted from one rancher's land to another's were driven back and this required not only "riding the line," but also keeping a rough count and checking the general condition of the cows. Here and there, a cabin of log or batten-board or hut of stone was set up along the perimeters to serve as a station for one or two men. Life at a "line camp" was a lonely vigil. Little wonder that when they did get to town the cowboys tended to raise a little hell.

The Posse, painting
by Frank Tenny
Johnson

ABOVE: *Fight in the Street*, engraving by Frederic Remington FAR RIGHT: *The Last Stand* by Edward Borein

Squatters and Nesters

A vexing problem for the rancher was the influx of "nesters" to the Great Plains. These were hardy and persistent men from the East, who hoped to grub a living for themselves and family from the soil. Some received 160 acres of land under the Homestead Act, others were outright squatters who held no legal claim to the land whatever.

The nesters erected shacks or rude houses of sod, and tilled the acreage to eke out an existence. As with the grangers of Kansas, the use to which they put the land was the opposite use to that of the rancher. In the eyes of the cowman, the nesters were ruining the grass with plows. These farmers on foot, wearing bib overalls, were objects of scorn to the free-roaming horseman. The fact is a cowboy is as different from a farmer as a hawk is from a chicken.

Matters were made worse by the invention of barbed wire by Joseph Farwell Glidden. By 1875 "sod busters" had run barbed wire fences around their gardens, their fields, even their little ranches, to the inconvenience of the cowmen, and also to their fury. Fencing the free grass to them was heresy. The enmity grew and many a nester would awake to find his fence cut, his gates dragged away, his livestock strayed.

Some big ranchers took even more decisive action to destroy the nesters. They sent armed cowboys to confront the intruders, and on more than one occasion to shoot to kill.

However, the cattlemen themselves could see one advantage to the new invention. The barbed wire fence could do the job of the outrider and no longer would a man's cattle stray and mix among his neighbor's herd. Miles and miles of "drift" fences were stretched; sometimes an entire gigantic ranch was enclosed. The days of free grass were doomed. "I tell you what ruined the West," one old cowman says. "Barbed wire and bib overalls."

Another Enemy

Cattlemen had yet another enemy: sheepmen. Sheep thrived particularly well on the western ranges. Legally, sheep herders had just as much right to the free grass as did the cattlemen. But to the rancher, sheep were a menace. Their grazing habits are different from cattle's. In

order to thrive, these animals must be kept constantly on the move. They crop the grass very close to the ground, and in the arid West this habit can endanger the plant by exposing the root system to the searing rays of the sun, which burns out the forage. An overgrazed prairie is ruined, and a ruined prairie means thin cattle and a low price for cows.

Other factors, as well, contributed to the cowman's loathing of the sheep herders. They tended to be little men, darting about on foot, with gypsy-like carts and busy dogs – in short, they were "foreigners." And the meat from their animals was considered barely fit to eat. A cattleman present when a diner would request roast lamb at a hotel or cafe would loudly refer to the order as a "plate of sheep."

The antagonistic attitude persists to this very day. One elderly cattleman, when offered his choice of roast beef or lamb by a kindly but unknowing hostess recently responded, "No thanks, I ate lamb once and gagged!"

Some Arizona ranchers set up "dead lines" beyond which the sheep herders might not pass. And the stockmen patrolled those deadlines, shooting to kill any sheep herder who transgressed it. In the Ten Sleep country of Wyoming it was not unheard-of for cowboys to spread saltpeter over the sheep range, thus killing the "bleaters." Even more directly, some cowboys simply murdered the sheep and shot and clubbed to death not hundreds but thousands of the little beasts.

Fatal Feuding

In Arizona, a feud between the cattle-raising Graham family and the sheep-herding Tewkesbury clan began in 1887 and ended five years later with 26 men shot down, bushwhacked, dry-gulched or lynched. This feud became known as the Tonto County War. It ended when the last of the Tewkesburys killed the sole remaining Graham.

The most deadly of all the enemies of the cowman was not the sheepman, but the rustler. Despite the penalty – hanging by the neck until dead – these daring thieves were, and are to this very day, a ceaseless scourge.

In the early days, the rustler was an individual trying to build a small herd by putting his brand

RIGHT: *Cowboy band*
from Dodge City,
Kansas
CENTRE: *The Magic of
the Drop*, painting by
Frederic Remington
FAR RIGHT: *Settler's
cabin* at meal time

on any maverick he could lasso, claiming a kind of right of ownership. Many a great herd was built on this basis and in times past when thousands of head of cattle ran wild, the animals were considered "fair game" for a free-enterpriser. Some big operators paid their ranchhands from two to five dollars for each maverick they branded, partly to discourage a cowboy from putting his own brand on the strays, partly to help the cowhand make some extra money. Later, the northern cattle barons agreed among themselves that the paying of commissions would cease and the cowboys would brand mavericks for the home ranch only.

Changing Brands

An even more heinous crime than simple rustling was the changing of a brand. This constituted the deliberate theft of marked property. It was accomplished by using a "running iron," or, better yet, a heated wire, not to deface the original brand but rather add to it and thereby alter its entire appearance.

For example: 10 became 701; or 70L became ЯoB; Ɔ—C, the wrench, could be altered to O—O, the bit, and so on. The rustler had to be ingenious.

A certain basic antagonism existed between the growing number of small ranchers and the great established spreads, many of which were controlled by distant Eastern financial interests. It had long been accepted among the "little fellas" that the big ranchers were too big, too

rich and too powerful. Some cowboys blatantly made their living stealing cows and many small ranchers on the same basis justified helping themselves by boldly cutting the barbed wire fences and driving the cattle home.

The big ranches really were too vast for cowboys to guard their lines effectively. And the little ranchers – the rustlers – gloated at the idea

of bringing the "big boys" to their knees. Many times small ranchers were helped by the very cowboys employed by the Eastern interests, who in sympathizing with the economic struggle of the underdog would themselves go a "little on the rustle." So determined were a great number of cowboys and small ranchers to destroy and ruin the huge ranches financed by absentee owners that rustling became a way of life. A cowboy loyal to his employer was sneeringly referred to as a "pliers man" on the basis that he had to spend so much time mending the wire fences which the rustlers cut.

Jury of Cattle Thieves

The big boys of course fought back. Between the years 1876 and 1886 dozens of Montana rustlers were either lynched or shot by vigilantes. Thirteen men were found strung up on a railroad bridge on one day alone. Many more were brought to trial. Bringing a rustler to justice, however, was a far cry from obtaining a conviction. In northern Wyoming, the home base of the rustlers, the jury and the judge were local residents. The judge himself had been elected by the very men who were doing the rustling; the jury was composed entirely of active cattle thieves. Acquittal was almost a foregone conclusion.

Range War

By 1892 the situation reached such a critical point that the cattle kings gathered in Cheyenne, Wyoming to take positive action. By now their change purses were shrunken to the size of a dead mouse skin from the loss of cattle. Their plan was to hire professional gunmen and proceed to clean out the rustlers in their Johnson County lair. And so, on April 7, 1892, a little army of men, calling themselves the "Regulators Association," boarded a train bound from Cheyenne to Casper. This army was composed of 40 cattle barons with their horses and gunslingers. In the early dawn, the men unloaded their horses at Casper, and led by a Major Wolcott, they rode north toward Buffalo, the county seat and very core of all the trouble.

Near the Johnson County line, the column came upon the Kay Cee Ranch, owned by Nathan Champion. Champion was known to be not only a rustler, but worse still, an organizer of the "Settlers" against the "Regulators."

Lying in ambush, the invaders captured an old trapper who had left the cabin to get water. From him they learned that with Champion was his partner, Nick Ray, and another trapper, Ben Jones. Not long after, Ben Jones came down toward the barns, and like his friend walked

straight into the barrels of the Winchesters.

Wondering what had happened to the two trappers, Nick Ray stepped out the cabin door and was instantly downed – riddled in the head and body. Valiantly he dragged himself back to the cabin as Champion thrust open the door and fired, wounding one of the hired Texas gunmen. In spite of the barrage, Champion was able to drag his wounded friend inside. Here, barricaded, Champion held off his assailants from early morning until about three o'clock. By then his partner had died, but Champion had wounded two more of his attackers.

Siege to the Death
At mid-afternoon a settler named Black Jack Flagg approached the Champion ranch. He was riding a horse, accompanied by his nephew driving a buckboard. As they drew near, they discovered the siege. Unharnessing the horse from the wagon and escaping the Regulators' fierce bullets, they galloped north to warn their friends and neighbors.

The cattle barons and their hired guns decided they must act quickly if they were to win their battle with the heroic Champion. Bravely they captured Mr. Flagg's abandoned buckboard, and piling it with sticks and hay, set fire to it and pushed it against the cabin. Soon flames consumed the side of the log house. Choked by smoke, Champion burst from his burning home, shooting as he came, only to die in a blaze of fire from a host of Winchesters.

Unbelievably, Champion had been writing in his diary throughout the entire siege. His last entry was, "The house is all fired. Goodbye boys, if I never see you again."

The Regulators left the Kay Cee Ranch, left the burning cabin, left the body of Champion with a big note stuck on his chest: CATTLE THIEVES BEWARE.

The Regulators Army then continued north. They had the names of some 70 rustlers to whom they intended to teach a little lesson. About fourteen miles south of Buffalo, at the T A Ranch, they were met by their forward scout, Phil Defrau. He reported that 100 or so angry and determined men were riding hard in their direction brandishing rifles and sidearms, as proof of their intentions.

End of the Johnson County War
Black Jack Flagg had been successful in warning the settlers. Red Angus, the sheriff of Buffalo, must have pretty well exhausted his supply of tin badges in deputizing volunteers. Recruits had been swarming in.

Now the tables were turned. In the shadows of the Big Horn Mountains, the Regulators, outnumbered two to one, frantically began to dig fortifications to attack the T A Ranch. Here the hunters became the hunted.

Barely had they got themselves readied when riders appeared along the horizon. Some shots were fired and returned. The siege had begun. The Johnson County men moved in, pushing bales of hay before them as shields. Meanwhile, as more and more recruits arrived, the settlers rigged up a moveable contraption to which they set fire, a sort of flaming smokescreen. The cattle barons were going to get a little of their own medicine.

And then, just as they were adjusting to the idea of being roasted, the sound of a bugle was heard in the distance. In no time, not one, not two, but three troops of United States Cavalry appeared, took matters in hand, stopped the fighting and spoiled all the fun. The comic-opera three-day Johnson County War had ended before if got started.

The Lincoln County War

Two men, John Chisum and Major L. G. Murphy, brought about another such infamous episode, the Lincoln County War, in New Mexico. Chisum and Murphy seemed destined to be antagonists; both were greedy, unscrupulous and willful men. The record suggests that Chisum perhaps smelled slightly more like a rose than Murphy.

Chisum was a Texan, who had been a trail driver, and tried his hand at the meat-packing business, only to run up debts amounting to $90,000. Unable to pay, he turned his back on his creditors and drove a herd of Longhorns west.

He decided ranching might be his forte and the Pecos territory of New Mexico might be his country. He was correct on both counts. Over the years he built up his herd until he had 100,000 head of cattle; he acquired land as well, much of it as a squatter, until his holdings were the size of the state of Pennsylvania.

So large was Chisum's ranch and numerous his Longhorns that his cowboys were hard pushed to patrol them. The rustlers were aware of this and reveled in the easy pickings. Despite his distinctive brand – a "long rail" which stretched from shoulder to flank and a split ear mark which gave a cow the appearance of having four ears – Chisum was robbed blind. As if to add insult to injury, when he was able to catch some thief red-handed, it seemed the culprit invariably escaped the Lincoln County jail with the greatest of ease.

Major Murphy, formerly of California, had settled in Lincoln where he owned a ranch, the general store, the saloon and the sheriff. Because his cattle herd was not extensive, people wondered how he managed to market so many steers each year. John Chisum didn't wonder. Angered at his losses, he flatly accused Murphy of rustling his cattle. Murphy sneered at the insult, but he did employ young Alexander McSween, an attorney, to represent him.

The Englishman

Another character in this drama was J. H. Tunstall, a very rich Englishman, lured to the

West by its rugged romance. He had bought himself a ranch near Lincoln. Tunstall's attire, like his speech, was very British and at first this made him an object of ridicule to the rough cowboys. But he was no weak cup of tea; he was straightforward and affable, so much so that he soon won the respect and even the affection of his own cowhands and of neighboring ranchers.

Among these cowhands who worked for him was an unprepossessing but likable boy only five feet seven inches tall, named William Bonney.

John Chisum's cattle losses were continuing and the rustlers were still escaping from jail. And then one day Chisum's cowhands caught some Murphy men red-handed with such incontrovertible evidence that the Murphy cowboys were held for trial.

Murphy ordered Mr. McSween to defend his men, but to everyone's amazement and Murphy's ire, the young lawyer flatly refused. The rustlers were so blatantly guilty that McSween's ethics overruled his legal training. Murphy was infuriated, but helpless.

Fueling the Feud

Shortly afterwards, John Chisum retained McSween to represent his legal interests. And Tunstall the Englishman opened a general store in Lincoln in direct opposition to Murphy's

to retrieve in cattle what he thought was due to him in the inheritance and to bring Tunstall in too. After considerable argument, Tunstall agreed to ride to town with the posse, accompanied by his ranch-hands. These included William Bonney, who rode ahead. Suddenly, without any reason (unless perhaps it was the drunkenness of the posse members) shots rang out. Horrified, Bonney watched as Tunstall, his boss, benefactor and friend, fell dead. He kept his head well enough to make a mental note of every posse member responsible for the crime. Little did Murphy or his men realize that the cowhand William Bonney was also the outlaw, Billy the Kid, who had killed his first man at the age of twelve and was one of the West's most deadly and ruthless gunmen.

Death of Billy the Kid

Chisum and McSween were fortunate to have Billy the Kid and his gunmen on their side, but Murphy balanced matters out by hiring gunslingers of his own.

The stage was now set for a pretty good war. As the months passed, little armies of cowboys ambushed one another, sheriffs were shot down, ranch-hands bushwhacked.

In a pitched battle in Lincoln, the Murphy men cornered McSween and his followers in his own house and then set fire to it. As the heat and smoke intensified, McSween's wife and some women friends were forced to leave. As they walked out of the door, not a shot was fired. But as for the men, when they ran out, each was met with a hail of bullets, including McSween himself.

Soon the choking smoke became unbearable and the remaining men burst out. Scurrying in bunches, racing hither and yon, they made a miraculous escape. Billy the Kid was the last to leave. As he blazed his way to freedom he killed one man and wounded two others.

With McSween gone, the war took on the spirit of a vendetta. The Kid began evening the score until nearly every man responsible for Tunstall's death was dead or about to become a corpse. Pat Garrett, the relentless sheriff of Lincoln County, who had doggedly tracked the Kid for months, finally surprised him in a friend's house on the night of July 14, 1881, and shot him dead. At that time Billy the Kid was said to have killed 21 men (and uncounted Mexicans and Indians). He was 21 years old.

With his death, the Lincoln County War came to a close. Murphy had died destitute before the Kid was killed. Chisum quit the whole business and he was buried in Arkansas three years later.

One Rotten Cowboy

When the West was young, there were undoubtedly a great many cowboys who were cleanliving, hardworking young men who lived

monopoly, hiring McSween to manage the business. When the Tunstall operation began to succeed, putting a crimp in Murphy's business, John Chisum, with Tunstall's money, opened a bank at the rear of the building and became its president.

To add fuel to the feud, McSween thwarted Murphy in an inheritance case. Murphy retaliated by charging McSween with embezzlement, whereupon the young attorney transferred his property to Tunstall.

This was too much for Murphy. He sent a deputized posse to Tunstall's ranch with orders

a lonely life on the trail and had a good time when they came to town. But some cowboys were plain rotten. John Wesley Hardin was one.

Hardin was born in Fanin County, Texas, in 1853, the son of a circuit-riding Methodist preacher. It was in 1868, in the post-Civil War period, that "Wess" Hardin first ran into trouble. According to Wess, he was being clubbed to death by a burly freed-slave named Maze, and to save himself he shot and killed the black man. Sure that his chance of acquittal in the Yankee-dominated courts would be nil, Wess ran away, pursued by two white officers and a black man. Wess got the drop on all three and buried them under the sand. Having wiped out four men at the age of fifteen, the boy was well on the road to his chosen career.

In 1869 he pumped lead into another white officer and shortly after claimed his sixth victim, Jim Bradley, in a gambling dispute. Number seven was a circus man who threatened to smash in his face; number eight demanded $100 from what he took to be a callow boy. Wess's slug hit the man squarely between the eyes.

Concealed Weapon

Wess was finally captured and jailed for killing a Mr. Hoffman. This was a murder, in fact, he did not commit. While being transported to trial, Wess escaped, killing Deputy Sheriff Jim Smalley in the process with a little pistol he had concealed in his armpit. Apprehended again, he was held under guard by three Texas state officers, Smith, Davis and Jones. All three died by Wess's gun, on which he could now put twelve notches.

Later, while driving 1,200 Longhorns on the Chisholm Trail toward Abilene, Wess shot two Indians, one for demanding a toll. A little farther along the trail he got into a row with some Mexican cowhands. He settled that squabble by spilling the blood of five of them all over the prairie.

In Abilene Hardin was confronted by Sheriff Wild Bill Hickok, who got the draw on him. Pointing his pistol at Hardin's head, Hickok ordered the boy to hand over his two weapons. Wess offered the pistols, handle first, with the barrels pointing toward himself. As Hickok lowered his hand to reach for the guns, Wess suddenly spun them and aimed both at the sheriff's head.

Strange Friendship

Somehow or other, Hickok talked Wess into surrendering his arms. Then on the boy's

FAR LEFT: *The Virginian*, painting by Charles Russell
ABOVE: *The Stone Hotel*, Oklahoma, offered more than just a bed

Saloon life
TOP RIGHT: The
"Varieties Saloon" in
Dodge City in the 1880s
RIGHT: Texas Cowboys
in a saloon during the
1890s
FAR RIGHT ABOVE:
Dodge City when it
was still the flourishing
cowboy capital of the
West
FAR RIGHT BELOW:
Cartoonists, like
cowboys, could be
cruel toward city people

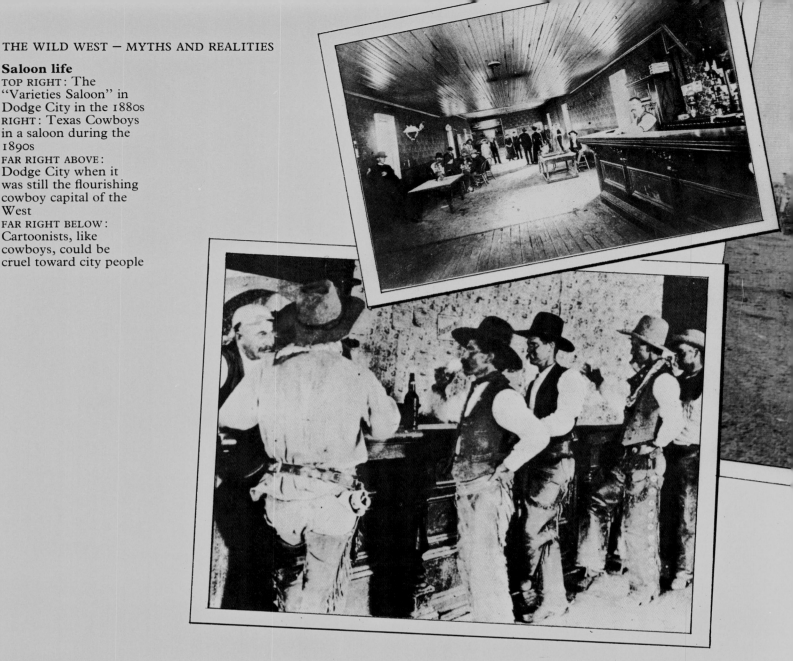

promise that he would behave himself, Hickok offered him friendship and a drink. Wess accepted.

Hickok showed the youngster a Texas warrant for his arrest but agreed not to serve it so long as they were friends. And friends indeed they remained. Hickok even deputized Hardin to apprehend a missing Mexican murderer. Wess punctured the Mexican in a cafe on the Kansas border. When the body was brought in, the cattlemen raised a $1,000 purse as Hardin's reward.

But Hardin couldn't stay out of trouble and didn't really seem to want to. Drinking in a saloon with a friend one day, he heard some ruffians making derogatory comments about Texans. Wess advised them he was a Texan. Shooting broke out. Wess settled the argument by plugging the leader, and left town at a gallop.

This was the way Wess Hardin lived his life. Either he was defending himself, avenging a friend's death, running and hiding from the law or catching odd jobs as a wrangler. As time went on, the list of his victims steadily grew. In addition to the first 21 men he had mowed down,

the bloody roster included two sheriffs, four Texas state policemen, J. B. Morgan, four black policemen, one Mexican holdup man, one sneak thief, one black gunslinger and two unknown roughnecks whom he shot in the dark. This made a grand total of 37 men by the time Hardin was 22 years old.

Up the River

That Hardin could for so long have eluded the authorities seems unbelievable. But in Texas of the 1870s he had many friends and relatives who were happy to hide him out.

In July of 1877, however, his luck ran out. Enjoying a big black cigar in a smoking car, he was captured from behind by Texas Ranger John Armstrong. At Hardin's trial he pleaded that he had never killed a man except in self-defense. With almost 40 killings to contemplate, the jury somehow saw it otherwise and sent him up the river for 25 years.

Hardin spent sixteen years in prison, where he busied himself studying law. Upon his release, he hung out his shingle in El Paso as a practicing attorney. On the night of August 19, 1895, he and a friend were gambling, when Sheriff John

Selman, with whom Hardin had quarreled earlier that day, walked in. Selman wasted no time. He ended Hardin's legal practice instantly by filling the back of his head with lead.

Belle Starr, Horse Thief

Not all the outlaws were men. Some, like Cattle Kate who got herself hanged for rustling, and Calamity Jane, an uncouth, tobacco-chewing slut enamored of Wild Bill Hickok, were of the so-called gentler sex.

One who has been considerably glamorized in the fiction of the West was Belle Starr, although a differing account had it that she was as "alluring as a hyena in heat with a face just like one to prove it." Belle was born in Missouri, and at the age of 24 eloped with one Jim Reed, who had a solid reputation as a horse thief and stage

Dance! you short-horn dance!

robber, besides at least one murder on his record. It was a real love match, it seems, for it lasted two years and might have gone on longer had Jim not got himself shot dead while resisting an arresting officer.

Belle then opened a livery stable in Dallas. Some of the horses she sold had a clean bill of sale, but the majority did not. Later she married a Cherokee Indian named Sam Starr and the two of them settled by the Canadian River. They ran a kind of hostelry in their cabin, a nice secluded place for cattle thieves or men running from the law to visit.

Belle herself was not above stealing a horse now and again. She and Sam were eventually caught at it, and for their clumsiness, they spent a quiet year in the hoosegow. Two years later, Sam got into an argument with a peace officer. Belle's marriage ended then and there as Sam and the lawman did each other in.

In 1889 Belle was riding her horse down a country road when a neighbor who had accused her of rustling his stock spied her and took a potshot. He was acquitted. Belle's daughter, Pearl, attended her funeral.

Pictures and Words

Several men who were not cowboys or outlaws or Indians or sheriffs played an indispensable part in the opening of the West. They were men who had talent and applied it in the right place at the right time; these men were artists, whose pictures did as much as any words to tell people of the glories of the West.

One of the earliest was George Catlin, a Pennsylvania lawyer turned artist, who had an inspired idea. He would set for himself a monumental project. As Audubon was painting all the birds of North America, so Catlin would paint all the Indians.

In 1829, Catlin was painting Iroquois Indians and the next year he was as far west as Fort Leavenworth making portraits of some transplanted eastern Indians: Shawnee, Delaware, Potuwatomi and Kickapoo.

In 1832 he was able to reach Fort Union on the steamboat *Yellowstone*. On this trip he painted portraits of the Sioux at Fort Pierre, Crow and Blackfeet at Fort Union. He also spent several days at the Mandan villages painting various ceremonial scenes. It was there he made his famous portrait of the chief, Four Bears.

The following year Catlin accompanied a troop of dragoons on an expedition to the southern plains where he sketched members of the Kiowa, Comanche and Wichita tribes.

Acclaimed in the Cities

By now Catlin's ambition to make a definitive collection of paintings depicting Indian life was becoming a reality. The first showing of his Indian paintings was held in Pittsburgh in 1833. New York gave his paintings a gala show in 1837. Now he was acclaimed. Later, exhibitions were held in other eastern cities, culminating in a London show which drew crowds for five years. His crowning glory was showing at the Louvre for the French King Louis Philippe.

Along with his art work, Catlin wrote copiously. His "Letters and Notes on the Manners, Customs and Conditions of the North American Indians" gave the public heretofore unknown information about the native Americans. Catlin's works form an invaluable ethnographic and historical contribution to the world.

Swiss Painter

Another who portrayed the Indians was Karl Bodmer, a young Swiss of a different temperament from Catlin. He had no ambition to create an Indian gallery. But he did.

Bodmer was commissioned as the official artist on an expedition to North America. Leaving St. Louis in the spring of 1833, the group traveled up the Missouri on the *Yellowstone*, making field notes and collecting specimens of plants, animals and Indian paraphernalia, of which Bodmer made detailed watercolor sketches. So superbly accurate were his paintings of the flora and fauna and of Indian life that they are unsurpassed both in ethnographic fidelity and dramatic portrayal of the Western scene. The expedition culminated in the spectacularly authoritative "Reise in das Innere Nord-Amerika in den Jahren 1832 bis 1834," filled with handsome plates of Bodmer's wonderful Indians, published in 1839.

Noble Scot Frontiersman

Captain William Drummond Stewart, a veteran of Waterloo, was bored stiff with his life as second son of a Scotch nobleman. The depres-

Wild women of the West
FAR LEFT: Belle Starr astride one of her horses, unlikely to have had a clean bill of sale
LEFT: Calamity Jane, prepared for anything

sing fact that his elder brother would inherit the family fortune while he at best would be left with a pittance was matched by the gloom of the family home, Murthly Castle.

To counter these doldrums, Stewart spent his time hunting game. Intrigued by word that reached him of distant Louisiana, he decided this rugged, untouched land would be the ideal challenge to his ennui. Off he went to become the West's first and most colorful sportsman, and an unusual patron of the arts.

Arriving in New York in the spring of 1832, Stewart made his way to St. Louis by canal boat and from there by riverboat to New Orleans. A year later, guided by the fur trader Robert Campbell, he was on his way up the Mississippi River heading West. His destination was the fur-trading rendezvous where Horse Creek flows into the Green River in what is now Wyoming. There, in a dazzling wilderness of rushing streams and grand mountains, Stewart was enthralled. The hunting was fabulous and so were the people. To him the Indians were proudly free, unspoiled creatures of nature, and the trappers were heroes of the frontier life.

He made friends with Jim Bridger and Antoine Clement, and with Bridger he went on an extended hunting trip, traveling as far north as the Big Horn Mountains and as far south as

Publicizing the West
FAR LEFT: Sculpture
self-portrait by Charles
Russell, one of the most
famous artists of the
West
LEFT: Charles Russell
and Will Rogers (in the
fur hat), the most
celebrated cowboy
showman
BELOW: Russell's
sketch "Cow Puncher
New Style AD 1896"
shows the artist's
disdain for the
"nesters"

Taos, New Mexico. In November, 1835, Stewart returned to New Orleans.

While there, he happened upon the paintings of an artist named Alfred Jacob Miller. Stewart so liked the painter's style that he suggested that Miller accompany him on his next trip. Miller was young and jumped at the idea. He didn't care what he painted, he just wanted to paint. In the spring of 1837 the two started out. Miller made dozens of watercolors along the way, and was having a great time. He made pictures of Fort Laramie and the Sioux, of the mountain men and the great rendezvous on the Green. And his impressionistic renderings were much to Capt. Stewart's taste.

Buffaloes to Scotland

The following year after the rendezvous of 1838 at the Popo Agie, Stewart learned of the death of his brother. But although he was now Sir William, he did not rush to claim his castle. First he gathered up his collection, which included two live buffalo, a grizzly bear, two young Indians and the trapper Antoine Clement. Then with this menagerie Stewart went back to Scotland. The buffalo wandered around the ancestral estate while the French trapper donned a kilt and tried his hand at waiting on dinner guests.

Meanwhile Miller worked on in New Orleans polishing his paintings for his patron. In 1839 he had an exhibition in New York which was much praised. Later he went on to become a virtual artist-in-residence at Murthly Castle before eventually settling in Baltimore as a successful portrait painter.

Except for his New York show, Miller's work of the West lay pretty well hidden for

ABOVE: *Wild Horse Hunters*, painting by Charles Russell
RIGHT: *Four Texan cowhands* of the 1890s keep a good grip on their Winchester rifles
FAR RIGHT: *A Dash for Timber* by Frederic Remington

many years in Scotland and in the private collection of another patron, William Walters, but were finally put on view at the Peal Museum in Baltimore after his death. Unlike Catlin's and Bodmer's pictures which received wide recognition during their lifetimes, Miller's endeavors saw little light until a century after their execution.

The Cowboy Artist

In good measure, however, it was the dramatic credibility and the untiring labors of two artists in particular, Frederic Remington and Charles Russell, that brought the romance of the West to the parlors of the East.

Charles Marion Russell, though born in St. Louis in 1864, almost qualifies as an indigenous Westerner. His father was a Yale graduate and president of a large brick company, and the family was a socially prominent one. As a boy Charles' interest was directed neither toward education nor business. He devoted his energies to playing Indians and trappers in the woods and filling his schoolbooks with sketches of wildlife.

To help redirect their son's interest into a proper and acceptable academic career, his parents sent him to a military school in Burlington, New Jersey. This lasted about six months.

The nobleman and the trapper depicted by the frontiersman-artist who was their companion both in the wilderness and in Scotland: Sir William Drummond Stewart and Antoine Clement portrayed by Alfred Jacob Miller

Instead of studying to get good marks, Charles spent most of his time doing guard duty, as a disciplinary measure. When he returned to St. Louis, his parents conceded that he had artistic talent and sent him to art school. He lasted there three days.

In the desperate hope of getting the spell of the West out of the boy's system, his father agreed to a Western trip. A friend of the family, "Pike" Miller, was part owner of a sheep ranch in Montana and he agreed to take Charlie on. At the age of sixteen, the boy went to tend sheep on the Judith Basin.

A Cowhand, Not a Sheepman

Charlie stayed at the Miller ranch for about a year, making many sketches. He also lost a lot of sheep and got himself fired. With not much else to do, he spent a winter with the Blackfeet Indians. Later, with even less to do, he sheltered with a hunter named Jake Hoover who took pity on him.

Charlie spent a year at Jake's cabin making drawings of the wild world around him. More by luck than intention, Charlie found his other life's work, when he hired on as a horse wrangler for a cattle roundup. This job he did well, and soon he was responsible for 200 cow ponies.

For eleven years Charlie worked as a wrangler, a cowpuncher and a ranch hand. And all the time he made drawings, sketches and paintings of what he saw. And the other cowboys approved his work.

After the great blizzard of '86, the owner of the OK Ranch, trying to write to a friend to describe the desolation, noticed that Charlie was drawing a picture on a small piece of cardboard. The owner tore up his letter and mailed instead Charlie's postcard-sized sketch titled "Waiting for a Chinook." His friend got the message.

Full Time Art

Charlie kept on drawing. In 1888, Harper's Weekly published his picture "Caught in the Act," and after eleven years of cowboying, Charlie gave it up to devote full time to recording the West. In 1893 he moved to Great Falls, Montana. He sold his paintings now and again, some to a family friend in St. Louis, some to Sid Willis, owner of the Mint Bar. Charlie thought a price of $25 was fair enough.

Russell's pictures were just right. Cowboys could pick out a particular horse, identify a well-known critter at a glance. That meant the pictures were good. And his stories of cowboying rang true. Wearing his old boots and a red sash at his waist, Charlie was a welcome addition at any bar.

In Great Falls, Charlie was introduced to a girl from Kentucky named Nancy Cooper. Nancy was only seventeen, but she became enamored of this 39-year-old cowboy and his paintings and when she was eighteen Nancy and Charlie were married.

Nancy became interested in helping her husband market his paintings to better advantage. She did this in two ways. First she was able to convince Charlie not to spend most of the day at the bar with his drinking cronies, but instead to paint all morning and visit with his friends in the afternoons, and limit himself to two drinks. And then she found more buyers for his paintings at increased prices.

National Recognition

In 1911 Russell's first one-man show was held in New York. By now, Charlie Russell, the

Sir W. D. S
vs Antoine (Cana
tt al

cowboy artist, was nationally recognized. In 1914 his works were shown twice in London. With his cowboy hat, boots and red sash, he cut quite a figure on the London gallery scene.

As the years passed, Charlie turned out hundreds upon hundreds of sketches and paintings, many as illustrations for popular magazines of the day. He also took up sculpting and turned out three-dimensional works of the same verve and simple freshness as his paintings. Nancy was successful at getting increasingly good prices for his work: in 1921 he received $10,000 for a small painting. Five years later when he was commissioned by a well-to-do Californian for a picture to fill a special place, Charlie charged $30,000.

But more than money, Charles Russell always loved the West he had known as a young man, and his pictures show it.

Transplanted Easterner

Frederic Remington, like Russell, was a member of an Ivy League sort of family; he himself graduated from the Yale School of Fine Arts. But although an Easterner, he too had a passion for both painting and the West.

At the age of nineteen he made his first trip to Montana, chiefly to get the taste of it. He also made many sketches. Two years later, in 1883, he spent his modest inheritance on a small sheep ranch in Kansas. This was hardly the wild West, and Remington was not much more of a sheepman than Charlie Russell had been, but it was useful experience.

Deciding to devote full time to art, Remington sold his ranch a year later. He moved to Kansas City, married his New York sweetheart and began work in earnest. As the years passed, Remington became prolific. His illustrations of Indians, cowboys and the U.S. Cavalry appeared in all the more popular magazines. He traveled widely throughout the West carefully studying costumes and equipment to ensure the accuracy of his work.

In 1891, before he was 30, Remington was elected an associate member of the National Academy of Design, an honor he had coveted.

**A Charles Russell
Gallery**
BELOW RIGHT and
BOTTOM: Paintings
depicting cowboys
rounding up steers and
bringing them in
FAR RIGHT: *Dangerous
Moment*

A Dude's Welcome,
painting by O. C.
Seltzer.

Overall, his diligence produced some 2,700 paintings and drawings and 22 bronzes. His career was cut short by peritonitis, which killed him at the age of 48.

Writers of "Westerns"

By the turn of the twentieth century, the West of the wild Indians and resolute explorers, the pioneers, the trappers, the gold-rush miners and the Longhorn drovers was pretty much a memory. No one date can mark the end of this fabulous era, but arbitrarily 1900 is as good a one as any. Well before that milestone year, however, men were already romanticizing the past glories in fiction and art and capitalizing on their own experiences or those of others.

Among the writers to popularize the West were Owen Wistar and Zane Grey, Emerson Hough, Charles Siringo, Ross Santee and Will James.

Owen Wistar was a Philadelphia lawyer who went West for his health. His novel, "The Virginian," published in 1902, won him immediate fame. As a best seller, it carried the aura of the West forcefully to the Eastern public.

Zane Grey was a melodramatic writer who turned out book after book, often fanciful and sometimes improbable. His "Riders of the Purple Sage" was to become one of the most popular "Westerns" ever written.

Emerson Hough, who also wrote novels of the West, was, on the other hand, a serious scholar. His "Covered Wagon" published in 1922 and "North of 36" of the following year were two of his best.

Charles Siringo, a former trail hand and sheriff, wrote narratives and a history of the West based largely on his own experiences.

Will James, like Siringo, had been a working cowboy and also wrote from firsthand knowledge. His poignant story of a cowpony, "Smoky," is a fine example of cowboy understatement; it was enhanced by his own sketches. Another book "Cowboy," by Ross Santee, is the wistful gentle tale of a real cow-puncher's life.

Wild West Show Biz

A different way of cashing-in on nostalgia for bygone days was developed by the former Pony Express rider, army scout and buffalo hunter, William Cody, known throughout the world as "Buffalo Bill:" he turned it into show business.

Cody's career as a showman began on a New York stage in 1872. A play called "Buffalo Bill, King of the Border Men," drew enthusiastic crowds, without Buffalo Bill himself in the cast. In fact, he was in the audience at one performance. Spotted by the promoter, Ned Buntline, he was brought to the stage. There he was loudly acclaimed and immediately became stage-struck. He swiftly signed a contract.

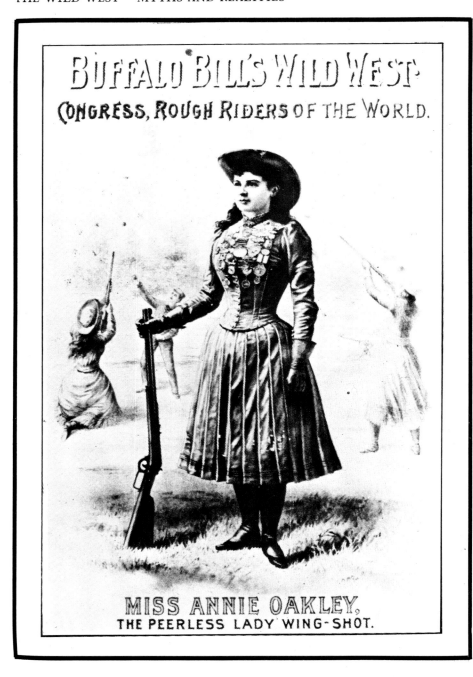

BUFFALO BILL'S WILD WEST
CONGRESS, ROUGH RIDERS OF THE WORLD.

MISS ANNIE OAKLEY,
THE PEERLESS LADY WING-SHOT.

PREVIOUS PAGES:
The Fall of the Cowboy
by Frederic Remington

Buffalo Bill
ABOVE and RIGHT:
Annie Oakley, the stage
heroine, and a portrait
from real life
FAR RIGHT: Stars of
Buffalo Bill's Wild
West Show of 1886

Cody's popularity as a hero of the West was not undeserved. He had begun his career at the age of fifteen as a Pony Express rider, a job requiring endurance and courage. Later he served as chief of scouts for the Fifth Cavalry. In an engagement with the Cheyenne, he had successfully rescued two couriers, and he gained fame with the killing of a young chief, Yellow Hand.

Employed by the Kansas Pacific Railroad in 1868 to supply meat for the construction gangs, Cody was credited with killing over 4,000 buffalo in the short period of a year and a half. It was this bit of mass butchery that earned him the name Buffalo Bill.

Soon after Cody's initial appearance in New York, Buntline gave him a part in a new play, "Scout of the Plains," and the showman in him emerged. In 1883, his famous "Wild West Show" had its opening in Omaha. Its success was meteoric. Now the public could witness, firsthand, live buffalo, real Indians attacking a stagecoach, genuine cowboys displaying feats of horsemanship and steer roping. Even the celebrated gunslinger Wild Bill Hickok was on display shooting up the arena.

Cody himself would open the show, leading a charging procession on a white steed. Dressed in buckskins and a big hat and with his white hair flowing, he was a dashing and colorful figure. He was an excellent marksman, and so was one of his co-stars, the beloved Annie Oakley. The two of them would shoot glass balls in the air. Annie even shot cigarettes from between the lips of her trusting husband. All in all it was a noisy "shoot-em-up" show and everyone loved it, even in England, where Cody took his show in 1887. He even gave two command performances for the Queen. Then he toured Europe and there, too, his popularity soared.

Buffalo Bill's Sad End
Unfortunately for all his flair as a showman, Cody was a poor businessman, and worse, he became a heavy drinker. These misfortunes led to the show's decline. Its last good year was 1910, and seven years later Cody died destitute. He was buried on Look Out Mountain near Denver.

By then the Wild West was, in reality, a thing of the past.

Dick Johnson.

Lillian F. Smith.

Annie Oakley.

Gabriel Dumont.

Young Chief.

Carter Coutrier.

W. F. Cody.

Jim Mitchell.

John M. Burke.

Buck Taylor.

Nate Salsbury.

CHAPTER X

Cowboys at Work

OVERLEAF:
Jerked Down, painting
by Charles Russell

BELOW: *Cowboys and
cowgirls* pose for the
camera, c. 1895
FAR RIGHT: *Sam
Maverick,* who gave his
name to innumerable
strays

THE ORGANIZER OF a cattle drive was a daring entrepreneur and he had to have a will to gamble. But the man who needed the real stamina and guts, determination and courage was the one who had actually to drive the herd of half-wild cattle over 3,000 miles. This was cowboy's work. In the early, pre-railroad days particularly, the cowboy's most important role was that of drover.

A Texas cattleman might decide to drive his own herd north to the mecca of the railheads, but more commonly the drover would take cattle from several owners. He himself would assume the financial risk by buying the cattle outright for a given price, with, of course the hope of great profit.

Collecting Cows for a Drive
Under such an arrangement, the cattle were collected at an agreed starting point. Each owner sent out his cowboys to gather the cattle.

Collecting the cows, often at a public corral, first involved finding them. Getting them out of the dense thickets was an almost impossible job. It meant knowing where they might be hidden, and then driving them through the mass of tangled underbrush that was often a maze of trails hidden by thorny bushes and prickly plant life. This was tough, hard work and the wild cows were quick and anything but co-operative. For that type of animal, roping was often the only method of securing them. The Texans carried especially short lariats, rarely more than 30 feet long, for a snare of greater length would tangle in the mesquite and chaparral.

As the cows were assembled – and all cattle were referred to as "cows," whether cow or calf, heifer or steer, even bulls – they were sorted by ownership according to their brands.

There was no selection for quality; the cows were all about the same. Each was a rangy, lanky, gaunt mass of beef and hide with an impressive set of horns.

The Peerless Longhorn

Despite the Longhorn's great size, he was thin-fleshed, lanky and slow to mature. His size did not equate with quality. His horns, sometimes measuring over seven feet from tip to tip, though possibly advantageous in self-defense, were a distinct handicap when it came to shipping. In a crowded boxcar, these sharp-pointed stilettos were a severe hazard to every other animal, for they tore up the hides, bruised the muscles and reduced the overall value of the carcass.

His ability to range, however, was phenomenal. Apparently unconcerned, a steer would graze as far as fifteen miles from water and go without drinking for over 48 hours. On cattle drives, Longhorns were known to go without water for four days and nights. This characteristic, combined with an inbred ability to

Cattle drive from New Mexico to Sterling, Kansas

withstand heat, to sustain themselves on the most barren of land and to remain immune to the ravages of tick fever, made the Longhorn peerless.

The term "beef" was applied to any animal over four years old, and a beef was worth from three to eight dollars at the roundup. All cattle were bought and sold by the head, not by weight.

In gathering the cows, it was only natural that many would be found to be without brands. These were known as "mavericks" and the determination of true ownership was absolutely impossible.

A Man Named Maverick

There are several versions as to how the term "maverick" came to be applied to unbranded cattle, but one, which seems most logical, will suffice.

One Samuel A. Maverick, a colonel and practicing attorney in San Antonio, Texas, in 1845 received as a fee not cash but 100 Longhorn cows. These animals were unbranded, nor did the colonel bother to see to it that his slaves put his mark on them. There is reason to believe the lawyer didn't even have a brand. There are plenty of records of lawyers who died not having had sense enough to make a will, and Maverick likely falls into that category.

At any rate, sometime later, as his herd multiplied, an interested buyer named Toutant Beauregard was quick to discover the cows were unmarked; he forthwith branded them with his sign and claimed Maverick's cattle and a great many other unbranded animals for his own.

The term "maverick" is still used today for any unmarked yearling or a calf that won't stay with its mother.

Dividing them Up

The general agreement among stockmen with respect to mavericks during the roundup was that the unmarked animals would be divided up, each man getting a fair share. Different rules applied at different times; sometimes it was a pro-rata basis depending on how many cows each owner was known to possess.

When the cattle belonging to the various owners had been sorted and counted, the buyer or drover received a bill of sale from each rancher for the cattle sold. With the exception of the mavericks, each cow carried the brand of its owner, but in releasing them to the buyer, all the cows were given a "vent" brand or "road" brand, a kind of additional bill of sale indicating the buyer as a "vendor" of the cattle in his charge. Some animals, which might have had three or four owners, would end up literally covered with brands.

Pushing the Cows Hard

In starting a drive, it was customary to push the cows hard for the first 25 or 30 miles; in some extreme cases it was as much as 100 miles. Men had learned that tiring the cattle reduced the risk of "coasters" turning back to the range they knew. By sundown, the cattle would be pretty tired out and no matter how strong their homing instinct might be, sheer exhaustion would overrule it.

After being pushed hard the first few days, the herd was allowed to move at a slower pace of between twelve and fifteen miles per day. This gave the animals time to graze and fatten on the way.

In a well-planned drive two "point riders," men most experienced in cattle driving, led the herd. At intervals along the main body rode the "line riders" while at the rear, pushing and coaxing the lazy cows ahead amid a dense cloud of dust, were the greenhorns, inexperienced cowpunchers equipped with nothing more than a loud "halloo" and a half-broke mustang to push the beasts along.

The first few days of a drive were especially difficult. The cows, particularly the young steers, were upset and nervous, ready to bolt at any opportunity. Some men made a point of including in their herd three or four old bulls. They found that the bulls' status and sobriety helped calm the herd and offset the antics of the exuberant young steers.

At dusk, when it became time to bed the cattle down, wise and fortunate was the drover who staked out a suitable watering place. Here

FAR LEFT: *Lonesome cowboy* by his camp fire
FAR LEFT CENTRE: *Cowboy in the Rain,* painting by Ace Powell
FAR LEFT BELOW: *Herding cattle* in New Mexico
BELOW: *Wichita cattle yards* in 1874; the cattle are being prodded into stock cars

ABOVE: *Cowboys with Pack Horse*, painting by Frederic Remington
FAR RIGHT: *Scattering the Riders*, painting by Joe Beeler

the cows could drink, rest and, hopefully, sleep through the night.

Wrangler and Remudas
The extra horses, too, had to be settled. Usually two "horse wranglers" were assigned to drive and herd the extra mounts, referred to as the "remuda." A rope corral was set up at each stop. Sometimes the men themselves served as temporary fence-posts until the horses were calmed down and the single rope could be tied to improvised posts and to the wheel of the chuck wagon. Occasionally, the horses were hobbled, but it wasn't a requirement; strangely, one single strand of rope formed a line beyond which the horses would not pass.

Now the cook, called "cookie," who had been hired solely for his ability to drive a team of horses, not for his culinary accomplishments, would serve the meal, usually baked beans, bacon, hard biscuits and rank coffee, from the back of the chuck wagon. More often than not "cookie" was an individual down on his luck. Otherwise, he would never have hired out for the job. In addition to his pots and pans, his equipment included one shovel, for his responsibilities included burying the dead. The one

attribute that "cookie" did not possess, according to any cowboy ever questioned about the matter, was an ability to cook.

"Come and get it!" or "Grub pile!" was the call, and every man responded.

Killing the Cook
Beans, bacon and coffee might not be much, but that was the fare. One cowboy, so upset at the rotten quality of the mess, flew into a fit of rage, and shot the cook dead. The other cowboys, realizing they might starve as a result, discussed lynching the murderer. But the drover intervened, and made a Solomon-like decision. He ordered that the killer should become "cookie" for the remainder of the drive. The meals were even worse than before.

The night-herders, men responsible for watching the cows, would select from the remuda a horse for the task. The men were given shifts, sometimes four hours, but usually two. The job of night-herder was not easy as the cattle had to be watched constantly lest they become "spooked" and stampede.

Songs Against Stampedes
Cowboy songs had great importance totally apart from recreation; a wrangler who couldn't

Relaxation for men
from the sun-soaked
Plains

striking of a match – might cause one timorous steer to bolt, whereupon the entire herd would most likely rush off in disastrous flight. To prevent this, the night-riders would sing to the cattle their soft, gentle, little lullabies. Some of these songs have come down to us today, others are lost in the starlit blackness of the great plains of bygone days. But the legend of the singing cowboy is very real.

This purposeful singing was unaccompanied by any instrument. A guitar would have been an impossible encumbrance on a cattle drive, and a mouth organ would have terrified the cows. A verse from one of these songs gives an idea of what the cowboy worried about:

Oh, say little dogies, when will you lie down
And give up this shifting and roving around
My horse is leg weary, and I'm awfully tired
But if you get away, I'm sure to get fired
Lie down, little dogies, lie down
Hi-yo, hi-yo, hi-yo

Follow the Leader

The mere thought of a stampede struck terror in every cowman, and while the songs were his best insurance, he took other precautions too. He could intersperse his herd with tame bulls, he could plan his drive in the early spring so that his cows would be fat and content on the greening grass, and he could make sure to rid himself of boisterous young steers. All too often there were one or two such animals that seemed

sing just might not get hired for the job. A stampede was frighteningly dangerous, a disaster which as often as not meant not only loss of cattle but injury and death to the men. Cattle were extremely nervous. And about the only way the cowboys could keep them calm was with their doleful little songs.

The least unexpected noise – the yipping of a coyote, a clap of thunder, even the mere

to enjoy the chance of bolting. The cowboys learned to spot these recalcitrants and cut them out of the herd, either by turning them loose or shooting them. If the latter case, "green" beef, or uncured meat, was at least a change from bacon.

No matter how diligent the night-watchers were, no matter how earnestly they sang their lullabies, stampedes did happen. A lightning or hail storm was frequently the cause; at the first or second crack of thunder, a steer might jump and start to bolt. Others would follow the leader and almost immediately the entire herd would be a rushing mass of pounding hooves and swinging horns.

The cowboys were more or less powerless to halt the onrush, but they would try. Every man except "cookie" was pressed into the chase, the object being to ride amongst the leaders and try to turn the herd in upon itself, thus causing the cattle to "mill" in a circling mass around and around until they would finally come to an exhausted halt.

Trampled to Death

Trying to get to the head of the herd often meant riding among the fast-moving cows, but in the black of night a cow pony's misstep in a prairie dog hole or a hidden ravine could mean instant death by trampling for its rider.

Often the cattle would run for many miles, only to be found scattered here and there, in little bunches, all over the prairie. The cow-hands had to collect as many as possible, for each lost animal reduced the drover's profit. Sometimes several days were spent searching for strays. But even so, many cows were lost for good.

If storms were particularly severe, or the cattle especially nervous, one stampede might follow another. It was common knowledge that if a herd once bolted, it was more than likely to do so again. It is recorded that one Texas herd stampeded eighteen times in one night and that another ran for over 40 miles before it came to a halt.

In addition to searching for cattle after a stampede, the men had the grim job of counting heads or reriding the trail in search of the trampled remains of a comrade. If, sadly, a mangled body should be found, the cook got out his spade. Over the simple grave the cowboys would hold their hats in tribute – nothing more.

From Plains to table
FAR LEFT ABOVE: Herding steers into stock cars, Abilene, c. 1868
FAR LEFT: The famous beast known as the Texas Longhorn
ABOVE: The midday meal, the chief one for the ranch hand; beef was always a favorite food

BELOW: *Chuck wagon scene* before the turn of the century
FAR RIGHT: *A single rope* was sufficient to form a corral from which horses would not stray
FAR RIGHT BELOW: *Brands* as listed in an old branding book

Under the Stars

Those cowboys who were not assigned night watch or who drew a later shift usually turned in after supper. There wasn't much else to do, and in any case twelve or more hours in the saddle induced fatigue. There were no tents on a cattle drive. Using his saddle as a pillow, the cowhand would simply roll up in a blanket beneath the starry heavens.

Rain was particularly unpleasant. Even though the men carried great yellow, oilskin slickers and might use a hat as a sort of umbrella, trying to sleep in mud and cold running water is never really comfortable. But when you are making a dollar a day, you accept inconveniences.

Fording the River

Whichever trail was currently popular, from the early Shawnee to the celebrated Chisholm, each traversed many rivers – the Colorado and Brazos and Red to the south, the Canadian and Cimarron and Arkansas farther north. These rivers, though shallow, were often wide, and if the season had been rainy they could become raging torrents. There was not one bridge over any of them, so each had to be forded.

It was considered good practice when approaching a river to keep the cattle moving, urging the lead steers to continue their pace, swimming the river to maintain the momentum. The men riding "point" and "flank" would swim their horses in the accustomed position to keep the cows in line. One old drover, Colonel Snyder, had two lead "swimming steers" who were trained, more or less, to plunge into the rivers ahead of the herd and lead it across. He used these animals on drive after drive.

It was not always easy, especially if the water was high, to get the cattle started. Once in, swimming with their heads just out of the water, many became caught in the swift currents.

There they might be sucked under or drown from exhaustion. The cowboys at all costs had to prevent such a disaster.

Most dangerous was the situation where the cattle, having already started across, became frightened, perhaps by a floating log or a sudden change in current, and trying to turn back would circle upon the herd. Now the cowboys had to swim their horses among the piercing horns, yelling and yipping to try to untangle the milling cows lest they be washed downriver and drown. If a man became dismounted in the river, he would be lucky to grab his horse's tail or that of a steer and be dragged to shore, or he might try swimming. Many a man met death by drowning.

Yet, remarkably, there is no record of any herd failing, ultimately, to cross a river.

Pintos, Piebalds and Palominos

The cow pony is a remarkable animal. As Texans introduced "hot-blooded" stallions from the East, the Thoroughbred, the Quarter Horse and the Morgan (which itself was very likely a Quarter Horse), the wild mustang was upgraded. The Quarter Horse was bred at first as a racehorse which with a quick start could run the quarter mile in record time. The cow pony inherited the endurance, surefootedness and toughness of the mustang, coupled with the speed and good disposition of the Quarter Horse, all of which made him indispensable to the cowboy.

In general, the cow pony is close-coupled, enabling him to turn very sharply. He tends not to be a large horse, rarely standing over fifteen hands high. Cow ponies come in a variety of colors from bays to blacks, from roans called "buckskins" to piebalds more commonly referred to as "pintos" or "paints." Some, like the Palominos, which are golden-

colored horses, and the Appaloosa, which sports spots and blotches, especially around the rump, are considered now to be separate breeds.

Breaking a horse is a difficult task requiring patience, skill and courage. An untamed colt is wild and nervous. There are many techniques used for breaking a raw horse and some cowboys become specialists.

One method is to wait until the horse is about four years old; by then it will have matured enough to have some horse-sense. First it must be petted and haltered and led around the corral. Next the cowboy shows it a blanket and then a saddle, all the time patting and smoothing the frightened colt from nose to hocks. A good idea is to wave a gunny sack around its face and between its legs to get the animal used to fluttering objects, so that later it won't shy. It's also important to acquaint him with a yellow oilskin slicker. A horse unfamiliar with this type of raincoat will most likely buck and heave, to the misfortune of everyone nearby, while on a rainy day a "slickered" horse is a pleasure to ride.

Busting Broncos

The colt is then gently, carefully saddled and allowed to spend the day walking around the corral to get accustomed to the feel of the weight. Finally, the cowboy gingerly mounts the horse, riding it around the ring, hoping not to get bucked off. Such an animal which has never worked cows, never really been tested, is known as "green broke." This method of breaking a horse may take several days.

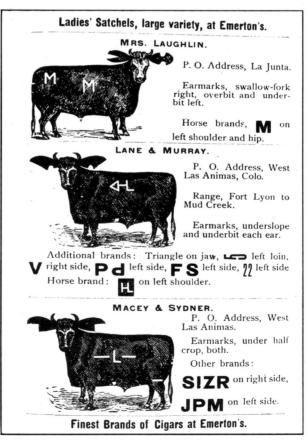

Not all cowboys have the time or patience to break a horse in this fashion. Some rope them, hobble them, saddle them, climb aboard and "let 'er buck." Such a "bronco buster" literally wears down the horse and "breaks" him. This is quick and effective, provided the horse is not so spirited as to be unbreakable.

A cow pony is quick, alert, willing, gentle and somehow, almost instinctively, knows how to cope with cattle. One that doesn't have these qualities isn't much use.

The stock saddle is heavy, weighing from 40 to 50 pounds. It must be of such sturdy construction that the horn, with a rope looped or "dallied" around it, can withstand the jerk and pull of a 2,000-pound bull. Its high cantle makes for easy, rocking chair-like riding; its heavy fenders protect the rider's legs. A wide latigo or girth, sometimes called cincha, ensures that it will stay secure on the horse.

With his saddle equipped with leather strings, the cowboy could tie his lariat, bedroll and yellow slicker for ready use. There were many styles of saddle, some plain, some elaborately tooled, but all, if they were good ones, built to withstand the toughest sort of strain. For many a cowboy, his saddle was his most cherished possession. Like Buck; when he goes by they say: "There goes Buck with his $100 saddle on his $10 horse."

While the saddle was the cowboy's prime piece of equipment, his hat and chaps, his boots and spurs were pretty important too.

A cowboy's hat was a combination of parasol, to shade him from the sun, and umbrella, to protect him from the rains. Sometimes it was even used as a pail to quench a horse's thirst. In the South, black wide-brimmed hats were favored; in Wyoming and Montana light-colored, narrower-brimmed hats were preferred. A wide-brimmed hat catches more wind and blows off more easily, but a narrow brim isn't much for shade.

The cowboy boot, high-topped and high-heeled, with a pointed toe, was designed for a very functional purpose. The high tops protected the cowboy's calf from chafing against the saddle's fender and from rattlesnake bites, should he have to dismount to tend to a sick calf. Most often the boots were stitched to form fancy patterns, especially on and about the tops, just to pretty them up.

The high heels kept his foot from slipping forward in the stirrup, and served as a brake, when, God forbid, he was roping cattle on foot. The pointed toe enabled easy entry into the stirrup. Mounting a frisky horse was enough bother in itself; fumbling around to get one's feet in the stirrups was more than bothersome, it was plain dangerous.

Throwing a Rope

The spurs the cowmen wore were fashioned from the old Spanish styles, most often with vicious rowels. There were many modifications, some fanciful, like the "gal-leg" spur, the shank of which was modeled after a woman's leg. A

good horseman used his spurs sparingly. A good horse behaved better because of their mere presence.

The bridle and the bit, like the spur, were derived from Spanish patterns. The bit took many forms, each designed to control the horse. Some bits, like the spade and the ring, were veritably lethal and some curb bits could

The trek to market
ABOVE: *Herd Swimming a River*, painting by A. Castaigani
RIGHT: Punching cows in Colorado
FAR RIGHT: Longhorns fording the Red River on a drive from San Antonio, Texas, to Dodge City, Kansas

be pretty authoritative. The idea of a harsh bit was to stop a headstrong horse, for all too often the half-tamed mustang or wild bronco was willful to the point of defiance.

The proficiency of a cowboy depended in large measure upon his ability to "rope." Throwing a rope required much practice and some men achieved a masterful skill.

The lariat was, in reality, a flying noose. Some 30 to 60 feet in length, the rope was threaded through itself between a smaller loop or hondo, to make a big loop. Thrown by the skillful cowboy it could capture the most wayward cow or mustang.

The Roundup

No one activity was more critical to the cattlemen than the roundup. It was thought of as the culmination of a year's work, but in reality it was the payoff of a daring gamble. It was the time to take inventory and to count the harvest. If the calf crop was high and the market was up, it was good times for the rancher. Conversely, if poor conditions, rustlers, blizzards or drought had taken their toll, the stockman could be badly hurt.

In the 1880s and 1890s, the roundup usually took place in midsummer. Very often neighboring ranchers joined forces. Despite the efforts of the line riders, cattle from one ranch invariably mixed with cattle from another and now was the time to "throw them over" to the land of the proper owner. A "captain" was chosen to supervise the round-up. He in turn selected "lieutenants," each with a group of cowboys. In general the lieutenants were the foremen of the co-operating ranches, for they knew best their own territory and their own men.

Originally, corrals were set up at a centrally convenient point where the cattle would be gathered, but since these were often at an isolated spot, rustlers discovered that they

Battle of wills as a
cowboy tries to control
a recalcitrant Longhorn

ABOVE: *Breaking a bronco*, as recorded by an early photographer
RIGHT: *"Slicker,"* or saddlecoat, as advertised in the 1902 Sears Roebuck mail order catalog
FAR RIGHT: *Lariat*, the indispensable "long arm" of the cowboy

made a most advantageous place to carry out their nefarious operations. The big ranchers learned quickly, tore the corrals down and used one or another's home ranch for sorting, counting, branding and steering.

The area of a roundup might involve as much as 4,000 square miles. Within the boundaries might be between 5,000 and 10,000 cows, scattered here and there in little bunches, hidden in watered draws, spread out on the "flats," secluded in the shade of the Ponderosa pines. It was the cowboy's job to bring them in – to sweep the range clean.

Gathering the cattle was no easy task. The cowboys were sent out to the far reaches of the range. At first a man might find four or five head, then possibly another ten or twelve. These he would drive toward the main corrals. Owing to the natural tendency for cattle to herd, the bunches would grow larger and larger. A cowboy driving one bunch would meet another and the two herds would combine. At length three or four men might be driving as many as 300 animals. When finally all the cows were assembled, which could take several days, the real work began – that of "cutting out" and branding.

From among the cowhands a "tallyman" was chosen, someone of reliable character who would keep count of which cattle belonged to each owner. Cattle were "cut out" or sorted for several purposes, first to brand the unmarked

calves, then to "beef cut" or ascertain the cowman's harvest so as to select the fat animals for market.

The Cutting Horse

Cutting out the calves for branding took skill, a quick eye and, the prize of every cowboy – the cutting horse. Almost by instinct, these little cow ponies seemed to realize which cow and calf were to be separated from the herd. A good

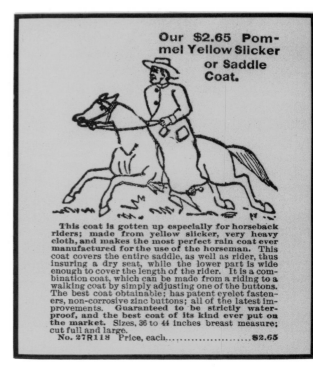

Our $2.65 Pommel Yellow Slicker or Saddle Coat.

This coat is gotten up especially for horseback riders; made from yellow slicker, very heavy cloth, and makes the most perfect rain coat ever manufactured for the use of the horseman. This coat covers the entire saddle, as well as rider, thus insuring a dry seat, while the lower part is wide enough to cover the length of the rider. It is a combination coat, which can be made from a riding to a walking coat by simply adjusting one of the buttons. The best coat obtainable; has patent eyelet fasteners, non-corrosive zinc buttons; all of the latest improvements. Guaranteed to be strictly waterproof, and the best coat of its kind ever put on the market. Sizes, 36 to 44 inches breast measure; cut full and large.
No. 27R118 Price, each.....................$2.65

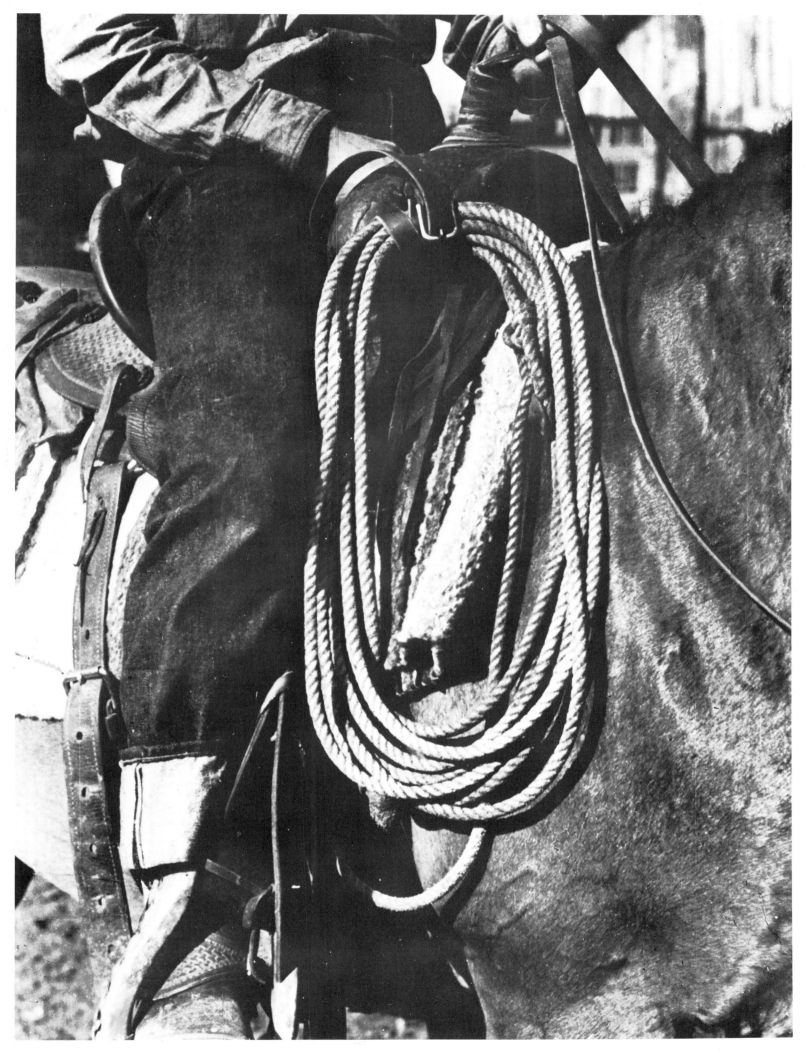

Our Olympia Heavy High Grade Cowboy Saddle.

$31.85

No. 10R8015

cowboy can indicate with the slightest motion of his body, the barest push of his knee, the gentlest touch of the rein, just which cow he wants separated and, as if by magic, the pony gets the message. He goes at his task with an uncanny spirit of enthusiastic loyalty. There is no more marvelous sensation for the working cowboy than to be on a good cutting horse – man and beast silently communicating to make the perfect team.

In separating a cow and its calf from the herd, the instinct of the calf to hang close to its mother no matter where she goes is of great help in determining ownership. When the pair were separated, the calf was branded with the mother's mark, and the little fellow added to the tally of the cow's owner.

As the pair was cut out, the calf was roped. Sometimes the cowboy would loop his lariat over the dogie's neck, often he would "heel rope" it and then drag the bawling critter toward the branding irons.

Branding the Calves

The irons were heated in a long fire pit, until they were scarlet red. Irons for each ranch were

278

readied and the tally-man totaled the branded calves belonging to each stock-man. As the calf was dragged to the fire, two men grabbed him, one at the head, the other by the tail. Holding the calf down by stretching it out, the brander could plant his iron hard on the sizzling flank of the struggling calf. With that stroke, the little animal became the legal property of a specific outfit.

If the men were holding down a bull calf, it was customary for one man, equipped with a sharp knife, to castrate him. In that painful instant of being "steered," as it is called, the calf became destined to be one of a future year's crop of beef. With the job done, the little steer was released to scamper off in search of its mother.

When the day's work was finished, the cowboys gathered around their respective camps – each ranch having set up its own chuck wagon and remuda. Here "cookie" might serve up a concoction of kidney stew, affectionately referred to as "son-of-a-gun stew," or maybe "county attorney," a stew made of veal, this complemented by canned corn, lead-weight biscuits and black coffee so strong a spoon was sure to float.

After nightfall, those cowboys not assigned to sing to the cattle might exchange tall tales or sing among themselves. With the cows safely coralled, a cowhand might even break out a banjo.

After the calves were branded and steered, the "beef cut" took place. It was now that cattle, especially the fat ones, were separated from the herd and held in readiness to be driven to the nearest railhead. The tally-man was busy keeping records of precisely how many beeves properly belonged to each ranch.

And so the roundup ended. Men were assigned to drive the steers to the railhead and here the tally was finally recorded. Each owner was now credited and often paid for what was due to him. More often than not there were buyers right at the corrals, but sometimes the ranchers waited for the money until the livestock, crowded in the drafty cattle cars, finally reached Kansas City or Chicago.

The Business of Ranching

The successful rancher had to be an astute businessman. Armed with a good knowledge of the economics of the business, he gambled against the odds of the elements, of disease and sudden death, of thieves and rustlers and of a fluctuating and often unpredictable market. His employees the cowhands were a motley lot of hard-working, hard-living and often soft-hearted men, who would care for a stranded calf with more compassion than a female Salvation Army officer could show toward a drunken bum on a blizzardy Christmas Eve.

Seasonal Work

Life on a working ranch changes with the seasons.

Winter is a time of feeding the herd and of repairing machinery. In the northern plains just getting the equipment operable in frigid winter weather can be a half-day's job.

The ranch-hand atop a wobbling hay wagon (known as a "hay rack") dumps off bales weighing about 85 pounds to the hungry cows, which follow along like strings of boys chasing an ice-cream vendor. If the wind is up to 30 miles an hour, the temperature down to ten below zero and the icy snow blowing diagonally to hit him full in the face like tiny needles, the general idea is to get the job done quickly. If the herd numbers 600 head, he must load, and in turn dump off, 150 bales of hay, for each cow needs a quarter of a bale, the equivalent of twenty pounds of grass. That is just about the amount of grass a cow consumes on summer pastures.

Mere hay is not enough if cows are to produce healthy calves. Feed must possess nutrients, particularly vitamin A, if the stockman's crop of calves is going to approach the ideal 100 per cent (that is, when every cow has a calf). Properly harvested alfalfa meets these standards; not all hay does. Thus commercial feeds, some in

XIT

Cortez's Three Crosses

Walking A

Flying W

Rocking Chair

Lazy K

Four Sixes

V Bar Backward L

Heart over Heart

J connected F over Mill Iron

Cow

Dinner Bell

Tumbling 3

2 connected 4

Quarter Circle, Upside Down Y,
Quarter Circle

Diamond Bar

FAR LEFT: *Assortment* of
branding marks
ABOVE: *Kansas city
stockyards* in 1874

pellet form, others as loose ground or rolled grains, are added to supplement the hay.

Feeding cattle begins in early winter in the northern country, before the snows. The winter's cold freezes the streams, the ponds and the stock tanks nestled under the windmills. Then a daily chore facing the cowboy is attacking the ice with axe and pitchfork to make a little waterhole. With the axe he chops the ice and with the pitchfork he removes the slabs so that the cows may drink. Chopping out a stream or stock pond is no major problem, but the cowboy can get pretty wet and cold if the chips fly in his face or the ice breaks through. But cutting the ice in a stock tank requires caution. Woe to the careless cowboy who chops right through the tank and loses gallons of precious water, bringing the wrath of the foreman.

Varieties of Mud

Spring, for a vast majority of ranches, is fence fixing time. If the rancher raises any crops, this is when he drills his oats or plants his corn. But perhaps most important, spring on a working ranch brings melting snow and that means mud.

There are various types of mud the cowboy contends with: red mud, cowpen mud – commonly called "crud" – and, worst of all, gumbo. Gumbo is light grayish in color and generally combines the slippery quality of vanilla ice cream with the sticky characteristics of bubble gum.

Pickup trucks are especially susceptible to being mired, for if the driver doesn't slip off the road into the ditch, his tires can gather so much of the stuff in a matter of minutes that it binds in the fenders and can stall him to a dead stop.

Spring is not all mud, for the cottonwoods do leaf out and in March and April the little calves arrive. When possible, climate permitting, the rancher allows the cows to calve on the range. This arrangement is more feasible in the southern plains where the winters are less severe and there is little danger of the calves freezing to death.

On a well-managed northern ranch, the cowboys must bring the cows to the barns to calve. Customarily, the cowboy will ride among the herd carefully observing the "heavy" cows, those that will give birth within twelve hours or so. These are gently cut out of the herd and driven home at a slow gait to prevent harm both to the mother and her unborn offspring.

Playing Midwife

The cowboys watch the cows intently, especially so-called "first calf heifers." These are young cows, very often no more than two years old, about to have their first calf. Frequently such new mothers need help. The good cowboy stays alert, always ready to "pull" a calf, if need be.

All sorts of trouble can develop at such a time and the successful rancher may have to be his own veterinarian. "Breech" births and Caesarean operations are not unheard of.

It is a happy moment for a cowboy when he hears the first tiny bawl of a new calf, and watches its mother lick it clean as it teeters on its wobbly legs, trying to nurse, searching by instinct for that warm, life-giving milk. This can make it worth having stayed up all night in a cold barn, playing midwife.

The cowman hopes for a 100 per cent calf crop, when every cow calves. This is not realistic, but he should be able to count on a 90 to 95 per cent calf crop. About half will be bulls. These little critters will, by autumn, become his saleable crop, the chief source of his income. It is in the late spring or early summer that the stockman readies his crop for sale.

Hoping for Rain

The spring roundup is an exhilarating time. Now is when a rancher begins to speculate on his profits as he counts his calves. He hopes for summer rains bringing lush grass so the calves will fatten. This, of course, is just hope. The eastern Colorado rancher, for example, knows full well that thirteen to fifteen inches of precipitation is the most he can expect for the entire year. It's a common saying among the stockmen of the arid West, as the sun rises bright and strong to the east, "Well, we've got another goddam beautiful day."

There is the sad yarn of the rancher who discovered a sick and bloated cow stuck in the mud at the edge of a stock pond. The cowboys roped the poor beast and dragged her out to the dried and crisp, withered grass. The men tried everything they knew to revive the poor beast, but soon saw they were losing to the old man with the scythe. Tex was sent to call the "vet" who, unbelievably, was instantly available and arrived within an hour. Among other things, the vet recommended that the cow be given an injection of glucose. Tex held the bottle of high-toned sugar water above his head to allow gravity to take effect and send the fluid down the tube through the needle poked into the unfortunate cow. Everything worked so well that the cow stood up. The cowboys cheered. And then the old cow stumbled, heaved an alarming sigh and dropped dead.

"What do you think killed her, Doc?" asked Tex.

"From the way she's bloated, I'd say lush grass."

"Lush grass?" yelped Tex. "We haven't had rain in ten weeks!"

Teamwork

Today rather than roping and throwing the calves that are to be branded, the cowboys generally run them through chutes into a "squeeze." This is a specially designed contraption composed of two parallel rows of bars which, when compressed, hold the animal

Roundup time

FAR LEFT: Just roped, the critter will be dragged off to be branded by the men near the gate

FAR LEFT BELOW: Branding irons hanging ready to be heated for use; the smaller ones on the left are intended for calves

LEFT: Flanking a calf, a job that can be done by one man but which is easier with two pairs of hands

BELOW: Branding, "steering" and inoculating a beast simultaneously, a process that takes as little as a minute

ABOVE: *Counting cattle*;
the "tallyman" is
standing in the alley
holding his fingers up
FAR RIGHT ABOVE:
"*Calf cradle,*" an easy
mechanism for
branding and
inoculating
BELOW: *The Fence
Builders*, painting by
Peter Hurd

firmly while it is worked on. Small squeezes, called "calf cradles," tip over so that the little animal lying prone can be treated more easily.

The cowboys push and prod the calves from a corral into the chutes and into the squeeze. Normally, five or six men are required for this job, two to drive the calves, one to brand, one to inoculate against the calf-killing diseases, one to castrate the bull calves, and another to keep the irons hot. A team such as this can work more than 500 calves a day – about one calf per minute.

In the summer the cowboy's time is divided between checking his calves, counting his cows and making hay. Hay is a prime crop, for it is the winter feed on a majority of American ranches.

Hay is cut and stacked in a variety of ways, due to the regional differences and variations of mechanized improvements. Essentially, haying involves mowing the grass or alfalfa at the proper time, allowing it to cure, and stacking it for winter storage.

Hay used to be stored loose in haymows or great stacks. With the invention of the baling machine, it could be put up more quickly, stored more compactly and preserved more effectively. Other labor-saving devices like the

swather, the accumulator and the automatic stacker have reduced the number of men required to make a ton of hay. It has not reduced the heat, or dust. Making hay, at best, is about as pleasant as cleaning out a chicken house in mid-August.

Feed alone is not enough to make a cow thrive. Water is essential. Clear, running streams, referred to as "live water," are ideal, but cool water pumped by windmills, and stock ponds (small, man-made dammed-up lakes) are also valuable sources of supply. In summertime, troubles arise in periods of drought. Creeks run low, wells go dry, the water in stock ponds recedes. During such periods, the cowboys may have to carry water in old oil drums to the animals. Even in good times, windmills must be oiled, pumps repaired.

Climbing Windmills

Oiling the windmill is a tedious task. A cowboy may be the epitome of confidence on a skittish horse, but put him atop the little windmill platform maybe 100 feet up with the wind blowing, loosening bolts and pouring oil in a gearbox with one hand while holding on for dear life with the other, and he can turn a bit shaky.

In autumn, when the grass dries up and the yellow cottonwood leaves begin to drop, the fall roundup takes place. This is the time of the auction sales where the calves are sold to the "feeders," the men who operate feed lots for the sole purpose of fattening calves to ready them for the slaughter-house.

Steers and heifers are sold separately at market, steers bringing a slightly higher price.

If the rancher plans to keep some of his heifers as replacements for his cow herd, the cowboys open and shut the corral gates culling the little females to determine which are best. Those heifers which meet a standard qualifying them to enter the herd are put in a special pen, later to be turned out with the cows, but only after they are completely weaned.

At this point too, the range bulls are separated from the cows and placed either in strongly built bullpens or in a distant pasture to await reacquaintance with the cows the next spring.

The calves that are to be marketed are weighed, which gives the rancher an idea of what price his calves may bring, but more importantly it tells him the rate of gain for each calf, which should be around three pounds a day.

Record Keeping

For those ranchers who keep accurate records, this is vital information. A careful stockman gives a number to each cow, either by means of an ear tag (a number tag on a chain) or a number branded on her side. The latter is the best method, for it can never be lost. By checking his

A land of contrasts
BELOW: A rancher on the northern Plains chops ice away from a water hole to enable his cattle to drink
FAR RIGHT: Main Street of Gold Field, Nevada
FAR RIGHT BELOW: Ranch in Colorado, where timber is plentiful

records with the calf's ear tag attached at birth, the cowboy can determine the cow's performance as a mother. If her calf does not measure up, she will be sent to the butcher as a "canner" or "cutter," to be replaced by a more efficient animal.

Sorting cattle in the fall is hard work. Either the corrals are filled with choking dust or they are a quagmire of mud and melting snow. To this is added the cacophony of bawling calves separated from their wailing mothers. The gates are heavy and must be opened and shut hundreds of times either to let a cow out or keep a calf in. Well-planned and sturdy corrals with adequate cutting pens and alleys make the job easier.

The cows and calves, of course, are anything but co-operative, and their desire to escape the pen and herd makes the job more exasperating. A cowboy on foot who is quick with the gate and a man on a good cutting horse are great assets. And it's also essential to have a ranch-hand who can keep the records straight, who can count cattle accurately and read the brands and ear tag numbers without mistakes. Otherwise the entire fall roundup can be an utter fiasco.

Just before the calves are ready for market, the ranchers must arrange for a brand inspection. In many Western states the brands are registered and printed in a record book. An experienced inspector knows pretty well all the brands in his region. He, together with the stockman, walks

among the calves to be sold confirming the marks and the tally. For a minimal fee, the rancher receives a certificate which indicates to the buyer that he is not purchasing stolen cattle.

A Sense of Humor
So it is clear that cowboying is not simply a matter of riding the range on "Old Paint." If a cowboy didn't have a sense of humor, he might go crazy from boredom over his mundane chores. The following anecdote illustrates the cowpuncher's flair for making jokes to lighten the monotony of his work.

It was a bitterly cold autumn day when Buck bundled himself in a parka, elk hide gloves and a brand new, fake fur, earflapped cap. Astride a huge diesel tractor, he and Tex dragged their pair of four gang plows round and round the 100 acre field. After about an hour or so, a little twister or whirlwind attacked Buck and blew off his fake fur hat. He quickly pulled to a stop, only to see his new hat plowed into a furrow. Climbing off his monstrous machine, he ran back to dig in the earth, hoping to retrieve it. Just then Tex arrived, stopped his rig and yelled, "Hey, Buck, lookin' for gold?"

"Hell no, I just plowed under my new cap and damned if I can find it."

"Don't worry," said Tex, "just wait till spring and you'll have a whole crop of little ones."

CHAPTER XI
Modern Times

WHEN THE LAST of the frozen bodies were dumped into the mass grave at Wounded Knee on a chill December day in 1890, an era ended for the American Indian. It was a period marked by skirmishes and battles and wars. For the Indian, it was a time of destruction, of death and dishonor.

370 Years of Destruction

From Cortez's arrival in 1520 until the massacre at Wounded Knee, the Indians had fought to defend themselves against white encroachment. Some, like the Calusa and the Natchez, Wampanoag and Massachusetts, were literally annihilated. Others, the Creek and Choctaw, the Shawnee and the Sauk and Fox and many more, were driven from their homelands. Some were grudgingly permitted to remain, tiny islands here and there engulfed by a sea of white men. Such were the Penobscot, the Iroquois and the Powhatans, the Cherokee and the Seminoles.

With the foregoing exceptions, the government's policy was one of complete removal. Andrew Jackson's determination to rid the East of all the Indians was, in fact, a chief executive's response to the nation's temper as a whole. In the 1830s the easy solution to the Indian problem was merely to push the tribes out of sight.

Far to the west of the Mississippi River, the government carved out a vast piece of land, called it "Indian Territory," and assigned blocks of countryside on which Indians might live. Little or no consideration was given to the Indians whose homelands these new settlers displaced. In the southwestern part of the Territory the "Five Civilized Tribes" were put.

It was the Cherokee, Creeks, Choctaw, Chickasaw and Seminoles who were called "civilized" – because, for one thing, the Cherokees had an alphabet, which had been developed by a scholar named Sequoya.

Other eastern tribes were later removed to

Indian Territory. Squeezed into lands reserved for the Five Tribes were Shawnees and Delawares, Sauk and Fox and Senecas, Potawatomis and Osage. And as the West burgeoned with more and more white settlers clamoring for land, the western states and territories were also anxious to rid themselves of Indians. Midwestern tribes, the Oto and Missouri, the Poncas and Pawnee were "given" land in Indian Territory. So, too, were some of the Plains tribes. The Kiowa and Comanche, the Cheyenne, Arapaho and Wichita were settled on reservations in what is now Oklahoma.

Considerable rhetoric rang through the halls of the United States Congress in the 1870s concerning the "Indian Problem" and the subject of removal. By now the Indians had their champions. Many were sincere do-gooders from Philadelphia and Boston, although perhaps their own forefathers may have helped to wipe out the Indian years before. But the policy of isolation on reservations prevailed. The Indians were never consulted as to what their own preferences might be.

The Least Disturbed

Some tribes were relatively lucky. The Pueblo tribes of the Southwest, and to a degree the Navaho, were the least disturbed of any Indians in the United States. After the revolt in 1680, which among other things taught the Franciscan fathers the advantage of allowing the Indians to retain their religion, the Pueblos were more or less unmolested. Nobody really wanted their desert lands. They carried on much as they had for generations and they still do.

Here the men still farm, the women fashion pottery. The Navaho men are still master silversmiths, their women still weave striking rugs. Today these are the colorful Indians of the "Land of Enchantment" whose dances tourists crowd to see. But most significant is the fact

RIGHT: *Song of the Talking Wires*, painting by Henry Farney
BELOW: *Indian craft skills*: from left to right, Santo Domingo jar; a Zuni bowl decorated with geometric floral and animal motifs; Pueblo jug with a spiral design several centuries old

OVERLEAF:
Outdoor feast on the
Flathead Indian
reservation in Montana

295

that these people have retained, and have been permitted to retain, much of their heritage. As such, they are a tribute to Indian determination and the will to survive.

Life on the reservations during the last half of the nineteenth century was grim. Unable any longer to feed themselves, the Indians were given rations. Beef cattle were supplied, which when released from corrals were shot and butchered by the Indians – the whole affair having the semblance of a rodeo buffalo hunt. Rations were often short, because of the graft of Bureau of Indian Affairs agents and dishonest suppliers.

But there was a more fundamental problem than the mere sticky fingers of some crooked officials and traders. The white man was handling the Indian as if he were made of clay, to be formed at will into something else. Industriousness and frugality were thought to be easily achievable for the Indian through farming, and this would make for self-sufficiency and prosperity. Fear of God through staunch adherence to Christian principles would produce men of upright morality and unimpeachable integrity. It was an approach that was clearcut and forthright. And today, hindsight tells us these ideas were disastrously wrong.

Diametrically Different

The Indians' concepts of property and wealth were diametrically opposed to those of the white man. For the majority of the tribes, tangible items were accumulated only to be given away. In the Plains, the horse became a standard medium of exchange and a man with a large herd was considered rich. But to obtain respect and status, he had to give his horses away.

For the Indian, the route to prestige lay in one's ability to acquire property and then share it with others.

The white man's approach to property and money was quite different. In the America of the nineteenth century, money was god. And, gloomily, things don't look very different in the twentieth.

Haircuts and Uniforms

Indian children were sent to boarding schools, often far from their homes. Here they were dressed in uniforms. The boys' hair was cut short. They were taught the conventional reading, writing and arithmetic. If they were caught speaking their native tongue, they were physically punished.

On the reservation, land was parceled out to each family head in 160-acre tracts. Reservation land not allotted was either retained in tribal ownership or sold to white settlers. Indian men were given plows and horses and told to farm their allotments. In spite of instructors provided by the government to teach the Indians

the techniques of agriculture, the plan never really worked. Crops failed and the men's interest waned. In these tribes, farming had always been woman's work.

Missionaries invaded the reservations, vying with one another to save souls. Church groups saw to it that ceremonies like the Sun Dance were banned and polygamy abolished. Shamans went into hiding. With such disruptions, Indian culture was all but killed.

Beginning in the latter part of the nineteenth century, governmental policy was administered by a specially created office, the Bureau of Indian Affairs, charged with the responsibility of transforming the Indian into a replica of the white man. The Bureau operated schools and hospitals, and also provided a series of social services.

Land in Trust

One branch of the Bureau concerned itself with the Indians' property – land. Early policy makers, aware that the Indians could be fleeced of their holdings by greedy white settlers, decreed that the land should be held in trust. Thus the Indians might not sell their land without permission of the guardian. Even the leasing of land was supervised by the Bureau. As the years went by, pressure from both Indians and whites

Show and reality
ABOVE: Calf-roping at a rodeo
FAR LEFT: Cowboys at work on the range

caused the Bureau to sell both tribally and individually owned portions. Today only some 55 million acres remain in trust.

In 1924, Congress granted Indians citizenship, a presumptuous gratuity indeed from a nation to the very people whose homeland it first was. In 1935, Congress passed the Indian Reorganization Act, another magnanimous bill, which recognized that the Indian tribes, as sovereign nations within the nation, were entitled to the right of self-government.

Self-Rule with a Flaw

In principle, the tribes were now allowed to rule themselves, draw up constitutions, elect councilmen, appoint judges and tribal police. There was only one flaw. The constitutions were prepared in Washington by well-meaning bureaucrats versed in the laws of the white man. No one thought of consulting the Indians. The idea was to do good for Indians whether they understood it or not.

Reservations were either situated on lands

originally occupied by Indians or lands they received in exchange for that which they had ceded. Treaty provisions specified that Indians might impose taxes on land or for other purposes if they so desired. None have done so to this day. Indians are subject to all applicable state and federal taxes, including income tax, and are eligible for all social services available to non-Indians, including aid to dependent children and unemployment insurance.

In an endeavor to compensate for the unconscionably low prices that had been paid to Indians for their lands, the government instituted an Indian Claims Commission. Here tribes could bring their cases for hearing and many were indemnified with millions of dollars. After a century of dishonor, the Americans were beginning to make restitution.

Beginning in the mid-1930s and continuing to the present date, studies and surveys were conducted in the field by teams of anthropologists, educators, psychologists, all to the end of understanding the Indian's problem, all in the hope of determining what might be done to im-

FAR LEFT BELOW:
Drying meat on the
Great Plains
FAR LEFT: *Indian dancer*
in a costume of striking
modernity
LEFT: *Pueblo craftsman*
drilling a bead

prove his lot. Books and reports were written, glowing programs of self-help were planned in Washington. But again, an important factor was overlooked, for seldom were the Indians consulted.

To the Cities

One such plan called for the urbanization of Indians. Since opportunities for employment on or near the reservations were all but nonexistent, it was believed that a program of relocation would enhance the Indian's chance of gaining a cash income through work in metropolitan centers. Indians were reimbursed to make the move and employment for them was arranged.

. Many remained in the cities; yet many more, ill-prepared emotionally for city life and poorly qualified for the jobs to which they were assigned, returned discouraged to their reservations.

Another Idea

Bringing industry to the reservations was also tried, to enable Indians to find employment at home. In some instances the idea proved success-

ful, mainly in the handcrafts area. The monotonous regimen required of belt line mass production was sometimes more than Indians were able to stand. The rate of Indian unemployment is the highest in the nation.

It almost seemed that in spite of the government's help, the services, the protections, the plans and programs, the Indians, in defiance, neither sank nor swam – they just floated. And neither the bureaucrats nor the social scientists, with all their resources and knowledge, could seem to grasp the reason.

The Indians, militarily defeated, their culture destroyed, were a people without a spirit, without a will. They could easily see that their way of life was no match for the militarily superior, industrially powerful nation of white men. Even their religion had failed them. Its "power" was weak, as evidenced by their defeat. They were a people embarrassed and ashamed. Pride in their heritage completely vanished. By the 1930s, Indians' knowledge of their own past was fading with the passing of the older generation, a group for whom the younger Indians had

Two good bulls, two good riders at modern rodeo shows

RIGHT: *Rodeo clowns* run a few risks along with the cowboys
FAR RIGHT: *The gate opens* and a bull explodes from the chute at a rodeo in South Dakota

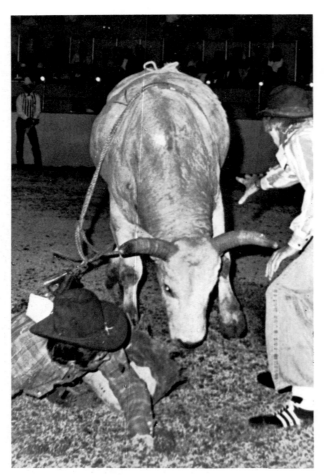

little respect. By now the plight of the Indians was a national tragedy and disgrace; that it was a direct consequence of a concerted effort at genocide, both physical and cultural, was even becoming apparent. No amends, however beneficent, no amount of governmental aid, no amount of scientific social planning, it seemed, could heal the wounds.

The Beginning of Hope

And then, starting in the 1960s, something happened. Here and there a handful of educated Indians, often independently, sometimes in concert with students of Indian affairs, began to recognize not only the value of Indian culture, but the desperate need for preserving Indian heritage in order that their people might once again enjoy a sense of self-respect. Only by a feeling of pride in his heritage could the Indian attempt to raise himself to an attitude of dignity.

When America was first discovered, it is thought there were approximately 1,000,000 native Americans. By 1900 their numbers were reduced to an estimated 300,000. Today with constantly improving health conditions over the last half century, the Indian population is again pushing toward the million mark. Conditions on the reservations are markedly improved since the 1930s. Many of the programs are taking effect at last.

It was the Indians themselves who conceived and spearheaded the drive toward renewed Indian self-respect.

D'Arcy McNickle, a Flathead Indian who once won himself a Rhodes Scholarship and has written several provocative books on Indian affairs, both fiction and nonfiction, formed an organization called American Indian Development.

Lloyd New, a Cherokee, whose forefathers had been removed to Indian Territory, agreed to take a job as director of the Indian School in Santa Fe, New Mexico, in the 1960s, on the condition that its curriculum emphasize American Indian culture in all its ramifications, Indian art in its broadest perspective.

Vine Deloria wrote an impressive book, "Custer Died For Your Sins," representative of the well-written books on Indian affairs being published by responsible Indian authors.

Other signs are encouraging. The Zunis have taken over complete control of all their tribal affairs. The Navahos have established a college with Indian administrators, faculty and students.

The Santa Fe school, now named the Institute of American Indian Art, offers, in addition to the regularly accepted academic courses, training in Indian painting, sculpture, weaving, music, dance, history, language – the entire gamut of Indian culture. Graduates are proving to be productive, positive, enthusiastic citizens, capable of functioning in two worlds – that of the white man and, with great pride, that of the Indian.

Red-Power Activists

But groups of young people, resentful of past wrongs, rallied themselves under the banner of Red Power. Other urbanized activists organized themselves formally as the American Indian Movement. They were convinced that the "Uncle Tomahawks" on the reservations were pawns of the Bureau of Indian Affairs, doing nothing genuinely for the well-being of their people.

In the late winter of 1972, the leaders of the American Indian Movement, in the hope of bringing the Indians' grievances against the Bureau before the American public, took it upon themselves to capture the little town of Wounded Knee. They chose the site of the massacre of Sioux ghost dancers in 1890 in bitter mood, Wounded Knee being the potent symbol of the white man's cruelty toward Indians, his past disregard for their way of life.

After taking over at Wounded Knee, the demonstrators made several demands including the removal of the duly elected Sioux tribal chairman and the return to the Sioux of all tribal lands as of the Treaty of 1868. This encompassed all the land of North Dakota and South Dakota east of the Missouri River, as well as parts of Wyoming and Nebraska.

Wounded Knee 1972

This action received widespread television,

newspaper and magazine publicity. Wounded Knee became an armed camp. Most of its residents, Indians and whites, were evacuated or fled, to be replaced by young armed Indians. The self-appointed spokesmen for the Sioux, and indeed for all Indians, continued their demands. Negotiations with federal authorities faltered, the government officials refusing to confer at gunpoint.

The tension mounted. Blockades were constructed, army tanks brought in, and the Indian occupiers were besieged. As days turned into weeks, two federal agents were shot, one permanently paralyzed, and two Indians were killed. Indians inside, tragically, took it upon themselves to pillage and burn the trading post, loot the small museum containing many valuable Sioux historical objects and, worse still, plunder the homes of the Sioux residents of Wounded Knee.

The overriding tragedy of the 1972–73 episode at Wounded Knee was that even after the 70 days of confrontation, little, if anything, was resolved.

For the Indian, the road to so-called civilization, with its mixed and very questionable blessings, has not been easy. The basic, brutal fact of life for the Indian is that he has no other choice than to exist within the world of the white man.

That the nation has at long last recognized the value of its Indian heritage, that Americans have finally assumed a rational and compassionate approach to the affairs of Indians – and even belatedly acknowledged the importance of a plurality of life-styles in America – is about the only ray of light in the whole picture.

Would-Be Westerners
The West has always acted as a magnet to adventurers, and this includes twentieth-century man. Today's adventurer may be a tourist, piling his wife and kids in the car and hitting the highway, to savor the wonders of a bygone day. Westerners know that the gold that was once in those hills is now in the tourists' pockets.

For those with well-lined pockets, the modern development known as the dude ranch offers a chance to play cowboy, to spend a week or more riding the range with real wranglers and singing cowboy songs around a campfire.

In the early days the term "dude" was applied to the "city slickers," Easterners seeking their fortunes in less rough-and-ready occupations than that of punching cows. To the cowboy, these men with their neat clothes and proper manners were a great source of merriment. And the cowboy often treated them in a bullying fashion, as has been illustrated by more than one equally scornful cartoonist.

All the fun of the rodeo
These bulky but oddly graceful animals rule at rodeos, often making spectators dodge them in a hurry

RIGHT: *A perfect circle* in the lariat twirling competition
BELOW: *Ponychuck wagon racing*, an exciting rodeo event
FAR RIGHT: *Driving Longhorns* through a Western town

By the turn of the century some farseeing stockmen observed the number of hunters and vacationers drawn to the West. And in this influx of urbanites they perceived the dollar sign.

Dollars to Be Made

Men with ranches in the wilds opened their headquarters as hunting lodges. Advertising a plentiful supply of big game – elk and bear, antelope or moose – the more hardy Easterners wearing ten-gallon hats and high-heeled boots ventured forth in search of a "he-man" experience and an antlered head to adorn their dens or trophy rooms.

The rancher would supply, at a cost-plus-profit basis, accommodation, pack-horses, and real wranglers who would make camp, do the cooking, and dress out the kill. On most of these so-called hunting expeditions the guest is led right to the quarry; all he has to do is pull the trigger. It's great for the ego development of certain temperaments.

Ranches for Dudes

Other stockmen opened their home ranches to vacationers, men and women who had enough money and spare time to spend two or three weeks in the genuine authentic, dude-ranch version of the "Wild West." Today dude ranching is a lucrative business.

The right costume helps one to get into the spirit: cowboy boots, tight Levis, a silk shirt and a big Stetson hat. These can instantly transform any city dweller into a cowboy who can ride among the cows on a mountain pack trip, eating beans from a pie plate and drinking coffee from a tin cup. Around the evening's campfire, a hired hand will sing a doleful song accompanied by a twanging guitar, and the dude can indulge in fantasy, imagining himself on the alert for an Indian attack, camped on the lone prairie surrounded by lowing cattle. This pastime is pretty thrilling, unquestionably romantic and completely safe.

The Rodeo Circuit

On the other hand, playing cowboy in the present-day rodeo circuit is an entirely different fame. This is gambling for pretty high stakes and a mistake can mean losing for keeps.

Rodeo, Spanish for "roundup," began long ago, but no one can quite agree when or where. Most likely, after a roundup when cowboys from two or three ranches were gathered, some buster decided just for fun to see who could sit a bucking bronc the longest or stay aboard a pitching bull without getting dumped, while some others, skilled at roping steers, were competing to see who was quickest at roping, throwing and tying a little critter all set for branding.

At these early rodeos the only spectators were probably the ranch-hands themselves, the only contestants the outfit's cowboys. The

fence making up the corral served as grandstand and whiskey was the refreshment. It was all very informal, all terribly rough.

Today the contestants are professionals. Urban spectators fill grandstands designed for thousands. Soft drinks are the standard refreshment and food is also served, in the form of a hot dog in a bun doused with mustard.

An Athletic Event

The modern rodeo is a well-organized athletic event drawing contestants from all parts of the country. The Rodeo Cowboys Association has set out rigid rules which the cowboys have to observe, partly to ensure that the contestants will be competing on an equal basis, but also to safeguard the cowboys and the animals.

At the big rodeos, with the stands filled to bursting, the announcer in a voice as silvery as his Stetson hat, calls over the public address system:

"Ladies and gentlemen, you are about to witness one of the great spectaculars of the West! Here the finest cowboys in America pit their skill and daring against untamed and dangerous animals.

"Each of these men has paid a fee just to enter this contest. This entitles him to compete for the prize money. That's all he'll get out of it – nothing more but your applause. So give them a big hand!

"And here they come – the Grand Entry – I give you, ladies and gentlemen, the Annual Western Rodeo!"

The opener at a rodeo is often a parade on horseback run at breakneck speed around the arena. Generally it's led by a "Queen" and her shapely female attendants, trailed by the cowboys whose gait seems more casual. The cowgirls follow, in tight, bright-colored pants, pale green, lavender or blue, often with matching shirts and hats.

The band will have sounded a frantic march as the horsemen tear around. When the entire group has circled the grounds, the Queen pulls her mount to a staggering halt before the grandstand. Now the band strikes up, the flag waves proudly, the spectators stand, the men hold their hats over their chests, and all sing the National Anthem. The show has begun.

Bareback Bull-Riders

The bareback bull-riders may be first to burst from the gates. Here the cowboy must stay on a writhing, twisting, bucking, grunting 2,000-pound beast for at least eight seconds, if he is to score. And the points he makes depend not only upon his skill, but equally on the viciousness of the bull. In other words, both animal and rider are rated, the bull on a scale of 25. A mild-mannered bull can pull a man's score down, no matter how able the man is. The cowboys do not

choose the beasts they are to ride; these are drawn for them by the judges.

A noisy buzzer sounds when the eight seconds are up. The rider who has managed to stay on now tries to jump clear. It is at this moment that the clowns – specially employed to distract the bull away from the staggering or fallen cowboy – begin their dangerous task. Carrying brooms, and a red rubber barrel, large enough for one of them to climb inside to hide, the clowns taunt the bull in all manner of ways. Often, amidst the shrieks of the crowd, the bull charges the barrel, rolling it hither and yon. Meanwhile the bull-rider has time to escape.

Bull-riding is considered one of the most dangerous of rodeo events and it takes a cowboy with steel guts to excel.

Bill Nelson, the 1971 bull-riding champion, won $21,000 in prize money.

Lariat Twirlers and Calf-Ropers

The rodeo events are frequently interspersed with special acts. The trick roper spinning and twirling his long lariat, jumping in and out of the big loops, is a favorite. Girls in flashy trousers more form-fitting than kid gloves straddling a pair of beautifully trained horses which gallop through a ring of fire add glamor and circus flavor to the show.

But the crowds' favorites are the real cowboy events, the bull-riding and calf-roping, the steer-wrestling, "bull-dogging" and bronc-riding. That's what they've paid to see.

Calf-roping is a contest of perfect teamwork between a cowboy and his horse and a runaway calf. The rider must wait behind a rope barrier until the calf is released. Then racing behind, the cowboy loops his rope over the fleeing calf's neck. Suddenly, the well-trained cow pony stops short, so that the rope, looped around the saddle horn, is kept taut, allowing the rider to dismount and run along the rope to grab the struggling calf and throw it.

The cowboy may either pick up the calf and

throw it on its side – called "flanking" – or wrench the calf to the earth by pulling on its foreleg – referred to as "legging." Now the roper must tie three legs securely with a "piggin string," a short length of rope which many cowboys carry in readiness in their mouths.

A good man can rope and tie his calf in fifteen seconds. The record time, seven and a half seconds, was set in 1967 by "Junior" Garrison, who was twice world champion. Phil Lyne of Texas, the 1971 calf-roping champion, earned over $28,000 by his consistent speed.

Steer-Wrestlers

Steer-wrestling requires brains and brawn and bravery. Here, chasing at a gallop a running steer, the cowboy must spring from his horse to grab for the horns. Locking them in his arms, with legs outstretched and high heels acting as a brake, he must wrench and twist the steer's head, throwing the animal to the ground. To score, all four feet and head must point in the same direction. The only help a steer wrestler gets is from a "hazer," a man who rides to the side of the running steer to keep it from veering away from the wrestler.

There's money in steer-wrestling, too. Billy Hale of Oklahoma, the 1971 champion, pocketed $23,000 for his skill. He threw some of his steers in just over five seconds. Steve Gramith toppled one in three and seven-tenths seconds to set a National Finals Rodeo record in 1971.

Bucking Broncos

Probably the most spectacular act, the one event that sums up in the popular imagination what a Western rodeo is all about, is the bare-back bronc-riding. Mounted on an untamed, cantankerous mass of wild horsemeat, whose single idea is to get rid of anything on its back, the cowboy starts out somewhat disadvantaged. He has nothing more to hang onto than a bit of rigging about the size of a suitcase handle as he explodes from the chute on an animal that packs the punch of dynamite.

The horse bucks and twists, twirls and lunges; the bronco-buster flays his legs, spurring the animal's shoulders and waving his free hand, for it is against the rules to touch the horse with his hand. For eight seconds the rider must stay aboard the bucking hunk of horseflesh if he is to win any points at all.

Many a cowboy is dumped long before the time expires and he acquires nothing but experience and some broken bones; others who do stay on may collect only a few points due to an infraction of the rules or the bad luck of drawing a mild bronco.

Despite the difficulties and disappointments associated with bareback riding, the rewards are

FAR LEFT ABOVE: *Steer wrestling*, or "bulldogging," the object of which is to wrench the steer to the ground
ABOVE: *"Bulldogging,"* at the beginning of the sequence
FAR LEFT BELOW: *Calf roping*

Riding the bucking broncos, the greatest crowd-drawer and the essence of rodeo

ABOVE: *Rodeo contestant* in difficulty
FAR RIGHT: *Larry Mahan* shows the form that made him five times World Champion All Round Cowboy, at the 1969 National Rodeo Finals

tempting. Joe Alexander, the 1971 champion, earned over $28,000 for the pounding he took.

The rodeo circuit is a grueling one, and if a cowboy is to make any money at it he must be willing to enter contest after contest. Rodeos are now held in all parts of the country, from San Francisco to New York City.

Many rodeo cowboys live out of their suitcases, several of them flying their own planes to get from city to city. Some of these men manage to have other interests too. Among them are a TV and movie actor, a veterinarian and a professional football player. Some train and shoe horses, others operate night clubs.

Barrel-Racing Cowgirls

Cowboying has not been the province of men alone. Women have at many times taken an active part not only in the work of branding and steering, but as early as the 1920s joined the ranks of rodeo contestants as bronco-busters and calf ropers. Today women particularly compete in a special event called "barrel-racing." Here three barrels are set up in a triangular pattern as markers. The cowgirls race their fast ponies against time around the markers, losing points if their horses tip over a barrel. The winner of this event is sure to produce cheers from the crowd.

While rodeoing is one of the roughest and toughest sports in America, it is also the cleanest one. Since each man competes as an individual against himself, gambling interests have little if any leverage. The cowboy as an independent cannot be bought and sold by a company of investors. He's not for hire and he can't be fired.

ABOVE: *"Rodeo queens,"* cowgirls of the 1920s who did not hesitate to tackle the bucking broncos
FAR RIGHT: *Exhibits* at a Western show include a silver-studded saddle and a chair made from bulls' horns

He's his own manager, his own employer, and one of the most respected sports figures in the nation.

So profoundly has the cowboy captured the popular imagination that a special museum, the Cowboy Hall of Fame, has been established in his honor at Oklahoma City, the capital of Oklahoma. Here one can see trophies won by champions, huge paintings and works of sculpture pertaining to cowboys and the life of the West.

The Cowboy Everyone Loved

Without question, the most unforgettable cowboy character on the American scene was Will Rogers, a man who punched cows and did rope tricks and best of all, talked. Although he was a man of few words, he talked his way into the hearts of just about every man, woman and child in America in the 1920s and '30s.

Will Rogers was raised on his father's ranch in Oklahoma, and later went to work on the famous 101 Spread, which among other things ran a Wild West show. Here he was taught much of his cowboying by Bill Pickett, a half-black, half-Choctaw Indian cowboy who is credited with having invented "bulldogging."

What made Will Rogers famous was his home-spun humor. It was his custom on stage, while twirling his lariat in complicated convolutions, to comment in his western drawl upon current events, the follies of man or the politics of the day. Later he went to Hollywood and became a movie actor.

While pictures and books, Wild West shows and humorists dramatized the West at the turn of the century, motion pictures brought it all to life. In 1916 the celluloid hero of the day was William S. Hart. He was eclipsed in the 1930s by a more up-to-date version, Tom Mix. While it seemed inconceivable that any actor could surpass these taciturn, brave, honest cowboys, there later appeared on the screen much like a silent comet illuminating the sky, the epitome of the folk-hero, Gary Cooper. It was largely through his roles in "Westerns" that he won the affection and respect of millions.

There seems to be no end to the persistence of the cowboy as a hero. The sort of cowboy character so often played by John Wayne has served as an ego-builder for a nation with his sincerity, his belief in the cause of right against wrong and strength against weakness. His is a wonderful world of stark contrasts, with no shades of gray, where the good guys wear white hats and always win. Only recently has any subtlety or irony, even a bit of black humor, been allowed to creep into movie "Westerns."

Cattlemen at work on
the range

For all their skill or glamor or romantic appeal, it is not the writer, artist, humorist or movie idol who made the cowboys; it is the real cowboys who created themselves. And it's happening this very day. Somewhere on the vast range country of America there is a cow-puncher climbing a windmill, branding a calf or pulling an old cow out of a mudhole.

As long as housewives buy hamburgers and restaurants serve sirloins, there will be the cowboy. Some may cut out cows on a motorcycle or "jeep," some may even check their cattle in an airplane, but on many an up-to-date ranch, there is no substitute for the cowboy on his horse.

British Breeds

That is not to say that cattle haven't changed. Replacing the Texas Longhorns have been various breeds from the British Isles, cattle that are more efficient, more compact and economically better suited to the times.

The Durham, now called the Shorthorn, has become popular because of its good beef quality combined with a propensity for producing large amounts of milk.

In 1910, the men at the King Ranch of Texas, owners of the largest spread in the United States, were given an unusual gift – a tremendous bull which was half Brahman and half Shorthorn. They were greatly impressed by its size and adaptability to intense heat and little water. They crossed Shorthorn cows with the offspring of this gift bull, whom they called "Monkey." Thus was created the famous Santa Gertrudis cattle, recognized as producers of very large calves peculiarly adjusted to a hot southern climate.

The most popular, and in many ways the most thrifty breed was the Hereford, familiarly referred to as the "whiteface." These hardy animals came to dominate the range country. They became *the* beef cow of the West.

The Aberdeen Angus, long popular among Eastern stockmen for their high percentage of usable meat to total carcass weight have only lately found favor with Western cattlemen. In recent years they have been in growing demand. They calve easily, which means a higher percentage calf crop, and their black skin makes them less susceptible to sun-burned teats and udders – an ailment so painful to the mother cow that she will not permit her calf to nurse. These characteristics, combined with the quality of the beef, make the Angus readily marketable.

Ed C. Lasater, a farseeing Texas and Colorado stockman, crossed some Brahman bulls with his Hereford and Shorthorn herds. After a rigid culling program, taking into account such factors as disposition, weight and confirmation, Lasater was so pleased with the results that he named his new breed "Beefmaster."

Charolais from France

In 1936, the men at the King Ranch bought two huge, white bulls from one Jean Pugibet, a French stockman operating a hacienda in Mexico. Pugibet had made a visit to France and was much impressed by this great breed called Charolais. In recent years, their popularity has increased, due in large measure to their great size (bulls weighing from 2,000–2,500 pounds) and the high amount of lean meat in proportion to excess fat.

Most recently, certain so-called "exotic" breeds are being introduced to American ranches. Without exception they are continental cattle of immense size. From France come the Simmental and Limousin, from Italy the Chianina and from Germany the Gelbvich. They are beefy and chunky and so long in the loin you can count the extra steaks in any one of them at a glance. For the stockman, that's where the real money is, in those tenderloins and sirloins. Each claim certain advantages such as low fat weight in proportion to red meat or high rate of gain in calves, matters of grave importance to the stockman whose chief aim, if he is to stay in business, is to sell the most steaks for the lowest cost of production.

Impressive Imports

The size of these European cattle is startling. There is a story of the Colorado rancher who bought twenty head of Charolais bulls, to begin a profitable cross-breeding program. The bulls arrived past schedule, a little after midnight. This, the rancher figured, was about par for the course. Cattle truckers, for some unknown reason, set their clocks differently from other people. The bulls were big and ranted around so violently in the corrals that the rancher decided to turn them loose in his 300-acre pasture rather than have them tear down his pens. He knew right then and there he'd bought himself a ranch full of big action.

Early the next morning, the Colorado stockman mounted his dependable cow pony, as experienced a buckskin quarter horse as you could ever set your saddle on, to check out his new high-priced purchase. He rode toward a ridge behind which he hoped to find the bulls. Suddenly, as the horseman reached the summit, several six-foot-high white beasts stood against the horizon. So impressive were they that the stockman's horse stopped dead in her tracks and trembled. It's one thing for a man to be impressed by cattle, but it's another thing for a seasoned cow horse to be stunned.

The upgrading of American cattle has been accomplished over a long period of time by mating average or "grade" cows with "pureblooded" or "registered" bulls. During the last quarter of the nineteenth century, a majority of cattle herds were composed of pretty nondescript animals, but as the buyers shifted from purchasing by the "head" to buying by the "pound," quality began to assume an economic importance. Now the aim of the stockman was to

ABOVE: *Driving cattle* across a river
FAR RIGHT: *The Empty Tank*, painting by Darol Dickinson

produce animals with good weight and tastier beef.

To achieve this, the cattle ranchers, the men who ran the great herds of commercial cows or so-called grade animals, saw the advantage of putting registered bulls with their cows. The breeders of pedigree Shorthorn bulls such as the Bates Duchess line promoted their stock as having such potency that the offspring inherited the same high-quality characteristics the sires themselves possessed.

On the basis of this theory, ranchers over the years have purchased high-quality bulls of various breeds to improve the standard of their calf crop and in turn increase the price the stockman receives for his product. These stockmen

work to produce the kind of beef which the consumers demand, all the beef eventually purchased by the housewife. These are the men who raise grade cattle, the great commercial herds that constitute the backbone of the American cattle industry.

Breeding Perfection

The men who specialize in pure-bred cattle, the registered Hereford or Charolais, Angus or Santa Gertrudis, are breeders in perfection. To be successful they must become superbly knowledgeable and accomplished in all aspects of animal husbandry. They are a combination of geneticists and showmen, animal lovers and salesmen, herdsmen and accountants.

ABOVE: *Grading the meat* ensures best quality for the housewife
ABOVE CENTRE: *Charolais crossbred steers* on exhibition at the Western livestock show in Denver
FAR RIGHT ABOVE: *Judging* at a cattle show
FAR RIGHT BELOW: *The ten best* of the breed pose for the crowd

They may operate a large spread or a small, entirely specialized farm. They carry out their programs in every state and in Canada and Mexico as well.

The herds of pedigree cattle may number from 25 or 50 head to several hundred. Sires are advertised with emphasis not only upon their confirmation, but upon records of their progeny. Other features which the breeders claim for their stock include statements that their bulls will settle more cows in a minimum of time, will cover more country and not "hang around the water hole."

The breeders go to considerable effort to present their stock to the "cow and calf" men, those ranchers who purchase registered bulls either to upgrade or maintain the quality of their so-called commercial herds. A good bull can produce fine calves which in turn bring more money at the market, and the quality of the herd itself can be improved by keeping the first-class heifers. By making them part of the herd while culling cows of inferior caliber, a rancher can improve his entire stock to meet the changing demands of the marketplace.

Intense Competition

The competition to sell the registered animal is intense. Full-page ads in color in such magazines as the *Western Livestock Journal* boast of the desirability of one breed over another, one strain against another. Handsome pictures show mas-

sive bulls, docile cows and alert calves. Even colored shots of a carcass showing mouth-watering, luscious rib eye steaks are presented to lure the stockmen into making a purchase.

Advertising also takes another tack in the cattle business, that of the great cattle shows. These exhibitions, held in the large cities of the West, give the breeder the chance to show his cattle in competition with the animals of other stockmen, as well as to sell them. For the show the cattle are greatly pampered, washed and brushed and curried to the point of loving perfection. Sometimes they are given a bottle of beer just before show time to fill them out and give them a "bloom." Ladies' hair spray is also effective to give the coat a sheen.

Ribbons and Cash

Judges, usually college professors who teach animal husbandry, award prizes in money and ribbons. To the exhibitor, the color of the ribbon is as important as the hardness of the cash. For a stockman, especially when he is exhibiting registered bulls, the award of a blue ribbon as first prize or a purple one to mark a champion is as valuable as the performance record of the bulls themselves.

In principle, the owner of such a champion does not sell his prize animal, but keeps it for breeding purposes and promotional advantage. It will be the offspring of these champions that are sold to the cow-calf stockmen.

When prizewinners are offered for sale, either on the auction block or by "private treaty" they bring excessively high prices. Today, the figure of $100,000 for a prize bull is not unheard of. The purchaser of these high-priced animals is a stockman running registered cows who makes such outlays to improve his herd.

Prices for Publicity

There's a joke among the men who run commercial herds about the high prices reported in the newspapers as paid for prize bulls.

"Yeah," said Slim, as he looked at the latest quotation of $103,000 for a pedigree Hereford. "I believe it sure helps to keep the values up."

"How's that?" questioned Tex.

"Well, it makes a fella think they must have pretty high-toned stuff."

"Right, but I never paid over $500 for a bull and I'm still in business."

"Tell you what let's do," barked Slim. "I'll just buy that gimpy six-year-old white-face bull of yours for $75,000 and send a notice to the *Daily Times*. We'll get a picture of you holding the check and me holding the bull."

"And then," croaked Tex, "I'll buy that stove-in four-year-old Angus sire of yours for $75,000 and we'll do the same thing. It's a sure way to pleasure and profit in the cattle business."

The point is, many of the registered beasts are overrated and overpriced.

It is true that the desire of stockmen to possess top animals very often reaches the level of absurdity. There is the amazing case of some investors who purchased a prizewinning Angus bull for around $50,000, only to discover the beast was impotent. They had no recourse, for in the cattle business, unless otherwise specified, the rule is you buy "as is."

Bulls, Bulls, Bulls

Cattle exhibitions give the cow-calf man an opportunity to see, all gathered in one place,

At the auction
Auctioneers must be fast talkers, whose voices can rise above the sound of hooves as the merchandise mills about

327

ABOVE: *Grand Champion* from Texas
RIGHT: *Early twentieth-century invitation* to negotiate "private treaty" purchases
FAR RIGHT: *Cows emerging* from the "squeeze" in which they are branded and inoculated

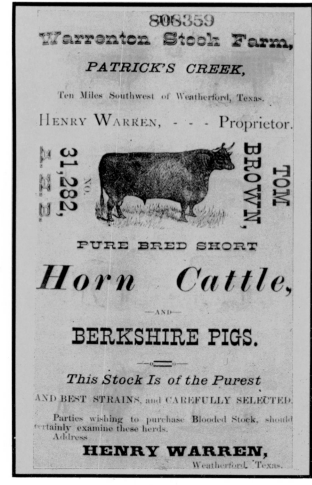

806359

Warrenton Stock Farm,

PATRICK'S CREEK,

Ten Miles Southwest of Weatherford, Texas.

HENRY WARREN, - - - Proprietor.

NO. 31,282, A. H. B.   BROWN, TOM

PURE BRED SHORT

Horn Cattle,

—AND—

BERKSHIRE PIGS.

This Stock Is of the Purest

AND BEST STRAINS, and CAREFULLY SELECTED.

Parties wishing to purchase Blooded Stock, should certainly examine these herds.
Address

HENRY WARREN,

Weatherford, Texas.

single bulls, pens of three and five, bulls of varied breeds and prices. From these he may select suitable sires for his herd. Many sales are made at these shows and, in general, honest ranchers obtain fine bulls from honest stockmen.

However, the stock shows in which prize animals compete for championships are in large measure for the benefit of the breeders of registered stock. Prize-winning steers attest to the quality of the breeder's line. Fashionable hotels, elegant restaurants and supermarket chains buy the fat animals for promotional purposes, thus placing their establishments before the public as purveyors of fine beef. While the rancher may expect to receive at auction 30 or even 40 cents per pound, the Grand Champion steer may bring many dollars per pound on the auction block. This wide gap in prices can make a cow-calf operator cry.

"Big Mac"

A case in point, one which is enough to raise the temper of every commercial cowman in the country, was the story of a 1971 Grand Champion, "Big Mac." This handsome Black Angus was bought at auction by McDonald's Hamburgers, a huge chain of drive-in restaurants, for eleven dollars and 40 cents per pound. Later, however, it was discovered that "Big Mac" was

losing his beautiful black color and, strange to say, was turning white. Close examination proved that the champion was not an Angus at all, but in reality a handsome, creamy colored Charolais steer which had been dyed. The sale was voided, the judges embarrassed and the owner's reputation jeopardized. For any student of the hoax, this was a wonderful one.

Stock Shows and Sales

The average stockman, the cow-calf operator, pays between $500 and $1,000 for his herd sires. And he goes about buying those bulls in a variety of ways. He may either attend the important stock shows held in such cities as Denver, Fort Worth or Kansas City. He may read the ads in trade papers and go to a dispersal sale where a breeder of registered stock is selling off his crop of young bulls, or he may just climb in his pickup truck and visit ranches where he knows the stockman has a reputation for raising high-quality bulls.

Buying a bull is no easy matter. A surprising number of factors must be taken into consideration. It's quite exciting, even though it is all done in a very low key, to observe a first-class rancher bargain for the purchase of a topflight sire from a reputable breeder. The rancher looks at confirmation, length of the loins where the beef steaks are located, strength of legs. A reputable breeder will guarantee fertility through a veterinarian's test, at the time of shipment only.

Acquiring a good herd of cows demands just as much care as purchasing the bull. Established ranchers need to obtain cows to replace those they have culled for one reason or another, those that have died, strayed or been stolen. Sometimes a man makes a purchase to increase the size of his operation or to improve the quality of his herd.

Cattle are graded for their quality. Consideration is given to the carcass classifications from the highest "prime" and "choice" to the lowest "canner" and "cutter." The stockman endeavors to acquire cows fitting the top quality. He is also interested in how easily she gives birth, her ability to give a good quantity of milk and her mothering instinct. It costs no more to keep a good cow than a poor one and her calves always bring a higher price on the market.

Private Treaties

Most cattlemen go directly to the ranch to purchase cows. Here they can walk among the herd and "fault" the animals, that is, point out the negative characteristics of this cow or that. If the cattle pretty much come up to the standard of quality the buyer is considering, and the asking

price, say $250 a head, is within the range of the going market, then a shrewd cattle buyer will take the faults into account, using them as leverage when he offers to buy the cows at $200 each. In such a transaction, called a "private treaty," cattle are bought and sold by the head, not by weight as calves are sold at the market.

Much dickering takes place when cattlemen buy and sell. Some crafty buyers dress in worn and shabby clothes, giving the impression that they can't afford to spend much. An alert seller, on the contrary, may wear the most stylish attire so that his well-groomed appearance will shed an aura of quality over his cattle. The buyer and seller may bargain for many minutes, or sometimes days, making counter-offers until one or the other gives in and they make a deal and shake hands.

Buying cattle is only one of the many activities of ranchers. Some of the work is seasonal, like making hay, while other chores such as feeding the bulls and horses are daily ones.

Many ranchers, particularly in the northern country, turn their bulls out shortly after branding time. The gestation period of a cow is 282 days or approximately nine months. Those cowmen wishing to have their cows calve, for example, in mid-March, will turn the bulls out on or about 15 June. Ideally a rancher wants his calves born as early in the spring as possible so that his calf crop will have a long growing season to reach maximum weight for the fall market. Ranchers in the southern regions do not necessarily follow this system since their cows can calve all year round without danger of freezing.

Artificial Insemination

Many cattlemen endeavor to have all calves born within a period of 30 to 45 days so that they will be uniform size and weight at marketing time. Evenness is a highly desirable quality which buyers reward by paying a premium price.

To ensure high-quality calves and evenness, cattlemen are turning to artificial insemination. By spending from five to fifteen dollars, a stockman can often avail himself of the genes of a proven sire. Such an animal may be a champion worth $50,000. For the cowman, it is a sound way to improve and upgrade his herd. And it has certain other advantages.

The stockman running 600 head of cows expects to keep about 30 bulls, at a cost of possibly $700 each, making an investment of as much as $21,000. If, on the other hand, he pays ten dollars for an ampule of semen for each of his 600 cows, he has annual expense of $6,000. A range bull's effectiveness is not much more than five years, so the stockman can figure an annual cost of about $4,200 for his 30 bulls. But the stockman must feed his bulls and winter and take the chance of his animals becoming cripped or infertile (and thus useless) or falling

The Denver stockyards
Each year cattle by the thousand pass through these pens, from the auction block to the meat packer

sick and perhaps dying. These factors must be entered on the debit side of the ledger.

Artificial insemination, when properly carried out, offers the rancher a better chance to get all his cows bred within the ideal period of 30 to 45 days. This requires a knowledgeable and observant cowboy, one who can accurately detect when a cow is in heat. There are only twelve hours during which the sperm can fertilize the ovum. The cowboy, often the technician who performs the insemination, must be skilful. Failure at any step in this delicate business means a reduced calf crop. Realistic stockmen using this method rarely expect the high rate of conception that a well-operated ranch with range bulls can achieve. Therefore, many combine the two methods, with a few "follow-up" bulls as a kind of insurance.

Airborne Rustlers

One problem that has plagued cattlemen from the beginning and has not been solved is rustling. Even with brand registrations and inspections – there are, for example, over 39,000 registered brands in Colorado alone – cowmen still lose many animals each year to thieves.

The modern rustler may actually survey a ranch in a small airplane to learn where the cattle are grazing. Then, under cover of darkness, he and his cohorts, secure in the knowledge that the cows he has spotted are pasturing far from the ranch headquarters, can open a gate or, with a pair of pliers, cut the fence. A cattle truck equipped with a portable loading chute can be pulled into the pasture where the cattle are rounded up and loaded in pretty short order. With the cows safely in the rig, the rustlers can be 200 miles away before dawn.

If a stockman's calves, or any cattle for that matter, are to be sold out of state, a health certificate must be secured. A veterinarian must make his inspection, attesting to the fact that the animals are visibly free from sickness and have been inoculated against such dread diseases as undulant fever. Some states have strict laws prohibiting the importation of unhealthy animals.

No longer are cattle driven to market. Rather, enormous semi-trailer trucks are backed up to the cattle ramps by skilful drivers. Cowboys push the calves into these huge latticed trailers, carefully counting as each one struggles into the conveyance.

Cattle Auctions

In most instances calves are shipped to public auctions. Formerly, these were held at the great cattle centers such as Kansas City, Fort Worth, Chicago and Denver. More recently, however, cattle auctions have moved to the country, partly to be closer to the feed lots, partly because many of the packing houses have left the cities, like-

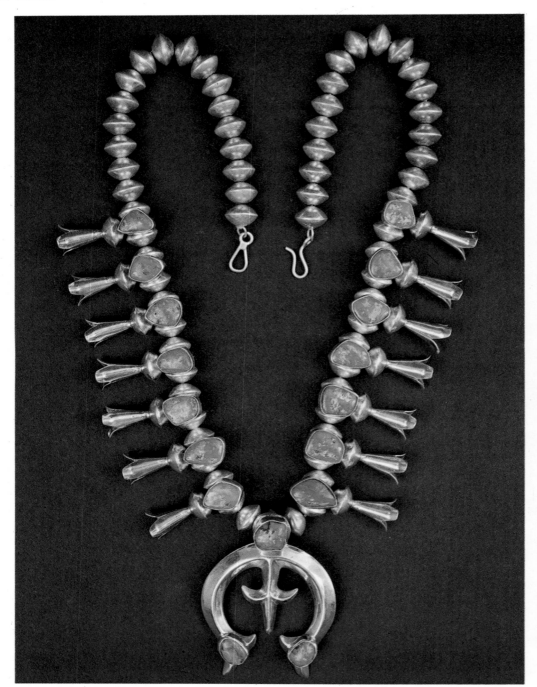

wise dispersing themselves to be nearer the feeders.

The buyers at the auctions are generally the operators of the feed lots. Here, in great pens, the cattle are fattened for as long as 360 days, getting ready for slaughter. Feeders purchase calves which they predict will fatten quickly and efficiently. Calves are sold to the highest bidder. If the market is high, say 45 to 50 cents per pound, the rancher will have a good year. If the market is low at 28 to 31 cents, the stockman may find that his year's operation has actually left him in the red.

The cow-calf operator has practically no control over what his calves will bring. At best he can gamble on the market, hoping either that by holding off a little longer prices will rise or guessing that the market is at its top and selling now. It's really less work and more fun to lose money at Las Vegas.

Suspense in the Arena

The auction house is a small semi-circular arena ringed by a grandstand with seats or benches facing the pit below. Here, on a sawdust-covered floor, the cattle are shown, having been brought in from the pens outside the building. Above the pit, facing the grandstand, secure behind a sturdy podium, sit the auctioneer and clerk. These officials nearly always wear white hats as a symbol of integrity.

There is a sense of suspense about a cattle auction. The sellers wonder how much they'll receive; the buyers wonder what they'll have to pay. The calves, ideally in bunches of twenty, referred to as carload lots, are pushed into the ring where the ring-man prods the animals around with a yellow cane so the buyers can get a view of the stock. As each lot is about to be auctioned, the auctioneer gets a price from the ring-man, the lowest figure at which he thinks the bidding

should start. The ring-man knows the local market, the auctioneer knows auctioneering.

"Hey, hey, boys," barks the auctioneer in a falsetto voice. "Looky here, looky here, steer calves from the Lone Star Ranch, top quality, high country, good stuff. Now who'll give me 34, 34, 34 a pound?"

"Thirty-four, 34," rasps the auctioneer in his singsong cry. "Now 35, I've got 35, 35, do I hear 36 cents?"

And so it goes, up at first by pennies, then by half cents, finally by less until the auctioneer finally pleads, "I got $38\frac{1}{4}$. Do I hear a half, who'll give me a half, a half, a half?" Bang goes the gravel. "Sold, sold for $38\frac{1}{4}$ to Killmore Feed Lots."

The calves are then pushed out of the ring and onto a set of scales. Here they are weighed and the total price calculated instantly. At that moment the stockman, watching his calves

Indian art and craftsmanship
FAR LEFT ABOVE: Navaho silver squash blossom necklace embellished with turquoise
FAR LEFT BELOW: Haida house post decorated with a killer whale and the figure of an ancestral chief
ABOVE: Navaho rug of intricate geometric design from Two Grey Hills

Stockyard scenes
ABOVE: In the feedlot, these animals will be brought up to weights of over 1000 pounds
FAR RIGHT: Cattle about to be sold at auction in the stockyards at Omaha, Nebraska

disappear from the ring, never to see them again, leaves his seat to pick up his check for a year's work. It may be a moment of joy or despair.

After the Sales

After the fall sale, the rancher's year begins again. This is the time to test the cows to determine how many are with calf. Pregnancy testing requires that each cow be brought into the squeeze and physically examined.

Those cows found to be pregnant are placed in one pen, while the "empties" are separated and put in another. A stockman is pragmatic and regardless of the quality of a cow which has not conceived he will dispose of her at auction. He knows that such a cow is possibly infertile and keeping her over for another breeding season, considering the price of feed, may cost him more than he will gain.

While the cow is in the squeeze is a good opportunity to check her teeth. This the cowboy does by prying open her mouth with a metal jaw-spreader. Teeth worn flat to the gums indicate age, but not necessarily old age. Teeth become worn from grit and sand in the grass. A cow without teeth cannot get enough to eat; she becomes gaunt, her milk supply diminishes and her calf begins to starve. In most cases, "gummers" are sent to market as "cutters," the lowest grade of beef.

Cows with False Teeth

On the other hand, if á cow has a superior record for producing excellent calves, the stock-man may decide to fit her with a set of false teeth. Now, with her mouth pried open, is the time to clip in the metal dentures. False teeth can add a couple of years to a cow's productive life.

The modern rancher is a businessman in work-clothes, a laborer, often with a college education. He's a gambling man, with the elements and the market his unpredictable odds. And perhaps most significant, he is a man with a fierce affection for his animals – his horse and his cows.

Still Indian Country

Today, the Southwest is one part of the country that retains much of its Indian flavor. The Pueblos still fashion handsome pottery and jewelry, the Navahos create striking silver pieces and weave beautiful rugs. Many tribes still carry on their colorful ceremonies. The Pimas and Papagos continue to practice their art of basketry. Though tarnished by early conquest and present-day commercialism, the land of the desert mesas is still most enchanting and still quite Indian. The aura of the Anasazi, "The Ancient Ones," continues to pervade the atmosphere.

A style of necklace conceived and especially favored by the Navaho is referred to as the "Squash Blossom." Silver beads are interspersed with silver blossoms, while at the base of the necklace an inverted horseshoe-shaped device called a naja is suspended. This striking piece of jewelry has a fascinating history, which

proves it to be, with the exception of the idea of beads, wholly European.

The art of silversmithing was learned from the Mexicans. The squash blossoms are in reality miniature pomegranates, a Spanish symbol of hope and devotion. The naja is an ancient Moorish emblem to ward off the evil eye, and was brought to the New World by the Spanish who used it as a horse trapping on their bridles. The Navaho combined these foreign concepts to create something completely Navaho. There can be no question that the Squash Blossom necklace is Indian.

Today, the Navaho men make not only necklaces, but also silver rings and bracelets and "bow guards" often set with handsome blue and blue-green turquoise. They have even mastered the art of sand casting, especially suited to massive openwork bracelets in geometric curvilinear patterns. And the Navaho make great use of their jewelry, bedecking themselves with silver, necklace upon necklace, rings on every finger, bracelets upon bracelets in gaudy display.

Navaho Rugs

The Navaho women are masterful weavers. Observing their skill, American traders during the late nineteenth century capitalized upon it by encouraging the women to adapt their weaving of dresses and blankets to the making of rugs. Bartering flour, cheap velveteen, canned beans or slab bacon for fine woven rugs the traders got rich. Without such exploitation, of course, the home industry which has produced some of the most unique and handsome rugs the world has ever seen might never have developed.

From the early native "Chief's Blankets" with their bold bars of red, black and white to the subtle geometrics and muted colors of vegetable-dyed yarns of the "Wide Ruins" design, the Navaho rug is indeed a masterpiece. Over the years different styles developed in the remote communities. At Two Grey Hills, for example, bold geometric forms woven with natural black, brown and white wool were made, while at Ganado the rugs are noted for their deep red backgrounds overlaid by stark black and white geometric patterns.

Curing Ceremony

The Navaho are still a highly religious people awed by sickness and death. Unlike the Pueblos whose ceremonies center around the forces of nature which affect the growth of their crops, the Navaho as a traditional hunting people seem more concerned with the well-being of the individual. Illness is a fearsome matter and their ceremonies are devoted to its cure. Cures are effected by employing the services of a "chanter" or priest versed in the songs of his people's

Artisans at work
BELOW: Maggie Osceda, a Florida Seminole, making a skirt in the same style as the one she is wearing
RIGHT: A Tlingit Indian named Wilson Wallace prepares a totemic plaque
FAR RIGHT: A Navaho named Bertha Stevens beats the weft in her ring with a wooden comb

mythology. The ceremony lasts eight days and when performed in accordance with tradition, a new lodge is erected. Here the patient is brought.

On the floor, the chanter and his assistant prepare a sand painting, reminiscent of the Pueblo, though far more elaborate and beautiful. Colored sands are sifted through the thumb and forefinger to produce exquisitely delicate symbols depicting the gods of mythological times. When complete it becomes, in fact, an altar upon which the patient is seated as the ceremony proceeds. Here offerings are made, songs are sung, all to the purpose of cleansing the patient and infusing him with the health-giving powers of the supernatural beings.

When this phase of the rite is finished, the painting is destroyed. On the final night, powerful masked dancers perform as spirits along with a clown. Other men perform tricks such as sleight of hand and on occasion an arrow-swallower may appear. The curing is not without its cost. The patient must offer a feast to the performers and guests and pay the chanter and his helpers in jewelry, sheep or other articles of

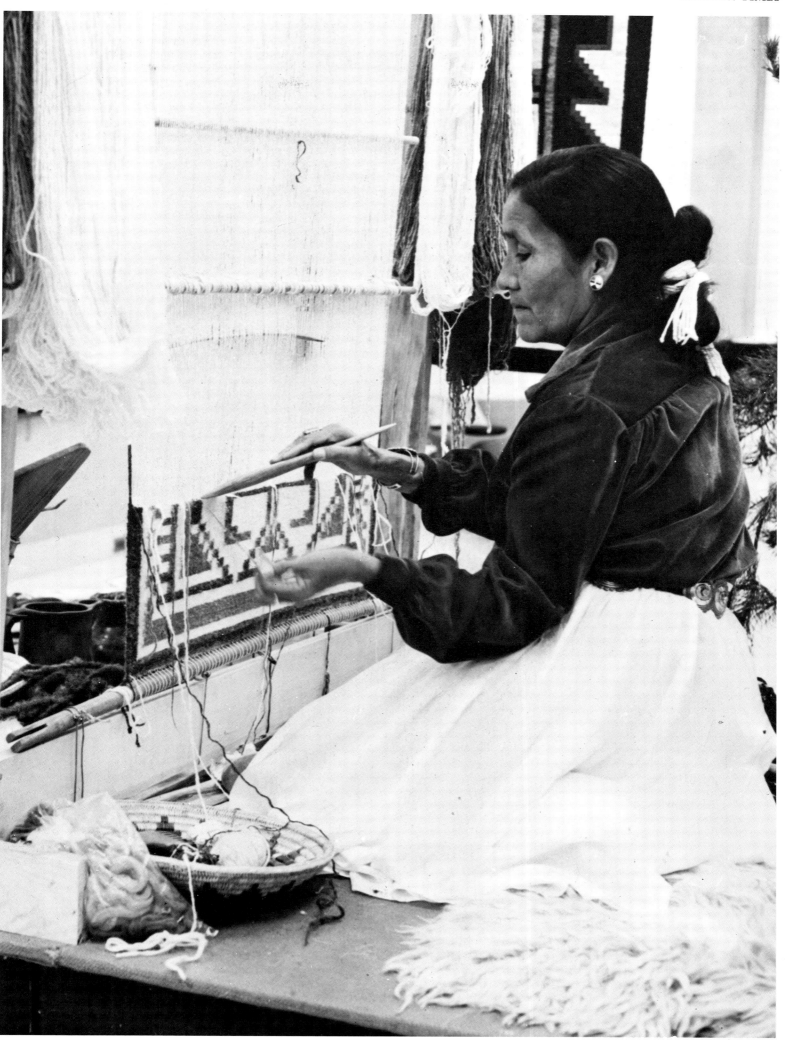

value. For the patient, this is a time of joy and celebration – the gods have shared their power and he is well again.

Modern Indian life
A trading post on the Sioux Reservation

The Westerners Endure

So there are still Indians in the West, today regaining a pride in their heritage and demanding their rightful place as proud contributors within the nation. There are still miners seeking riches, many of them these days people who have been technically trained in specialized universities to supervise sophisticated mining operations. There are still cattlemen trying to make money running ranches, and cowboys branding calves with red-hot irons. The road agents holding up stage-coaches have vanished, but bank robbers and cattle rustlers still ply their nefarious trades. Sheriffs still get paid to wear badges and hunt down criminals. The smooth-talking horse traders are now used-car dealers, and, sadly, judges no longer keep bars.

Today the West has much of what the rest of the country has. Its cities of skyscrapers, its handsome churches, its fine museums and libraries and great universities are the attributes of what we call civilized society.

Preserving the Habitat

And what of the land itself, in the present day? How well is it being preserved?

The West, we can see now, was destined for exploitation. At first it was the trappers who depleted the beaver. They were followed by the miners scarring the hills for gold and silver. Settlers from the East felled the forests and broke the sod. Later, men grazed their cattle and sheep on the free grass. Within 75 years, the seemingly inexhaustible resources were running out. No longer was it profitable to mine the precious metals. The discovery of rich coal and oil deposits in the later part of the nineteenth century did add a new dimension to the country's wealth, yet within a century they too were severely drained.

Not until the 1930s did farmers and ranchers start to practice sound conservation techniques. Prior to that, much range was damaged by over-grazing, wind erosion caused great dust storms in sodded regions which should never have been plowed. Strangely, even the agriculturists – who represent the chief contributors to a true production economy – were zealously destroying the very resource upon which their life depended. The lumbermen, like the farmers, after nearly destroying their rich resource finally began taking care of it, with the practice of cutting on a sustained-yield basis which they combined with a program of reforestation.

Now, in the last quarter of the twentieth century, Westerners are still exploiting their land. Cursed by overpopulation, misled by the fallacious notions that because things are bigger

they must be better, that only through growth can an economy function, the inhabitants have gone far to destroy the beauties and riches of the West. A combination of factors brought this about.

A rapid growth in population has strained housing facilities of many Western communities. Much of this growth has been promoted by state governments and Chambers of Commerce frantically seeking new industries to expand economic productivity and increase the tax base. Real estate developers have been quick to capitalize on the ever-expanding urban sprawl by buying up parcel upon parcel of valuable agricultural land at prices ranchers and farmers cannot afford to reject. As a result, many productive agricultural areas are all too rapidly being displaced by an unproductive and unattractive suburbia.

Destruction by Dam

Water has always been at a premium in the West. Water rights have been jealously guarded and theoretically protected by law. The vast amounts required by new industry and an expanding population have plunged the supply to a dangerously low level. Water tables drop, demanding deeper and deeper wells, more and larger dams.

Proponents of these gigantic reservoirs claim various benefits including hydroelectric power, increased irrigation, flood control and added recreational facilities for fishermen and boating enthusiasts. The engineers who design these reservoirs often fail in their cost-benefit calculations to foresee that they may become useless through silting.

And as they demolish irreplaceable farmland and wildlife habitats, they destroy untold natural beauty. As more monuments to man's engineering achievements are built, it is at the expense of nature's beauty. The short-sighted dam builders have succeeded in spoiling much of the Western landscape.

Today the rugged character of the West has been transformed into one of safe and soft gentility. It is as though a chemist had converted strong whiskey into lukewarm tea. The vastness of the plains still remains, it is true, the grandeur of the lofty mountains and the brilliance of the Western sunsets still inspire awe.

Deer and elk, black bears and grizzlies may yet be found in wilderness areas. Coyotes still prey on sheep, and antelope roam the plains. And here and there hawks and eagles wheel high above the blue horizon as beavers build their dams in cool wooded streams far below. But their numbers have been decimated and their habitats severely reduced. A few buffalo remain, and a handful of wolves are confined to reserves. The wilds that once were the West are now very tame indeed.

The National Parks

The National Parks System offers to an enormous and ever-growing public the West's natural wonders – geysers and wild animals, Indian artefacts and forests of petrified trees. Associated with the parks are all manner of camping and motel accommodation, cafeterias and gasoline stations to attract thousands of visitors. Concessionaires get rich selling food and supplies, cheap novelties and gimcracks. Emphasis on comfort and safety of visitors has reached what some consider to be ridiculous proportions and when it is a choice between protecting a human or an animal, park authorities, naturally enough, don't hesitate.

Recently in Yellowstone Park in Wyoming two young men deliberately camped in an area plainly marked as off limits, and one was mauled to death by a grizzly bear; park rangers promptly shot the bear. It is becoming clear to everyone that if the parks and their wonders are to be preserved some way of restricting the number of visitors will have to be found. As matters stand, not only are the parks being worn out, but they are about as appealing as rush hour on a Manhattan subway.

Hunting, Fishing and Endangering

Sportsmen, too, such as hunters and fishermen, do their share in destroying the environment, although quotas are placed on most wild game so that only specified numbers of deer, elk or antelope may be shot. But some evade the wardens, either shooting animals out of season or in numbers beyond the legal limit. Today more and more animals – the grizzly bear, the mountain lion, the golden eagle – are being placed on the endangered list.

In the face of the onslaught of too many people and the inevitable forces of progress and change, a growing number of men and women are working to retain something of the

Dudes in fancy dress
Outfitted like Daniel
Boone, visitors at a
dude ranch enjoy a
pack trip

quality of the nation's Western heritage.

Groups have been formed to restore historic landmarks and preserve natural wonders. Ecologically concerned organizations are active in developing wildlife preserves and sponsoring statutes for the protection of endangered species. Their endeavors supplement federal and state programs for wilderness areas, parks, monuments and shrines as well as the activities of local and state historical societies.

A Westerner's Smile

But the preserving of the true flavor and character of the West is not to be achieved in pickling history. Rather, it is to be found in the attitude of its people. When parting company, instead of "Good night" or "So long" or "See you later," people out West are likely to say, "Have a nice day." And their smiles are genuine.

The story of the American West would appear to have been the saga of daring explorers and flamboyant military men, of wilful lusty entrepreneurs, of robber barons, and outright brigands. But that's not accurate. The West was settled by a stalwart and determined people. Most were law-abiding, hard-working, God-fearing citizens. In addition to farmers and doctors, lawyers and ranchers, their ranks included all categories of endeavor – preachers and schoolteachers, blacksmiths and bankers, coopers and shopkeepers. They were the "salt of the earth."

Their lives were often drab and dull. Rarely did they make the headlines in the annals of history. And yet it was they, with their simplistic view of life, who would prove to be the effective conquerors of the West.

Their contribution, while neither sensational nor profound, was solid and sustained. It was they who made the West a valuable and integral part of an expanding and prosperous nation.

Further Reading

Adair, James *The History of the American Indians*
Beaudoin, Kenneth Lawrence *The Caddos*
Belden, Josiah *1841 California Overland Pioneer*
Bogart, W. H. *Daniel Boone and the Hunters of Kentucky*
Boon, Captain Daniel *Life and Adventures of Colonel Daniel Boon, The First White Settler of the State of Kentucky*
Brown, Dee *Bury My Heart at Wounded Knee*
Brown, Dee *Trail Driving Days*
Brown, Mark, and Felton, W. *Before Barbed Wire*
Browne, J. Ross *Adventures in the Apache Country*
Brownell, Charles de Wolf *The Indian Races of North and South America*
Buchanan, James *Sketches of the History, Manners and Customs of the North American Indians*
Dale, Edward Everett *The Indians of the Southwest*
Deloria, Vine *Custer Died for Your Sins*
Derbec, Etienne *A French Journalist in the California Gold Rush*
Dobie, J. Frank *The Longhorns*
Eshelman, Henry Frank *Annals of the Susquehanna and other Indian Tribes of the Susquehanna Territory*
Ewers, John *The Blackfeet: Raiders on the Northwestern Plains*
Foreman, Grant *The Last Trek of the Indians*
Freuchen, Peter *The Book of the Eskimos*
Green, Ben *Wild Cow Tales*
Grey, Zane *Riders of the Purple Sage*
Grinnell, George Bird *The Cheyenne Indians: Their History & Ways of Life*
Harris, Benjamin Butler *The Gila Trail*
Hassrick, Royal B. *I and Tex*
Hassrick, Royal B. *The Sioux: Life & Customs of a Warrior Society*
Hill, Douglas *The Opening of the Canadian West*
Hough, E. *The Story of the Cowboy*
Ideizer, Robert Fleming, & Whipple, Mary Anne *The California Indians*
James, Will *Smoky*
LaFarge, Oliver *Laughing Boy*
Leighton, D. C., & Kluckhon, C. *The Navaho*
Lourie, Robert Heinrich *Indians of the Plains*
Lowie, Robert *The Crow Indians*
Marriott, Alice *The Ten Grandmothers*
Mathews, John J. *Osages: Children of the Middle Waters*
Morgan, L. H. *The League of the Iroquois*
Nichols, Frances S. *Index to Schoolcraft's 'Indian Tribes of the United States'*
Sandoz, Marie *The Cattlemen*
Santee, Ross *Cowboy*
Siringo, Charles A. *A Texas Cowboy*
Speck, Frank G. *Creek Indians of Taskigi Town*
Swanton, John *The Indians of the Southeastern U.S.*
Tax, Sol(ed.) *Indian Tribes of Aboriginal America*
Thompson, L., & Joseph, A. *The Hopi Way*
Underhill, Ruth Murray *Red Man's America*
Verrill, Alpheus Hyatt *The Real Americans*
Vestal, Stanley *Warpath and Council Fire*
Wallace, Ernest, & Hoeble, E. Adamson *The Comanches Lords of the South Plains*
Ward, Don, & Dykes, J. C. *Cowboys and Cattle Country*
Ward, Fay E. *The Cowboy at Work*
Wellman, Paul I. *The Trembling Herd*
Wissler, Clark *Indians of the U.S. Four Centuries of the History & Culture*
Wister, Owen *The Virginian*

Acknowledgments

The publishers would like to thank the following individuals and organizations for their kind permission to reproduce the photographs in this book:

University of Alaska Museum 97; American Museum of Natural History 36 centre right, 45 right, 81, 100-101; Philip Anschutz Collection 226-227; Arizona State Historical Society 216 above right; Bancroft Library, University of California 109 below; Barnabys Picture Library 9 below, 186-187, 235, 308 below, 309, 344-345; Bizzell Library, University of Oklahoma 215 right; Boatmans National Bank, St. Louis 128-129; British Museum 27 above, 47 right, 66-67; S.O. Butcher Collection 222 below; Butler Institute of American Art 166-167; Camera Press 188-189, 306 below; Amon Carter Museum 2-3, 20, 74-75 above, 74-75 below, 106-107, 119, 150-151, 202, 203 above, 203 below, 206 below, 207 above, 207 below, 224 above, 234, 237 below, 240, 241 below, 242 above, 243, 247, 248-249, 250-251; William L. Clements Library, University of Michigan 153; Colorado Cattlemen's Association 325 above; State Historical Society of Colorado 112-113, 118 below, 204, 256-257, 266 above, 269 above, 272 above; Corcoran Gallery, Washington DC 145 above left, 145 above right; Crown Publishers 276 below, 278 above right, 278 centre right, 278 below right; Denver Art Museum 36 below, 49 above, 50-51, 102 below, 103 below, 106 below, 114 below, 118 above, 270 above, 294, 295, left, 300 right, 344-345; Denver Museum of Natural History 36 above, 39 below; Denver Public Library 1 left, 1 right, 8-9 above, 12-13, 25 below, 28 above, 41, 46-47, 52 above, 58 below, 59, 60-61, 63, 64 above, 68 above, 68 below right, 69 above right, 69 below right, 70 above, 70 below, 71 below, 75 above, 75 below, 76-77, 86, 91, 95 below, 96 above, 96-97 below, 102-103, 104 above, 105 above left, 105 above right, 108 right, 109 above, 113 above, 116, 117 above, 130-131, 142, 144 below, 156 above, 173, 179 below right, 181 above, 181 below, 188 above, 194, 206 above, 212 below, 214 above left, 216 above left, 216 above centre, 217 above left, 217 above right, 222 above, 232, 257 above, 261, 267, 268, 269 below, 270 below, 272 below, 276 above, 277, 278 left, 279 above, 279 below, 283, 284 above, 284 below, 285 above, 285 below, 287 above, 289 below, 310 above, 316, 317, 320 above, 321, 324 right, 328 below, 332-333, 337; Denver Public Library (E. Curtis) 57, 93, 137; Denver Union Corporation 326-327; Carl Shaefer Dentzel 138; Detroit Club, endpapers; Detroit Institute of Arts (Joseph Klima) 42-43; Darol Dickinson 18 below, 323; Mary Evans Picture Library 117, 121 above, 121 below, 124-125, 160, 172, 180, 200 above, 205 above, 218, 220-221, 228, 230 below, 231, 252 below, 253, 260 above, case; Phil Fahs Photo 14 below, 21 above, 327; Werner Forman Archive 37 below, 38 left, 39 below, 66 below left, 67, 73, 98, 99, 290-291, 295 below, 334 below; Alan Frank 198-199; Thomas Gilcrease Institute of American History & Art 114-115, 162-163, 244-245, 254-255; Glenbow Alberta Institute, Calgary 94-95 above; Globe (John R. Hamilton) 14 above; Susan Griggs Agency 260 below, 306 above, 318-319, (Adam Woolfitt) 6-7, 10-11; William Harmsen Collection, Denver 71 above; Royal B. Hassrick 34-35; J. Jerome Hill Reference Library, St. Paul Minnesota 26 above, 205 below; Historical Picture Service 305; Anne Horton 132 left, 176-177; Hudson's Bay Company, Winnipeg 98 below; Idaho Historical Society 211 right; Bureau of Indian Affairs, U.S. Department of the Interior 25 above, 56, 296-297; Indian Arts & Crafts Board 292, 334 above, 338 above, 338 below, 339; International Harvester Co. NY. 185; Mack Jones 288; Kansas State Historical Society 134, 148, 215 left, 230 above, 237 above, 264-265, 280-281; Library of Congress 29 below, 37 above, 58 above, 236 below; Municipal Art Dept., Los Angeles 287 below; Gordon Macgregor, Jekyll Island, Georgia 293, 300 left, 340-341, 342, 343; The Map House, London 78-79; University of Michigan Museum of Art 170-171; Nina Hull Miller, Lexington, Nebraska 217 below; Minnesota Historical Society 178-179 above, 193; Missouri Historical Society 129, 139 above; Montana Historical Society 182-183, 239; J. Maxwell Moran Collection, Time Inc., New York City 174-175; Museum of the American Indian 34, 62 above, 62 below; Museum für Völkerkunde 52-53 below; Ruth Koerner Oliver 208-209; National Gallery of Canada 24 above, 127 right; National Museum of Canada 92; National Western Stock Show 324 left, 325 below, 328 above; Nebraska Historical Society 168-169; Nevada Historical Society 289 above; New Britain Museum of American Art 30-31; Museum of New Mexico, Santa Fé 217 above centre; New York Public Library 26-27 below, 143 below; New York Historical Society 145 above centre; North Carolina Museum of History 139 below; Oklahoma State Historical Society 238; Old Lincoln County Memorial Commission 233; University of Oregon 224 below; Kipp Parker 18 above; Peabody Museum, Harvard University 82 above, 82 below, 107 below; Pennsylvania Academy of Fine Arts 149; Picturepoint 308 above, 314; Popperfoto 38-39; Fred Rosenstock Gallery 15 below, 229, 260 centre; Royal Ontario Museum 68 below left, 100 above centre, 103 above, 145 below; Rodeo Information Foundation 304, 307, 310 below, 311; Jerry Sinise Photo 19, 266 below, 286, 320 below, 329, 336; Smithsonian Institution 24 below, 28 below, 29 above, 32 above, 44, 45 left, 48-49 below, 54, 55, 64-65 below, 69 above left, 69 below left, 80, 84-85, 87, 88-89, 94 below, 104-105, 108 left, 158-159, 161, 164-165, 190 above, 301; St. Louis Art Museum 27 below right, 72; St. Louis Color Postcard Company 144 above; Shelburne Museum Inc., Shelburne, Vermont 194-195; Southwest Museum, Los Angeles 155 inset; Stovall Museum of Science and History 32-33 below; Taft Museum, Cincinnati 294-295; Union Pacific Railway 196-197; U.S. Forest Service 192-193; U.S. National Archives 157 above, 214 above right, 216 below; Utah State Historical Society 178-179 below, 191; Walker Art Studio 330-331; Walters Art Gallery 124-125, 132 right; Warner Bros. 15 above, 298-299, 322; Washington University Gallery of Art, St. Louis 126-127; Wells Fargo Bank 210-211 below, 212 above, 213; Western Americana 22-23, 40, 110-111, 112, 113 below, 120, 131, 135, 136, 140, 141, 143, 146-147, 184 above, 184 below, 190 below, 192 left, 210-211 above, 214 below, 219, 223, 225, 236 above, 241, 242 below, 246 above left, 246 above right, 246 below, 252 above, 258-259, 262, 271 above, 271 below, 273, 274-275, 278 below centre, 281 below, 312, 313, 315, 345; West Point Museum Collections 152; W. F. Whitfield 263; Whitney Gallery of Art, Cody, Wyoming 154-155, 200-201; Woolaroc Museum, Bartlesville, Oklahoma 156-157; Yale University Library 100 above left, 179 below left; Yale University Library/Western Americana 133; ZEFA (M. J. Pitner) 4-5, 299, (W. L. Hamilton) 302, 303.

Index